Living a Jewish Life

ALSO BY ANITA DIAMANT
The New Jewish Wedding
The Jewish Baby Book
What to Name Your Jewish Baby

Anita Diamant
Howard Cooper

Living a Jewish Life

A Guide for Starting, Learning, Celebrating, and Parenting

HarperPerennial

A Division of HarperCollins*Publishers*

PERMISSIONS:

Letter to the Front, © Muriel Rukeyser, used by permission of William L. Rukeyser.
"How difficult for me is Hebrew" © 1976 by Charles Reznikoff. © 1977 Marie Syrkin
Reznikoff. Reprinted from The Complete Poems of Charles Reznikoff with the permission
of Black Sparrow Press.
Blessing the Children © Danny Siegel. Reprinted with permission of the author.

BOOK DESIGN: ADRIANNE ONDERDANK DUDDEN

Library of Congress Cataloging-in-Publication Data
Diamant, Anita.
    Living a Jewish life: a guide for starting, learning, celebrating, and parenting/
Anita Diamant, Howard Cooper.
    p.   cm.
    Includes bibliographical references and index.
    ISBN 0-06-271508-9—ISBN 0-06-273025-8 (pbk.)
    1. Judaism—United States—Customs and practices. 2. Jewish way of life.
I. Cooper, Howard, 1956– . II. Title.
BM700.D48   1991
296.7′4—dc20
                                                                90-56092

        95   DF/HC   10   9   8   7

For my daughter, Emilia
"She is a gift and a wonder"
Psalms
A.D.

For Annette S. Cooper, of blessed memory
"My mother was a perfect *tzadik*"
H. N. Bialik
H. C.

CONTENTS

COMMUNITY

OBSERVANCE

ACKNOWLEDGMENTS

This book is the collaboration between a writer and a teacher. *Living a Jewish Life* had its genesis in an adult education class taught at Congregation Beth El of the Sudbury River Valley in Sudbury, Massachusetts. Howard Cooper, then director of education, was teaching "Making a Jewish Home Now That You Have a Family of Your Own," which offered people the opportunity to peruse the menu of Jewish practice without "prior knowledge or experience." Howard, who holds an undergraduate degree in Judaic Studies and a Master's degree in Education, is the kind of teacher who inspires students with his obvious love for the subject. His sense of humor doesn't hurt either. His approach to Jewish tradition suggested this book.

The process of creating *Living a Jewish Life* began with and regularly returned to long conversations between Howard and myself—many of them held at an ice cream shop halfway between our respective homes. Over endless cups of watery coffee (and, okay, a few sundaes), we hammered out the contents of each chapter, discussed philosophy and vocabulary, and worried about what to leave out.

Howard collected the source material from a variety of Jewish texts, as well as from anecdotes and bibliographies, which became the backbone of my research. He also drew heavily on his personal experience. Some original material in this book came from a questionnaire we sent to people around the country, asking about their holiday and Shabbat observances. But even more information and ideas came from conversations with colleagues, teachers, and friends. We polled many rabbis, but also listened carefully to lay people—the people who we imagined as our readers, people with varied levels of Jewish knowledge who are interested in making more meaningful Jewish choices.

Chapter drafts were sent to a group of readers—experts and novices, rabbis and lay people. Their comments were invaluable, not only in terms of accuracy and erudition, but also in their sensitivity to language, nuance, and style. Without the careful, thoughtful input of Rabbi Herman Blumberg, Rabbi Devorah Jacobson, Cantor Riki Lippitz, and Rabbi John Schechter, this would be a very different book.

There were three people who read every single chapter, and who were extraordinarily generous with their time. Rabbi Neil Cooper (Howard's brother) was our "on-call" rabbi. Always available to clarify questions of Jewish law or custom, cite a verse, or check a source, Rabbi Cooper was both a source of support and of ballast. We depended on Leslie Tuttle, a student of Judaism who is now raising two Jewish children, to point out places that needed better definition or further amplification. Rabbi Barbara Penzner's contributions were practical, creative, spiritual, learned, loving, and always on target.

Many others read, criticized, and suggested changes in one or more chapters, including: Fran Addison and Rob Gogan, Marsha Feder, Rabbi Lawrence Kushner, Joan Kaye, Billy Mencow (also a great source of bibliographic information) Rabbi Nehemia Polen, Jenique Radin, Brian Rosman, Danny Siegel, Larry Sternberg, Rabbi Gerald Teller, Moshe Waldoks, and Jonathan Woocher.

The following people answered our questionnaire, made comments on specific chapters, engaged in helpful conversations, or provided other kinds of support during the research and writing of this book, for which we are most grateful: Velda Adams, Rabbi Lester Bronstein, Debra Cash, Betsy Cohen, Rabbi Richard Israel, Sherry Israel, Jay Fialkov, Lev Freidman, Rabbi Janice Garfunkel, Ora Gladstone and Mitchell Silver, Rabbi Stuart Weinberg Gershon, Karen Kushner, Maddy and Peter Langmann, Jeff Liberman and Joni Levy Liberman, Rabbi Norman Mendel, William Novak, Joel Rosenberg, Marion Ross, Arthur Samuelson, Ella Taylor, Craig Taubman, Scott Tepper, Betsy Platkin-Teutsch, William Whalen, Susan and Marty Wieskoff, the staff of Kolbo in Brookline, Massachusetts, and the office staff at Temple Emanuel in Worcester, Massachusetts. Carol Cohen, our editor at HarperCollins, was both wise and helpful.

Howard Cooper wishes to thank Rabbi Gerald Teller, a life-long teacher and mentor, and the man most responsible for his career as a Jewish educator. He also acknowledges the support of his father ("Who taught me that I could do anything I set my mind to, and to finish what I began."); his sister, Marsha Feder ("Who provides me with an on-going example of effective Jewish parenting."); his daughter, Hannah Evy ("In her eyes I see the bright light of the future, and the warm glow of the past."); and his wife Janet Sokoloff, ("My life-mate and friend, who held my hand, helped me clarify my thoughts, and has taught me so much about what it means to 'do Jewish.' ")

I would also like to thank my family and friends for their support and patience during the writing of this project, especially my husband, the one and only Jim Ball.

Finally, a word about Larry. Rabbi Lawrence Kushner of Beth El in Sudbury has had the most profound influence on both of us—as Jews and as people. His imagination and his erudition continue to inspire us to learn and to teach. He is the godfather of this book. And we thank him with love.

Anita Diamant

PREFACE

Dear Readers:

While I was writing this book, I kept you in mind. I thought a lot about who you might be, and why you might pick up this book, and what you needed from an introduction to Judaism. I did this because I wanted to write a book that you would be comfortable with, a book that you could really use.

Because my image of you guided the contents, the organization, and the tone of *Living a Jewish Life,* I think it's only fair to tell you who I think you are.

I think you are North American, and most likely a member of the baby-boom generation. I also think you have two children under the age of 5—and that children are not part of your life-plan. I think you went to Hebrew school as a kid and hated it—and that you grew up knowing you were Jewish but never belonged to a synagogue or any other Jewish organization. I think you cherish memories of your mother lighting candles every Friday night—and that you've never seen anyone do that in your whole life. I think you are interested in Judaism because the person you are in love with is Jewish—and that you have been a Jew-by-choice for many years. I think you are not Jewish at all but are raising a Jewish child with a Jewish spouse. I think you are the Christian grandparent of Jewish grandchildren.

I think you know not a single word of Hebrew—and that you can still read Hebrew from the days of preparation for your *bar* or *bat mitzvah.* I think you believe deeply in the existence of a Holy One— and that the question of religious faith is meaningless to you.

I think you are married and divorced, single and happy that way, straight and gay, active in the Jewish community and alienated from it.

I think you are intelligent, thoughtful, and genuinely interested in Judaism as a way of life. I think you are curious about how to make Jewish choices in ways that do not deny the importance of all the other parts of yourself and your world. I think you are eager to learn from tradition and confident of your own ability to interpret ancient sources and ways.

I think we have a lot in common.

I was born to Jewish parents, both Holocaust survivors, who gave me an undiluted and positive Jewish identity. Yet, I consider myself a "Jew-by-choice" and a relative newcomer to making Jewish choices.

It was not until I was nearly 30 years old and fell in love with a non-Jew that I realized how little I knew of my tradition and my heritage. So I joined a little Jewish reading group and discovered the vastness of the Jewish library. I wrote a few newspaper articles on the Jewish community, and learned how varied and vital a world that is. I started to light candles on Friday night and made a place for meaningful ritual in my life.

When my fiance decided to convert to Judaism, we found wonderful teachers and studied together. And we started making Jewish choices, a process that includes finding teachers as gifted and generous as Howard Cooper, my collaborator on this book, a process we continue day by day, year by year. Indeed, for me writing this book has been part of that process.

Living a Jewish Life is filled with choices that only you can make. Howard and I think of this book as a doorway, a threshold that is wide and inviting enough to welcome everyone who cares to enter into an exploration of living a Jewish life in these times. We hope you will find this a good place to begin. We hope you find a place for yourself inside.

Anita Diamant
August 1, 1990
10 Av 5750

For the modern Jew, observance is no longer a matter of "the all or the nothing." One only has to start. Nobody can tell where this beginning will lead.

Franz Roszenweig
(1886–1929)

Introduction

"To be a Jew in the 20th century is to be offered a gift," wrote the poet Muriel Rukeyser.

For most American Jews, accepting the gift means making choices—Jewish choices. It means figuring out how to be Jewish, and how Jewish to be. Opening this book and reading these words might constitute your first Jewish choice as an adult.

Your reasons for exploring Judaism are uniquely your own. Perhaps they have something to do with the desire for a more examined life, or the need to acknowledge spiritual or religious feelings. Maybe you are looking for an honest way to provide your children with an authentic sense of their place in a great religious, ethical, cultural, and ethnic tradition.

Whatever your motivation or background, the first goal of *Living a Jewish Life* is to open the door of that tradition to you; the second goal is to help you make your own Jewish choices.

Based on the experiences of contemporary American Jews, this book takes a descriptive rather than prescriptive approach to Judaism. The word "should" does not appear in these pages. Because Jews do things—everything—in many different ways, this book contains many menus: lists of choices about the hows, whens, and whys of modern Jewish life.*

Living a Jewish Life is an introduction to liberal Judaism, or more precisely, the broad range of religious practices of non-Orthodox North American Jews. The term *liberal* is used to describe people who identify themselves as Conservative, Reform, Reconstructionist, traditional/egalitarian, secular, humanist or New Age. What all these different kinds of people have in common is that their Jewishness is largely a matter of their own choice. In other words, they do not necessarily practice Judaism on God's authority or because their parents would be horrified if they didn't, but because they have found meaning and

* While the "menus" do include offerings from the cultures of Sephardic (Spanish, Mediterranean) Jews and the Jews of the Middle East, much of what appears in this book reflects the fact that the vast majority of American Jews are descended from Ashkenazic, or Eastern European, ancestors. Unless noted, customs described in this book derive from Ashkenazic sources.

strength and life in the gift that is Judaism. *Living a Jewish Life* is an expression and celebration of the diversity that comes from this choosing.

Although not a book of "do's and don'ts," *Living a Jewish Life* does have a point of view and an agenda of sorts—to encourage interested readers to make Jewish choices and to try some of the rituals, observances, and customs described in the following chapters to see how they feel and to explore what they can mean. Thus, *Living a Jewish Life* contains a great deal of practical information, complete with suggestions, instructions, and menus for everything from prayers to arts and crafts projects. However, the "how-to" materials are not presented as ends in themselves.

One of the hallmarks of liberal Judaism is its insistence on meaning, on considering the "why" of everything: Why light candles on Friday night? Why forego shrimp? Why get married under a canopy? Why join a synagogue?

For liberal Jews, answers to these questions are not fixed, but open, dynamic, and personal. The answers come from many sources: from the process of studying traditional Jewish texts, such as the Torah and the literature of Jewish law and imagination; from Jewish history; from discussion with teachers and peers; from a sense of God's presence; and from personal reflection and experimentation informed by the insights of psychology and feminism.

This is a "how-to" book that acknowledges the complexity and the difficulty of its premise. Making Jewish choices for the first time can feel awkward, even for people who were born Jewish. There is a sense that you ought to know Hebrew, and when Passover begins and what the Talmud is. Being uncomfortable in a synagogue or with the ritual of lighting Hannukah candles might seem to confirm the suspicion that you will never "get it," that you never will fit in.

Starting to "make Jewish choices" as an adult can be especially awkward for people who were not born Jewish. Jews-by-choice and non-Jews may not carry the same emotional baggage as those who are Jewish by birth, however, there is a greater danger of feeling overwhelmed by the sheer amount of history, customs, rituals, traditions and languages to be learned. And there is the fear that no matter how much you learn, you will never be comfortable or accepted.

Living a Jewish Life can help overcome the sense of inadequacy that virtually everyone feels when he or she begins to "do Jewish" as an adult. First of all, this book provides some essential Jewish vocabulary that is more than just a list of words to memorize, because living a Jewish life involves learning concepts contained in words that do not translate very well—words like *tzedakah*, which means "righteous giving," not "charity;" and *mitzvah*, which is not well served by a definition like "good deed" or "commandment." Shabbat, Torah, kosher, Reconstructionist: these and other terms are explained in the context of Jewish practice. Because—and this is the key—Judaism is not just a contemplative or abstract system of thought, but a blueprint for living fully and honorably in the world with other people.

Living a Jewish Life is divided into four sections: "Making Jewish Choices," "Home," "Community," and "Observance."

"Making Jewish Choices" takes a step back to explain some of the basic concepts and underlying assumptions of *Living a Jewish Life*. It starts with how "Liberal Judaism" is expounded in this book, with a discussion of how liberal Jews approach the idea of "Mitzvah," and some advice about "Starting." This is followed by some ideas about "Jewish Parenting," and a reassuring "Note about Hebrew."

Part Two, "Home," describes the physical, intellectual, and ritual elements that define the Jewish home, which is the heart of Jewish life. Part Three, "Community," introduces the range of agencies and institutions that support and complement Jewish home life, with information about how to find a niche in the community, through synagogues, educational institutions, and other kinds of organizations. The fourth and final section, "Observance," provides an overview of the Jewish calendar, the annual holiday cycle, and the events that celebrate the human life cycle.

While the book is arranged and written to be read as a whole, chapters are self-contained so they can be used in any order, according to the interests and needs of the reader. Each chapter includes an annotated list of books that the authors recommend for further reading, with entries for children wherever possible. You will also find marginal notes scattered throughout, quotes culled from a range of Jewish sources, grace notes to the text.

In order to make *Living a Jewish Life* as accessible as possible, Hebrew words and references have been kept to a minimum. Every non-English term used in this book is defined at least once in the text. However, because some terms are not translatable, and because the

Hebrew and some English words may be unfamiliar, both a glossary and index are provided for easy reference. Similarly, a timeline is included to provide both Jewish and secular reference points to dates and historical events mentioned in the text.

The Jews have often been called the Chosen People. They have also been called the Choosing People: The people who chose to establish and choose to maintain a relationship—a convenant—with God. Today, American Jews are accepting the gift that is Judaism, but instead of relegating it to a cupboard as though it were a delicate antique vase to be used only on special occasions, they are using it as they would a sturdy earthenware pitcher that is always on the table, sometimes taken for granted, but missed when misplaced. An everyday object. Necessary. Full.

---

from LETTER TO THE FRONT

To be a Jew in the twentieth century
Is to be offered a gift. If you refuse,
Wishing to be invisible, you choose
Death of the spirit, the stone insanity.
Accepting, take full life. Full agonies:
your evening deep in labryinthine blood
Of those who resist, fail, and resist: and God
Reduced to a hostage among hostages.

The gift is torment. Not alone the still
Torture, isolation; or torture of the flesh.
That may come also. But the accepting wish.
The whole and fertile spirit as guarantee
For every human freedom, suffering to be free,
Daring to live for the impossible.

Muriel Rukeyser, 1913—1980

Making Jewish Choices

This book is for people who are interested in making Jewish choices at many different levels of Jewish expertise. *Living a Jewish Life* contains definitions for people who are new to the fundamentals, and creative ideas to intrigue those who are at home with Jewish practice. Regardless of your level of expertise or particular interest, however, this chapter is most important because it explains and amplifies key terms and themes that are used throughout.

Liberal Judaism

There is no Jewish Vatican, no ultimate arbiter of Judaism. Ever since the destruction of the Temple in Jerusalem in 70 C.E.,* Jewish life has been changing, pluralistic, and contentious. Liberal Judaism is part of that venerable tradition of diversity.

But in truth, the term "liberal Judaism" pleases no one. For one thing, "liberal" is so strongly associated with politics and politicians. And "liberal Judaism" is extremely vague, indicating such a broad spectrum of beliefs, practices, and institutions that it is barely descriptive. "Liberal Judaism" is, however, the most widely recognized alternative to "non-Orthodox Judaism," which is even less palatable: a self-

* Jews use C.E., (Common Era), and B.C.E. (Before the Common Era) rather than the designations A.D. and B.C., which refer to the divinity of Jesus (Anno Domini means "in the year of our Lord.")

abnegating term, a definition in opposition to something rather than in affirmation of anything.

In fact, it is easier to define liberal Judaism in terms of what it is not because it is so dynamic, so responsive to the present, so multiform. It is not static or rigid enough to describe categorically, so it is impossible to honestly complete any sentence that begins, "Liberal Jews believe that God is. . . ." or "Liberal Jews observe the Sabbath by. . . ." The use of the word "menu" in this book is not intended to be cute; it expresses the crucial element of liberal Judaism, which is choice.

Liberal Judaism is some 200 years old, which in the context of Jewish time is relatively young. Before the late 18th century, virtually all Jews experienced birth, education, marriage, family, work, recreation, worship, and death, mediated by Jewish law and custom. The non-Jewish world perceived of and treated Jews not as individuals, but in accordance with prevailing attitudes, laws, and prejudices.

That reality was fundamentally transformed by the Enlightenment —a cluster of 18th century philosophical propositions and political movements that challenged previously accepted ideas and institutions with their belief in individual liberty, equality, democracy, and rationalism. The Jewish world responded to the radical changes in secular society with its own Enlightenment, called the *Haskalah*.

The doors to the ghettos and the great universities of Europe were unlocked. Jewish men shaved their beards; Jewish women removed their traditional head coverings. More Jews worked and even socialized with Christians. But alternatives to an all-encompassing Jewish lifestyle were limited: Jews could abandon their traditions altogether and convert to Christianity, or they could try to live a kind of double life, an existence that Jewish reformers of the time described as, "Jews at home, but men (like all others) on the street."[1]

A few generations later, life in America and the drive to assimilate pushed this paradigm much further; one was a Jew precisely the way the neighbors were Presbyterian. What had once been an all-embracing view of life shrank to nominal affiliation with a once-in-a-while or once-a-year observance and a general lack of interest in—and often discomfort with—Judaism. In other words, one was a Jew on the street but a man or woman at home. For several generations, this was the model of liberal Judaism, which was by and large equated with choosing to do as little as possible, or nothing at all; to abstain totally from traditional Jewish practice.

Since the 1960s, liberal Judaism has begun to forge a new synthesis of tradition and modernity, identity and practice, which allows for an encompassing yet flexible Jewish consciousness. Thus, liberal Jews, fully at home in the secular world and participating in every aspect of public life and culture as equals and as leaders, also light candles on Friday nights, study Jewish books, and belong to Jewish institutions. From this integrated perspective, there are Jewish dimensions to many of the seemingly value-neutral choices of daily life: everything from donating blood to planning vacations, from deciding how much to give the United Way campaign to ordering lunch, becomes a Jewish decision.

Less is no longer more. Increasingly, contemporary liberal Judaism is embracing once-rejected traditional customs and rituals at home, in synagogues and in other institutions. Often they are reimagined, reinterpreted, and reconstructed to reflect the powerful insights of the present, particularly those of psychology and feminism, which have challenged and invigorated virtually every aspect of modern Jewish life. Liberal Judaism is, in fact, busy creating new traditions, customs, and rituals; finding new words for old wisdom.

Liberal Judaism—expressed in Reform, Conservative, Reconstructionist, or alternative settings—can be a rich and engrossing way of life, although not necessarily an easy one. It is, for example, not as straightforward as Orthodoxy, which mandates behavior according to clearly defined laws and traditions.* Liberal Judaism demands choice at every turn, and requires a degree of self-consciousness that does not appeal to everyone. But for those who feel intellectually, communally, and spiritually nurtured and fulfilled by the dialectic—the tension and resolution—of making Jewish choices, it is "a tree of life."

---

* The scope of this book is liberal Jewish practice. The absence of discussion about Orthodox Judaism and why some people choose to embrace a much more traditional lifestyle is not intended as an insult or slight. For those interested in exploring Orthodoxy, there are outreach programs and workshops run by various synagogues and organizations. *To Be a Jew* by Rabbi Hayyim Donin (Basic Books, 1972) articulates an Orthodox approach to Jewish practice.

Mitzvah

"Making Jewish choices" is traditionally expressed in the concept and execution of *mitzvot,* the plural of *mitzvah.* The word *mitzvah* does not translate well. It derives from a military term for "command," and it is often translated as "good deed." But Jews don't perform *mitzvot* like so many good Scouts. A *mitzvah* is a commandment from God, but a command that exists only when put into action by people. A *mitzvah* is an idea that is given form. It is value-action—praxis.

Obviously, the word "commandment" immediately raises the essential theological question. Because a commandment implies a Commander, the whole notion of *mitzvah* seems to rest on the existence of God—on a God who gives orders. For Jews who believe the Bible was divinely revealed, the authority of *mitzvot* is unassailable; God commands, so people must obey. From an Orthodox perspective, all *mitzvot* mentioned in the Torah are binding.*

Liberal Jews, for whom the authority of the Bible does not necessarily reside in the idea of divine authorship, tend to emphasize the fact that *mitzvot* are subject to human response—to a sense of being commanded or directed—and thus to human interpretation.

> Moses asks God to explain the laws for keeping kosher:
> "THOU SHALT NOT SEETHE A KID IN ITS MOTHER'S MILK."
> "Does that mean we should have two sets of dishes?"
> "THOU SHALT NOT SEETHE A KID IN ITS MOTHER'S MILK."
> "Does that mean that we should wait six hours between eating milk and
>   meat?"
> "THOU SHALT NOT SEETHE A KID IN ITS MOTHER'S MILK."
> "Does that mean we should check the label of everything we buy and use
>   only those items made with pure vegetable shortening?"
> "THOU SHALT NOT SEETHE A KID IN ITS MOTHER'S MILK."
> "Does that mean . . ."
> "OKAY, HAVE IT YOUR WAY!"[2]

Some of the *mitzvot* elaborated in this book include: lighting candles on Friday night, giving money to the poor, refraining from eating pork and shellfish, entering sons into Jewish life through the covenant of circumcision, teaching children the story of Passover, and treating the dead with the utmost respect.

---

* However, the opportunity to perform some of them (e.g., the commandments related to the rituals in the ancient Temple in Jerusalem) is not available.

For liberal Jews, not all *mitzvot* have the same weight because not all *mitzvot* provoke the sense of feeling commanded. As one rabbi has written, "There will be *mitzvot* through which my forebears found themselves capable of responding to the commanding God which are no longer adequate or possible for me, just as there will be new *mitzvot* through which I or my generation will be able to respond which my ancestors never thought of."[3] Indeed, for liberal Jews, the increasingly complex modern world may suggest new and binding *mitzvot* regarding everything from the proper application of medical technology for the terminally ill to the ecological imperative to recycle.

Because each *mitzvah* is the occasion for reflection and choice, liberal Jews take on *mitzvot* for many reasons. For some, there is a compelling argument in following a particular discipline simply because it has been and remains a part of Jewish identity. Many commit themselves to fulfilling *mitzvot* that are consistent with a personal sense of right and wrong, such as giving to the poor and working to fulfill the prophetic call for justice. Some find *mitzvot* a way of maintaining a relationship with what is holy in life: "While I have and retain the freedom of choosing my specific means of response at a given moment, the essential fact of my life will be my intention to respond [to God through *mitzvot*]."[4]

The Hasidic masters discerned a relationship between the Hebrew *mitzvah* and a similar Aramaic word that meant "together."[5] Thus, a *mitzvah* can be thought of as an act that unites people, and as an act that unites people with God. Doing *mitzvot* can knit together the dichotomy between holy and profane. Doing *mitzvot* can be a way to discover the sacred in the mundane.

In whatever way the idea of *mitzvah* is understood, and for whatever reason a *mitzvah* is undertaken, the concept defies the rationalist, Western approach to the world, which posits that understanding should always precede action. (In other words, we tend not to open doors until we know what is behind them.) Doing *mitzvot* requires setting aside that world view. In the Bible, when the Israelites are given the Torah, their response was, "We shall do and we shall hear."[6] In other words, they promised to act first, and hear (or understand) second. To leap before looking.

The logic to, benefits from, and understanding of *mitzvot* may be compared with human experiences that are endlessly described but ultimately available only through living. Such as making love. Such as becoming a parent. Or burying your own parents. Doing *mitzvot* is how you experience and practice Judaism, how you "do Jewish."

Starting

It is helpful to think about beginning to make Jewish choices the same way you approach any life-altering, life-enhancing discipline, such as taking up an exercise regimen, changing your eating habits, learning to play a musical instrument, or studying a new language. In other words, you need forethought and patience.

Especially patience. Without patience for the beginner's inevitable awkwardness—whether at the piano, on the tennis court, or in the synagogue—there can be no mastery of any new art, game, or language. Starting to make Jewish choices requires a suspension of the kind of standards (for competence if not excellence) to which many adults hold themselves. You must allow yourself to learn as a small child learns: without grades, deadlines, or too many expectations.

However, as an adult, impatience is inevitable. And, as with any discipline, there are times when the rewards just do not seem worth the effort. Sometimes you just don't feel like jogging. Sometimes you really want sour cream and butter on your baked potato. Sometimes, the last thing in the world you want to do is leave the warmth of home for Friday night services.

The rewards of Jewish living are a little more difficult to measure or explain than dieting or jogging. For one thing, there is little support for liberal religious practice in American culture. Indeed, in a society that celebrates immediate gratification, many Jewish choices seem downright countercultural. By choosing them, you declare yourself to be at least one step outside mainstream American culture. In some cases, it is relatively easy to explain that step. For example, most people—Jews and non-Jews—immediately understand the idea of preserving one day every week for rest and family. It is much more of a challenge trying to explain that you don't eat lobster or beef stroganoff because that's what Jews have done for centuries, or because it is a way of reminding you of your own Jewishness.

But even with as familiar and appealing an idea as the Sabbath, when you try to explain that *Shabbat* is sacrosanct to you (with no exceptions for basketball games or theater tickets) even supportive friends and family members can become suspicious or defensive: What are you? Some kind of fundamentalist kook? Besides, if you're too Jewish to go out with me on Friday night, why are you eating that cheeseburger? Do you think you're better than me because I don't light candles on Friday night?

Because liberal Jews tend to undertake *mitzvot* only when they can be done honestly, willingly, and not strictly by rote, there may be apparent inconsistencies in practice: not everyone who lights candles on Friday night maintains a kosher home; not everyone who keeps kosher goes to synagogue services, and so forth. Configurations of *mitzvot* vary enormously, and sometimes change. Over the course of a lifetime, practices that seemed alien sometimes become deeply meaningful, whereas others that were once very important are later abandoned.

Liberal Judaism's response to the *mitzvot* is neither automatic or defensive, but personal and open-ended. At the heart of exploring Jewish choices is the sense that, "This is how I do Judaism. It's not that my way is the only way or the 'right' way. But it is my Jewish way—for now."

Jewish Parenting

Many people do not begin to make serious Jewish choices until they become parents. Then, the question "What are we handing on to our children?" becomes a primary motivation for exploring Jewish questions: from selecting a religious education to figuring out how to impart a sense of Jewish identity. Although *Living a Jewish Life* is not a book only for parents, it addresses the concerns and needs of adults who are facing these questions. And although this book is non-prescriptive, it does reflect one basic pedagogic truism: children learn the most from their own parents.

The essential goal for Jewish parents through the ages has always been to raise a child to be a *mensch*. Taken literally, *mensch* is Yiddish for "person"; figuratively, a person who cares and shares, loves and studies, and acts righteously in the world. Just as it is difficult for children to grow up as *menschen* (the plural of *mensch*) without *menschen* for parents, children rarely learn to cherish their Jewishness without witnessing their parents' commitment to Judaism.

No child learns to make Jewish choices in after-school programs or even at a full-time Jewish day school, if Judaism has nothing to do with the life of the family. Jewish identity cannot be entirely learned in a classroom because Jewishness is not simply a function of the intellect; it is an expression of heart and soul, and also of the psyche and senses.

To raise children who will care about their Jewishness, parents need to establish their own relationship to Judaism in ways that stimulate and satisfy them as adults. (And this is equally true for families where both parents are Jews and interfaith families where the non-Jewish parent is committed to raising Jewish children.) Parents often begin incorporating Jewish choices into family life by lighting candles on Friday night, or by joining a synagogue, or by celebrating holidays "for the children." If those practices remain essentially meaningless to the adults, children will see that Judaism is merely a matter of going through motions. If, however, those rituals and commitments that were originally undertaken "for the children" become important and fulfilling for parents, children will learn their Judaism as naturally as they learn their native language.

One of the great discoveries of parenthood is how much children can teach adults about life, time, joy, and tenderness. American Jews are often unfamiliar and uncomfortable with the gestures of ritual, such as lighting candles and singing in public. Kids, however, are experts at learning through pretending and can make it much easier for adults to suspend their disbelief in the "magic" element of rituals, and make the leap to non-utilitarian language and actions. "Playing *Shabbat*" may be the best way to approach experimenting with Sabbath customs and rituals.

Raising Jewish children also means adding a whole new set of goals to the list shared by all parents (good grades, good manners, and so on). In two-parent families, Jewish parenting requires agreement on a long list of choices that may include the selection of a Jewish name for a new baby, or looking for a house in a neighborhood that is reasonably close to a synagogue and where there will be other Jewish children to play with yours. Jewish parenting also means making decisions that may not be entirely popular with kids: like no television on Friday night, or the decision that religious school takes precedence over soccer practice. And these mean Jewish conflict.

Because children grow up to make their own decisions, perhaps the most important task for parents is to give children practice at making Jewish choices: appropriate to their age, of course. Youngsters can be asked *how* they would like to participate in Friday night rituals: by setting the table, by singing, by saying a blessing, by drawing a picture. Older children can be included in family decisions about where to send charitable contributions. A child who announces he does not want to attend services with the rest of the family might be offered some alternatives for those hours, such as reading a Jewish book, babysitting for pre-schoolers whose parents are attending services, or doing volunteer work during those hours. In other words, the options presented require a Jewish choice.

At the birth of a baby, Jews have always prayed that their sons and daughters grow up not to "be Jewish" but to "do Jewish" in three particular ways: "May he/she grow up to a life of *huppah*, Torah, *ma'asim tovim.*" The Hebrew words refer to marriage under the Jewish wedding canopy, love and respect for Jewish learning, and acts of righteousness. In order to see that prayer becomes a reality in the 21st century, parents are exploring and experimenting with Jewish observance in ways that are described in this book.

A Note About Hebrew

Hebrew is the language of the Torah, the prayerbook, the Passover *haggadah*, and the land of Israel. Although it is not the only Jewish language,* it is the universal and sacred language of Judaism. The ma-

---

* In addition to Hebrew, there are three other languages written with the Hebrew *alef-bet* (alphabet), that are part of Jewish history and culture: *Aramaic* is an ancient Semitic language, the language of the Talmud, and also Jesus' spoken tongue; *Yiddish,* a combination of Hebrew, German, and words borrowed from other languages, is still spoken by Jews of Eastern European descent (Ashkenazic); *Ladino,* a combination of Hebrew and Spanish, is still spoken among Jews of Mediterranean (Sephardic) background. Both Yiddish and Ladino have a rich literature that includes poetry, lyrics, prayers, and fiction.

jority of American Jews cannot read or speak Hebrew, which makes many people feel not only illiterate (a kind of powerlessness in itself) but also inauthentic as Jews.

In one sense, Hebrew is not essential. Almost all commonly-used Hebrew texts and prayers are available in good English translations. And, of course, any home ceremony can be performed entirely in English. (It goes without saying that God understands.) If you do not know any Hebrew but want to incorporate its sound and flavor into home observances, most prayers are transliterated (the Hebrew sounds spelled out in the Latin alphabet) and available on audio tape.

Although Hebrew is not "required," learning its alphabet, vocabulary and grammar is a way of experiencing Jewish empowerment. And as every bilingual person can testify, something always gets lost in translations. Which is why basic Hebrew courses are so popular.

Outside of spending some time in Israel, the best way to learn spoken Hebrew is by attending an *ulpan,* the intensive Hebrew language instruction course developed for immigrants to Israel. If, however, your main interest in Hebrew revolves around synagogue practice and ritual observances, adults can learn Hebrew as an access language—for reading purposes only—with a modest commitment of time in a weekly or biweekly classes. Many people learn by following along with their children's Hebrew lessons.

Synagogue and community center adult education programs offer prayerbook Hebrew courses on a regular basis. To learn spoken Hebrew

---

1.
How difficult for me is Hebrew:
even the Hebrew for mother, for bread, for sun
is foreign. How far have I been exiled, Zion.

2.
What are you doing in our street among the automobiles, horse?
How are your cousins, the centaur and the unicorn.[7]

Charles Reznikoff, © *1976*

(which will also make prayerbook Hebrew accessible) check Jewish community centers and local colleges.

FURTHER READING

Contemporary Jewish Religious Thought, edited by Arthur A. Cohen and Paul Mendes-Flohr (Charles Scribner's Sons, 1987) A collection of fascinating and very brief essays on a wide range of subjects, from "Aesthetics" to "Mitzvah" to "Zionism."

The Book of Letters by Lawrence Kushner (Jewish Lights Publishing, Woodstock, VT, 1990) An introduction to the Hebrew alphabet, the tradition of Jewish scribal arts, and the imaginative and mystical possibilities of each letter.

Teach Yourself to Read Hebrew by Simon & Anderson (EKS Publishers, Oakland CA, 1985). Written for adults, it lives up to its title.

Home

The Jewish home has been called a *mikdash ma'at*, a little sanctuary. It is an evocative image. From the moment you walk through the doorway of a sanctuary, you know you are entering a place that defies the idea that space is always neutral.

A sanctuary looks different from other places. It is defined and ornamented by ritual objects, books, and art. A sanctuary feels different from the workplace and the marketplace. In a sanctuary, the mundane criteria for success and failure fall away. What matters is not what you do but who you are.

A sanctuary is a place of safety and asylum. It is where the dispossessed go for shelter, where the hungry go for food, where the weary find rest. Sanctuaries are filled with voices, sometimes singing in unison, sometimes raised in disagreement. And sometimes, a sanctuary is as still as a garden.

Today, when many American families feature two wage-earners and a constant juggling of roles, needs, and schedules, making a home into a sanctuary seems more difficult than ever—and more important. The tools for making a home into a *mikdash ma'at* are the *mitzvot* described in the following pages.

"A Little Sanctuary" elaborates the Jewish vision of the peaceful home as a place of hospitality and beauty. "*Shabbat*—The Sabbath" is an introduction both to Judaism's core insight and to creating a personal and family day of rest. "Good Deeds" explains the Jewish view of charity and social justice, and how they can be incorporated into daily life. "The People of the Library" is divided into two sections: the first defines and explains some of the major Jewish texts, such as the Bible, Torah, Talmud, and Midrash; the second contains suggestions for building a home library. "What Jews Eat" explains the Jewish dietary

Behold, how good and how pleasant it is, when people live together as one.
Psalm 133

laws and their contemporary relevance and practice. Finally, "Travelling Jewish" discusses the portability of the insights and practices of the Jewish home.

No sanctuary is perpetually filled with all the beauty or meaning it might contain. No home is ever fully or finally a sanctuary. But the on-going process of making Jewish choices is what makes a home into a *mikdash ma'at*, a little sanctuary, an island of peace, a safe harbor, a beautiful Jewish place.

A Little Sanctuary

With the destruction of the Second Temple in Jerusalem in 70 C.E., the focus of Jewish religious and ritual life had to change. The Jewish home became the new center of Judaism. But this little sanctuary—this *mikdash ma'at* —is not a museum for vestigial rituals and ceremonies. It is home, the place where basic human needs are expressed and met. According to the Jewish paradigm, home is the primary source of identity and education, as well as affection, recognition, and sexual fulfillment. This chapter introduces a few of the fundamental ideas-in-action, or *mitzvot*, that Jews traditionally have considered essential to making a home into a little sanctuary: peace, hospitality, beauty, and the *mezuzah*.

Peace at Home

One of the primary reasons for adding a consistent Jewish dimension to family life is to create opportunities for sharing moments of peace. The Hebrew name for the goal of a "peaceful home" is *shalom bayit*.

In these times, family peace and harmony are the province of psychologists and counselors, who regularly prescribe that couples and families under stress make appointments to share relaxed time, to talk, even to have fun. Furthermore, all sorts of experts have written about the importance of rituals to children. Morning and bedtime routines, annual holiday celebrations—these are powerful and positive ways of grounding and reassuring kids about the predictability of the world and their place in it. At its best, sharing family life in Jewish ways is a technique for making peace.

Jewish tradition has always been quite explicit about the duties and obligations of family life. These are not meant to impose an external order on individuals and families, but rather are a guide to creating *shalom bayit*. The Jewish laws on family matters go into great detail and extend into the most intimate aspects of life. In matters of sexuality, for example, the rabbis codified the rights of women, making it clear that wives could expect their sexual needs to be met, and that husbands could not force physical attentions on unwilling wives. Family violence of any kind is condemned in the traditional sources. Indeed, many of the rabbis even frowned on disciplinary spanking.

The biblical call to honor parents, *kibbud av v'em,* was elaborated into a web of intergenerational obligations. Whereas it is a child's duty to behave respectfully to elders, parents are responsible for educating their children, and not only in religious matters. For example, the Talmud tells parents that they should teach their children how to swim as well as how to read.

The Sabbath or *Shabbat* has always been and continues to be the basic building block of family peace. Creating a restful island of time—turning off the television and turning to one another—is not just a nice family custom. It can actually prevent injury from the wear and tear of the week. It can heal wounds that were not even apparent.

I am a father. I have a daughter and I love her dearly. I would like my daughter to obey the commandments of the Torah; I would like her to revere me as her father. And so I ask myself the question over and over again: what is there about me that deserves the reverence of my daughter?

You see, unless I live a life that is worthy of her reverence, I make it almost impossible for her to live a Jewish life. So many young people abandon Judaism because the Jewish models that they see in their parents are not worthy of reverence.

My message to parents is: every day ask yourselves the question: "What is there about me that deserves the reverence of my child?"

Rabbi Abraham Joshua Heschel, 1907–1972

The peace of the house is really the health of the house. Traditionally, on *Yom Kippur,* the Day of Atonement, family members turn to each other and apologize for their hurtful words and thoughtless actions of the previous year. Today, the concept of *shalom bayit* can be extended to include support for family therapy and other forms of counseling whenever it is needed.

However, the concept of family peace or *shalom bayit* is *not* a call for seriousness. The idea expressed in the Hebrew word *shalom* is not the same as that of the Latin *pax,* from which the English "peace" derives. *Pax* means "quiet." *Shalom* comes from the root *shalem,* which means "complete" or "whole." *Shalom bayit* is not a quiet home, but a whole one. Quiet, somber observances miss the point. Laughter and foolishness are pretty good indicators of family harmony. With very few exceptions, the goal of Jewish observance is to open people to the experience of joy—in Hebrew, *simcha.* In one family, *Shabbat* is greeted with a top-of-the-lungs cheer: "Gimme an S. Gimme an H. Gimme an A. Gimme a B. . . ."

Hospitality

In every neighborhood, there is one house where children know they are always welcome to play. These are households where it seems that the couch is forever being made up for an out-of-town visitor. And these are homes where it just isn't Friday night without guests at the table. Children who grow up in these homes learn the challenging pleasures of serving and sharing, and the joys of offering hospitality.

For Jews, hospitality is not simply a matter of good manners; it is a moral institution. Judaism defines hospitality as a sacred obligation; it is the *mitzvah* called *hachnasat orchim,* literally, "the bringing in of guests." The patriarch Abraham is the biblical exemplar of hospitality; it was said that he kept his tent open on all four sides so that strangers would always know they were welcome. In the desert, of course, the offer of water, food, and a place to sleep could be a life-saving act.

In the Middle Ages, Jewish communities ran charitable associations that provided meals and shelter for Jewish travelers who were unwelcome, if not in danger, in the non-Jewish world. Likewise, it was considered a special honor to provide a bed and meal for scholars studying at a *yeshiva,* an academy of Jewish learning.

In the small communities and tight-knit ghettos of the past, everyone knew which families could be counted on to make room for one more guest, and these people were considered praiseworthy and holy. There is a rich folk literature about poor folk who, because they provided shelter and a crust of bread to a stranger, were rewarded with great wealth. The prophet Elijah, the legendary harbinger of the messiah, is often portrayed as a beggar in search of a meal and a place to sleep, testing the practical morality of the Jews he encounters.

Today, hospitality tends to be the work of institutions. Jewish organizations provide help to newcomers to town, to Soviet immigrants, and to college students. However, there are still many opportunities for individuals to perform the *mitzvah* of hospitality for strangers. For example, volunteering at a shelter for the homeless can be seen as an extension of *hachnasat orchim*—as can helping to settle a Soviet Jewish family, or inviting students from a local college or university for a Friday night meal or a Passover *seder.*

Beauty and Holiness

Home decoration is part of all known human cultures. But Judaism's tendency to blur the distinctions between sacred and secular, and its definition of the home as a holy place suggests a special set of aesthetic considerations. Displaying Jewish art in a home or office is an act of identification and connection. Shopping for ritual objects and artwork can be a way of exploring Jewish identity, a way of deciding how to express Jewishness in concrete terms.

There is a long tradition of Jewish art, based both in custom and

---

Hospitality is more important even than encountering God's Intimate Presence.

Talmud: Shabbat 127a

religious tradition. According to the rabbinic principle of *hiddur mitzvah*, when a physical object is needed to fulfill a commandment, the object should be made as beautiful as possible. Thus, while it is perfectly alright to make a blessing over wine in a paper cup, it is even better to use a beautiful goblet especially created for that purpose. Over the centuries, Jewish artists and artisans fashioned ritual objects not only for large synagogues, but also for the homes of ordinary Jews. Embroidered and brocade cloths have covered loaves of *challah* used in weekly Sabbath home rituals as well as synagogue Torah scrolls.

Generally speaking, there are two kinds of Jewish decoration for the home: ritual objects and works of art.

Ritual objects have a religious as well as purely decorative function. They include: the *mezuzah* (a small container affixed to the doorposts of a home containing a piece of parchment inscribed with biblical text); the *hannukiah* (the candelabra or *menorah* used at Hannukah); Passover *seder* plates; candlesticks used for *Shabbat* and holidays; and special goblets for blessing wine *(kiddush)*.

Some families use ritual objects as decorative elements, for example, displaying the family *hannukiah* year-round, or framing the *challah* cover grandma embroidered in the old country. Some people collect and display spice boxes or the elaborate braided candles used for *havdalah,* the ceremony that marks the end of the Sabbath.

The presence of ritual objects in a home, though not necessarily a sign of observance, acknowledges the religious and ritual aspects of Judaism. A *mezuzah* on the door, no matter how beautiful in its own right, says more than "this family enjoys lovely things." It is a sign and a symbol of identification.

Jewish works of art are more difficult to categorize and far more varied than ritual objects, and include everything from fine art photographs of Israel to framed examples of Hebrew and English calligraphy, from coffee table art books and illustrated calendars to fine oils, lithographs, and sculpture. Although the works of Marc Chagall, Ben Shahn, Chaim Gross, and others have been identified as "Jewish art," many other Jewish artists produce work that would never be labeled "Jewish." On the other hand, works on a theme from the Hebrew Bible might be considered Jewish art, regardless of the artist's religion.

And of course, Jewish art exists in the eye of the beholder. Some pieces might be immediately identified as Jewish, e.g., a painting of Moses. However, an abstract rendering of the creation story may appear like nothing but a pleasing collection of shapes and colors to a guest unless you choose to explain your understanding of it. Perhaps the best definition of Jewish art is that which engages the viewer not only on an aesthetic level, but also in particularly Jewish emotional, intellectual, or spiritual ways.

There is a large and growing selection of Jewish art created especially for children, including special *mezuzot* (plural of *mezuzah*) decorated with kites and Teddy bears, mobiles that feature Jewish symbols, and posters of the Hebrew alphabet illustrated with bright, funny pictures. Children can help create their own Jewish ambiance by being permitted to buy a poster, or by having one of their own Jewish drawings or paintings framed and hung.

The *Mezuzah*

The little box or cylinder affixed to the doorways of Jewish homes is a clue, a reminder, a sign of welcome, a decoration, an amulet, and a sentry box. The practice of hanging *mezuzot* on the doorposts of Jewish homes dates back to biblical time and they have been used virtually everywhere Jews have lived ever since. These ubiquitous objects have been assigned many meanings: they are reminders of God's presence, reminders for peace, a way of marking the difference between Jewish and non-Jewish space, a signal that Jews live there, an opportunity for *hiddur mitzvah* and a good-luck charm.

Inside the container is a piece of parchment, called a *klaf,* containing the biblical reference to *mezuzah,* which means "doorpost." The words come from the book of Deuteronomy: "Write these words upon the doorposts of your house and on your gates." Also written on the parchment is the *Shema,* the proclamation of God's oneness, and biblical verses which follow it in the prayerbook: [1]

> Listen, Israel, Adonai the Eternal, Adonai is One
> You shall love your God with all your heart, with all your soul, and with all your might. And these words, which I command you

this day, shall be upon your heart. You shall teach them diligently to your children, and shall speak of them when you sit in your home, when you walk by the way, when you lie down, and when you rise up. You shall bind them for a sign upon your hand, and they shall be for frontlets between your eyes. You shall write them upon the doorposts of your home and upon your gates.

And it will come to pass, if you will listen diligently to My commandments which I command you this day, to love your God and to serve Me with all your heart and with all your soul, that I will bring rain to the land in its season, rain in autumn and rain in spring and harvest rich in grain and wine and oil. And there will be grass in the fields for the cattle and abundant food to eat. But you must take care not to be lured away to serve gods of luxury and fashion, turning away from Me. For I will turn My face from you, and I will close the heavens and hold back the rain and the earth will bear no fruit and you will soon perish from the good land that I am giving you. Therefore impress My words upon your heart and upon your soul; bind them as a sign upon your hand and let them serve as frontlets between your eyes. Teach them to your children and talk about them when you are at home and when you are away, in the evening and the morning. Write them on the doorposts of your home and upon your gates. Then will your days be multiplied, and the days of your children, upon the land which I promised to give to your ancestors, as the days of the heavens above the earth.

Mezuzot and their scrolls are sold, usually separately, by Judaica shops and Jewish bookstores, and through mail-order companies. According to tradition, the scrolls are written by a *sofer*, a trained scribe. Thus, the parchment may cost as much as the *mezuzah* case.

Why do we affix the mezuzah to the doorposts of rooms within rooms? This is necessary so that no one should think that only in public must one avoid doing wrong.

Moses Alshekh, 16th century Safed

According to tradition, *mezuzot* are hung not only on the front door of a home, but on every doorpost inside, except for doors to closets and bathrooms. A *mezuzah* is affixed on the right-hand side of a door (as you enter), at eye level, on the upper third of the doorway. It is hung at an angle, with the top facing in toward the house or room. Two simple blessings mark the occasion:

בָּרוּךְ אַתָּה, יְיָ אֱלֹהֵינוּ, מֶלֶךְ הָעוֹלָם, אֲשֶׁר קִדְּשָׁנוּ בְּמִצְוֹתָיו וְצִוָּנוּ לִקְבּוֹעַ מְזוּזָה.

Baruch ata Adonai Eloheynu Melech Ha-olam asher kid'shanu be-mitzvotav vitzivanu likboa mezuzah.

Blessed be the Eternal One, Source of Life, by Whose power we sanctify life with the *mitzvah* of affixing this *mezuzah*.

בָּרוּךְ אַתָּה, יְיָ אֱלֹהֵינוּ, מֶלֶךְ הָעוֹלָם, שֶׁהֶחֱיָנוּ וְקִיְּמָנוּ וְהִגִּיעָנוּ לַזְּמַן הַזֶּה.

Baruch ata Adonai Eloheynu Melech Ha-olam
sheheheyanu v'key'manu v'higianu laman hazeh.

Blessed be the Eternal One, Source of Life, Who has given us life, helped us to grow, and enabled us to reach this moment.

(affix *mezuzah*)

Some Jews celebrate the hanging of a *mezuzah* with a brief ceremony called *Hanukat Habayit*, "dedication of the home." *Mezuzot* are usually hung within 30 days of moving into a new house, but any occasion—a newly renovated attic, or even the purchase of a new *mezuzah* for a "naked" doorway—can be an excuse for gathering friends and family for a little celebration.

Hanukat Habayit—Dedication of a Home
adapted by Rabbi Barbara R. Penzner

We face the Eternal every moment we live.
We stand before God in every action we take.

The presence of the Holy One fills the whole world.
There is no place in the heavens or the earth that is not touched by holiness.

If we but open our eyes we would recognize that the gateway to fulfillment is wherever we stand. It is to open our eyes to the holiness everywhere about us and within us that we perform the *mitzvah* of *mezuzah*.

We place the *mezuzah* on the gateway to our home, to remind us of the Holy when we enter and when we leave.

"Blessed shall you be in your comings and blessed shall you be in your goings."

Love Adonai with all your heart, with all your soul, with all your might. Take this teaching to heart. Transmit it to your children. Recite it at home and away, morning and night. Bind it upon your hands that your deeds be just. Keep it ever before your eyes that your vision to daring and true. Inscribe it upon the doorposts of your homes and upon your gates, that your going out and your coming in be for peace.[2]

(*Challah* is passed around)

When the Temple in Jerusalem was destroyed twenty-five hundred years ago, the rabbis ordained that the Jewish home would replace the Temple. It would become a *mikdash ma'at,* a little sanctuary, and our table would be the altar, our bread and salt the sacrifice and every meal a holy occasion.

בָּרוּךְ אַתָּה, יְיָ אֱלֹהֵינוּ, מֶלֶךְ הָעוֹלָם, הַמּוֹצִיא לֶחֶם מִן־הָאָרֶץ:

Baruch ata Adonai Eloheynu Melech Ha-olam hamotzi lechem min ha'aretz.

Blessed be the Eternal One, Source of life, Who brings forth bread from the earth.[3]

(Holding the *mezuzah,* members of the household say:)
May our house be a place of holiness, by welcoming guests, *hachnasat orchim,* in the bonds of family, with deeds of loving kindness, gifts of *tzedakah,* and words of Torah.

בָּרוּךְ אַתָּה, יְיָ אֱלֹהֵינוּ, מֶלֶךְ הָעוֹלָם, אֲשֶׁר קִדְּשָׁנוּ בְּמִצְוֹתָיו וְצִוָּנוּ לִקְבּוֹעַ מְזוּזָה.

Baruch ata Adonai Eloheynu Melech Ha-olam asher kid'shanu be-mitzvotav vitzivanu likboa mezuzah.

Blessed be the Eternal One, Source of Life, by Whose power we sanctify life with the *mitzvah* of affixing this *mezuzah*.

בָּרוּךְ אַתָּה, יְיָ אֱלֹהֵינוּ, מֶלֶךְ הָעוֹלָם, שֶׁהֶחֱיָנוּ וְקִיְּמָנוּ וְהִגִּיעָנוּ לַזְּמַן הַזֶּה.

Baruch ata Adonai Eloheynu Melech Ha-olam
sheheheyanu v'key'manu v'higianu laman hazeh.

Blessed be the Eternal One, Source of Life, Who has given us life, helped us to grow, and enabled us to reach this moment.

(affix *mezuzah*)

Bruchim Ha'ba'im.
May all who enter be blessed.

FURTHER READING

Abram Kanof, *Jewish Ceremonial Art and Religious Observance* (Harry N. Abrams). A lushly illustrated history of ritual objects.

Shabbat—The Sabbath

We all have moments when the perfection of the world is revealed to us. A walk on the beach. A spectacular sunset. Our lover's eyes. A sleeping child. Sometimes, these moments take us by surprise, like rainbows. Sometimes, we engineer them: we plan vacations in the mountains, or tiptoe into the baby's room.

Shabbat is the way Jews arrange their lives to stay in touch with what is perfect in the world on a regular basis. It is Judaism's essential insight, its backbone, its methodology.

Shabbat, the Hebrew word for Sabbath, has been described a thousand ways. It has been called shelter, palace, fortress, bride and queen. *Shabbat* is the only day of the week with a Hebrew name at all; the others are merely numbered in relation to *Shabbat:* the first day, the second day, the third day. In Yiddish, it is pronounced *Shabbes.*

The apparently simple idea that one day out of seven should be devoted to rest and reflection has always been a radical concept. Its earliest practice challenged the ancient world, where labor was the lot of beasts and slaves, and leisure was the privilege of the rich and powerful. Today, when the hum of the machine never stops, when everyone has too much to do and not enough time in which to finish, *Shabbat* continues to pose fundamental questions about values and the value of life. For Jews looking toward the 21st century, the challenge of *Shabbat* is literally radical, recalling our imaginative roots—the biblical story of creation.

> The heaven and the earth were finished, and all their array. On the seventh day God finished the work and stopped. And God blessed the seventh day and made it holy, because on it God rested from all the work of creation.[1]

To the Talmudic rabbis who interpreted these words, the story does not mean that on the seventh day God rolled over, pulled up the covers, and went back to sleep. In their view, only after the seventh day—Shabbat—came into being, was the world completed, and perfect.

The Meaning of *Shabbat*

"The meaning of the Sabbath," wrote Rabbi Abraham Joshua Heschel, "is to celebrate time rather than space. Six days a week we live under the tyranny of things of space; on the Sabbath we try to become attuned to holiness in time. It is a day on which we are called upon to share in what is eternal in time, to turn from the results of creation to the mystery of creation; from the world of creation to the creation of the world." [2]

Millions of words have been written about the meaning of *Shabbat* in language ranging from legal to ecstatic. It has been associated with virtually all the great themes of Judaism: freedom, covenant, peace, and redemption. Sections of the *Shabbat* liturgy recall the time when the Jews were slaves in Egypt. [3] And although *Shabbat* celebrates freedom, it is also a reminder of the contrast between slavery and freedom. The Jewish notion of freedom entails both political and personal responsibilities; the mandate to work for the liberation of all oppressed people, and the task of remaining free from enslavement to false idols, such as wealth, power, and fame.

Shabbat is called a covenant between God and the Jews. Relationships among people cannot be verified by the senses or by reason; we give each other tokens like wedding rings. *Shabbat* is the token between God and the people of Israel. ("I have given them my Sabbath to be a sign between Me and them, so they will know that I am the One that sanctifies them." [4])

The essence and responsibility of this covenant is to create wholeness—in Hebrew, *shalom*. *Shabbat* is about making peace with everyone: business associates, strangers, and especially within families. The highest priority is given to reconciliation and loving kindness. Intimacy and sexuality are among the blessings of *Shabbat*.

Finally, *Shabbat* embodies the Jewish vision of redemption. Observing *Shabbat* fully means behaving as if the world were redeemed—complete, safe, perfect—right now. *Shabbat* is the opportunity to focus on what is right with the world, and thus to be refreshed to do the work of redemption: repairing the world *(tikkun olam)*. Indeed, the Talmud says that if everyone on earth were to observe two consecutive Sabbaths, the whole world would be redeemed.[5]

History

The word *Shabbat* appears almost two hundred times in the Bible.* The earliest mention of Sabbath rest is found in Exodus, when the Israelites who have escaped from Egyptian slavery are told to gather a double portion of manna on the sixth day so they do not have to work on the seventh.[6] By the time of the first Temple, (the 10th century B.C.E.), *Shabbat* was associated with joy as well as rest. The prophet Isaiah said, "And you should call the Sabbath a delight."[7]

During the second Temple period (the first century C.E.), the nature of *Shabbat* was the subject of an intense and passionate debate whose outcome has shaped subsequent Jewish practice. Among the sect known as the Sadducees, *Shabbat* was given an extremely ascetic interpretation: virtually all movement and all indoor illumination were forbidden. However, the Pharisees (forerunners of the rabbis) permitted far more latitude, declaring *Shabbat* laws moot in cases of helping the sick or saving a life. The Pharisees also made the lighting of candles on Friday night a precept that developed into the most evocative of all Jewish rituals.[8] After the destruction of the second Temple by the Romans in 70 C.E., *Shabbat* observance came under the purview of rabbis, who have been interpreting and debating its meaning and practice ever since.

Although *Shabbat* has been a constant feature of Jewish life throughout history, its observance changed over time, and varies among Jews living in different lands. For American Jews, most of whom have Eastern European roots, *Shabbat* associations—smells, tastes, sounds, and

---

* In this book, Bible refers to the Hebrew Bible, which consists of the Torah (or Pentateuch), the Prophets, and the Writings. See "People of the Library" for a discussion of these terms.

images—tend to come from *shtetl* life and Yiddish culture of the last century, mediated through American popular culture. Thus, *Shabbat* conjures up memories of chicken soup and braided *challah* and scenes from *Fiddler on the Roof*. Less familiar to most Americans are the customs of Sephardic Jews, who lived near the Mediterranean and in the Middle East, whose *Shabbat* associations include the aroma of lemons and dishes seasoned with fresh mint and garlic.

Regardless of the particulars, however, *Shabbat* has always been experienced as different from all the other days. *Shabbat* is the day for wearing new clothes, for inviting guests to share the best meal of the week, for singing at the table, and for giving and receiving blessings. Jewish life and Jewish time are oriented around *Shabbat*, which takes precedence over almost everything else. Jewish weddings are not permitted on the Sabbath and neither are funerals; *Shabbat* is meant to be savored on its own, undiluted by other celebrations—unclouded, as much as possible, even by death.

Jews have often suffered for their loyalty to *Shabbat*. Antiochus Epiphanes, the villain of the Hannukah story, outlawed *Shabbat* and many Jews died defying his order. Marranos (Jews who publicly converted to Christianity during the Spanish Inquisition but practiced Judaism in secret) lit *Shabbat* candles in their cellars.[9] And there are heart-wrenching stories of Sabbaths remembered and observed in the darkness of Hitler's death camps.[10]

Choosing *Shabbat*

The first appearance of *Shabbat* in the Torah is as a verb, *shavat*. "And God ceased/rested/stopped."

Shabbat is recreated weekly; Jews make *Shabbat*. The first verb for

---

More than Israel has kept the Sabbath, the Sabbath has kept Israel.
Ahad Ha-Am, modern Hebrew essayist

most Jews today, however, is not "make" but "choose." And choosing *Shabbat* is not one decision, but many. Choosing *Shabbat* means making a commitment to a weekly period of rest and peace. It means making distinctions between activities that are *Shabbat*-like from those that are work-week-like. It means avoiding things that might violate a sense of ease and peace, and planning ways to enhance that feeling.

These choices vary from one household to the next. Many Jews unplug the telephone or turn on their answering machines during *Shabbat*, but some people find telephone conversations with family members and friends are relaxing and appropriate. Though traditionally money is not handled on *Shabbat*, some people make a distinction between shopping at the mall and taking the kids out for ice cream.*

Because *Shabbat* is often defined in terms of prohibitions against certain kinds of activities, many American Jews have come to think of Sabbath observance as a series of restrictions, a weekly sentence of self-denial.[11] But *Shabbat* is not a retreat from the world or an exercise in asceticism. Making *Shabbat* is not a matter of refraining, but of doing. The Talmud says "the affairs of heaven" are permitted on the Sabbath; specifically teaching children and arranging weddings. Resting, eating, and praying are not only permitted, but mandated. There are other verbs for *Shabbat*, too; sleeping, reading, thinking, studying, talking, listening, meditating, visiting the sick, laughing, singing, welcoming guests, making love.

But it is not entirely easy to choose even so pleasant and life-giving a discipline as *Shabbat*. All choices have consequences. If Friday night is going to be time at home, that means turning down invitations for dinner and a movie with friends or family. And for chronically over-scheduled people, sitting still for an hour, much less an afternoon, can be a real challenge. However, these are precisely the reasons that many people view *Shabbat* prohibitions less as sacrifices than as opportunities to reorient an overly hectic life around the need for rest, relaxation, and time with family and close friends.

This is not a simple change. The decision to start making *Shabbat* requires thought, discussion, planning—and it may entail discomfort

---

* This kind of decision-making is a feature of liberal Jewish practice, which tends to be informed more by the spirit than the letter of the law, or *halachah*, which regulates Orthodox life more strictly.

and disagreement. Although it is common for one member of a family to be both instigator and guiding force behind a commitment to making *Shabbat*, it is important to include as many family members as possible in the idea. This is rarely a problem with young children, who tend to enjoy the specialness of *Shabbat* for its own sake, and quickly come to look forward to Friday night's magic. For older children, however, beginning *Shabbat* observance may seem restrictive or just plain weird. Parents need to be quite secure in their desire and enthusiasm for *Shabbat*, and they can ease the transition to it by emphasizing the playful and joyful aspects of the day and encouraging children's input as well as their participation.

It is essential for family members to talk not only about *how* to make *Shabbat*, but also *why*. Reasons can range from the practical to the mystical: *Shabbat* is something constructive and pleasant the family can do together, it is an opportunity to learn, it is something Jews have done for thousands of years and connects us to our heritage, it creates an opportunity to visit with friends and family we otherwise don't see, it is something beautiful and positive we want our children to remember, and it is a way of finding and building community with other Jews.

Regardless of the whys or the ways, however, a commitment to consistency and regularity is essential for *Shabbat* to work. And it is crucial to remember that *Shabbat* is not something you do for or to your family. It is something you make together.

Making *Shabbat*

While it would be difficult to overemphasize *Shabbat*'s intellectual and theological significance, the Jewish Sabbath is not an abstraction or

---

The real and the spiritual are one, like body and soul in a living man. It is for the law to clear the path; it is for the soul to sense the spirit.

Rabbi Abraham Joshua Heschel

disembodied idea that can be attained through revelation or prayer. *Shabbat* must be understood in its uniquely Jewish form—as a *mitzvah*.

A *mitzvah* is a command from God, chosen and enacted by people. The *mitzvah* of *Shabbat* is being human in the most humane context that people can imagine and create.

The rest of this chapter is a kind of cookbook for making *Shabbat*. Just as it would be self-defeating for a novice in the kitchen to attempt an elaborate, multicourse dinner, it is not a good idea to take on every aspect of *Shabbat* observance all at once. Most people begin with Friday night table rituals: lighting candles, eating *challah*, singing songs. It may take weeks before even simple acts feel natural, but after a few months of repetition, comfort and a sense of expertise will come.

And just as cooks learn through apprenticeship, the best way to learn how to make *Shabbat* is with and from others. Sharing Friday night meals, attending services at different synagogues, and getting together with friends on Saturday afternoon can provide you with ideas, models, and support for developing a personal *Shabbat* observance. Some synagogues run *Shabbat* retreats, usually a weekend at a camp, inn, or estate, where people study, pray, relax, and practice the fine art of making *Shabbat*.

On the following pages, *Shabbat* observances are divided into four sections. The first part is devoted to preparing for the seventh day. The second describes Friday night, the eve of the Sabbath *(erev Shabbat)*, where the focus is around the dinner table. The third describes *Shabbat* morning, which includes a synagogue service that features the reading of the Torah. The last part is *Shabbat* afternoon, which begins with a special lunch; continues with studying, resting, napping, and enjoying friends and family; and ends with *havdalah*, the ritual that separates *Shabbat* from the new week.

Preparation

Shabbat is a vacation from the demands of the week. Like any vacation, it creates a shift in orientation to the whole week. For some people, preparing for *Shabbat* starts with avoiding late-afternoon appointments on Friday and trying to be home early.

Shabbat creates a deadline for finishing up things, for example, getting the house clean, making sure that essential errands have been run, and that *challah*, wine, and flowers have been purchased. A traditional analogy compares making *Shabbat* with inviting a Queen to your home for dinner. In other words, if Queen Elizabeth of England were coming over for the day, you would probably run the vacuum, take out the good china, and fuss over the dinner menu.

FOOD

Although Jewish law calls for three "feasts" on *Shabbat* to ensure a sense of celebration, it also forbids the lighting of fires, which traditionally means no cooking. Thus the biggest job of preparing for *Shabbat* tends to be food preparation. Although many Jews do cook on *Shabbat*, preparing even part of Saturday's meals in advance can create more time for relaxing, resting, and playing.

Historically, Friday night dinner has always been the gustatory highlight of the week for Jews, no matter what their financial circumstances. Making it special does not necessarily mean making it elaborate or conforming to the chicken soup and brisket menus of Eastern Europe. Some people find that making the same special meal every Friday night has its advantages; not only is it easier for the cook, it also reinforces the soothing, repetitive ritual nature of the meal and establishes a family tradition. But any menu can be made special with a tablecloth and flowers on the dining room table. Ritual objects such as an embroidered cover for the *challah*, candlesticks, and special wine goblets will immediately make a meal an event.

SLOWING DOWN

Shabbat releases us from the usual patterns of doing and being and celebrates the sensual, creative parts of us that may be sacrificed during the work week. Celebrating the sensual can mean lowering the lights, taking time to smell as well as taste food, and making sure to hug and kiss the people you love.

In the rush to prepare home and table for *Shabbat*, it is easy to forget the importance of readying yourself. Nothing accomplishes the major shifting of gears from work to rest better than a hot shower or bath. If there is time, meditating, listening to music, and reading something that helps you get "in the mood" are also good ways to unwind. Even a few minutes to wash hands and face, shave, comb your hair, put on perfume, or change clothes can help. Some people get into the spirit of *Shabbat* by listening to Jewish tapes and records.

Traditionally, one's best and/or new clothes are worn on *Shabbat*. However, if wearing a good dress or suit and tie are the trappings of work, a change into comfortable casual clothes might better facilitate a shift into *Shabbat*-mode. Some people put on the traditional skullcap (*kippah* in Hebrew, *yarmulke* in Yiddish) before beginning Friday night rituals.

CHILDREN

Shabbat can easily become a focal point of anticipation and fun for children. The celebration can begin with a baking session or a trip to the bakery for *challah* and other goodies. Setting the *Shabbat* table with children can be both a game and a reward, assigning special jobs to each child: candlesticks and candles for you, the *kiddush* cups for you because you're so grown up and responsible, and so on. Kids can also create *Shabbat* centerpieces of *Legos*, paper flowers or dandelions from the yard.

Shabbat can inspire all sorts of arts and crafts projects. Because most small children love wearing hats, *kippot* (the plural of *kippah*) can be part of the fun. Some children collect them, and a "custom" *kippah* can be created with some felt, a little glue, and a plain rayon *yarmulke*. To make a Sabbath plate or set of dishes, apply Jewish symbols and lots of imagination to one of the melamine kits available in many toy stores. (Special pens are provided, and the dishes are then sent to a factory where the child's design is permanently baked on.)

Finally, when everything and everyone is ready, remove your watches. Empty your pockets. Unplug the phone for a while. You are going to a party. And remember, *Shabbat* is not a solemn occasion. Along with the candles, wine, and *challah*, smiles and laughter belong at the table.

Friday Night

The four core ritual elements of a home *Shabbat* evening *(erev Shabbat)* celebration are: blessings over candles, wine and bread, and the eating of a meal. Friday night rituals vary enormously from one Jewish household to the next. In some there are many songs; in others, there is no singing. Some families recite all the blessings in English; others do them in Hebrew. Some people discuss the weekly Torah portion at dinner; other people use the time to reflect on the week past. Some eat earlier than usual in order to attend services; others eat later than usual and linger at the table as the candles burn down.

The various elements of Friday night, listed first and then explained, are a menu from which a personal *Shabbat* home ritual can be created. As with any menu, all sorts of combinations are possible. Once you find a comfortable way to proceed, it can be very helpful to make a one-page guide to the order and blessings in English, transliterated, and/or in Hebrew. This *''Shabbat seder''* can then be decorated, laminated, and given to guests.

Even with fairly detailed explanations, however, *Shabbat* is not entirely comprehensible solely from the page. The best way to learn it is to live it—by watching and participating with others who are experienced at making *Shabbat*.

Friday night rituals consist of:

Giving *tzedakah*
Singing
Lighting candles
Blessings for children
Blessings for husband and wife
Blessings for wine *(kiddush)*
Blessing over hand washing
Blessing for *challah*
Eating the meal
Focused conversation
Blessings after the meal *(birkat hamazon)*
More singing
Going to synagogue
Making love

GIVING TZEDAKAH

Giving money to the poor is associated with nearly all Jewish celebrations and festive occasions. In moments of great joy, *tzedakah* is a way of both sharing happiness and of recalling that the world requires our attention.

It is traditional to put aside money for *tzedakah* before candles are lit. Many people cherish childhood associations of *Shabbat* with little tin cans called *pushkes* which represented different Jewish charitable organizations. Making a collection box by decorating a can or jar, or making a container out of clay or paper is a great project and a wonderful way of introducing children to the concept of *tzedakah*. (See the chapter called "Good Deeds.")

SINGING

Beginning a meal with a song breaks the week's routine and inaugurates *Shabbat* as a special kind of time. Although almost any song will accomplish this, many Hebrew songs *(z'mirot)* are associated with the *Shabbat* table. One of the simplest and best-known is *"Shabbat Shalom,"* whose lyrics consist only of those two words.

But words are not really necessary. According to one tradition, a wordless melody or *niggun* is itself a prayer, and one of the purest forms of prayer at that. *Niggunim* (the plural) are usually fairly simple, repetitive, and easily taught.

One song closely associated with Friday night is "Shalom Aleichem," which is an invocation of angels thought to hover close on *Shabbat*.

Shalom aleichem
malachei hasharet
malachei elyon
mi melech malchei hamlachim
Hakadosh Baruch Hu

Peace be yours, angels of peace
Angels of the most high
Angel of the King who is King of kings
The holy blessed One.

LIGHTING CANDLES

In all cultures throughout the world, fire is considered one of the basic elements; it is a universal symbol of power, mastery, and divinity. Friday night candle lighting dates back to the first century C.E., and the blessing is as old as the eighth or ninth century.[12] For Jews, the lighting of candles is the act that formally ends the week and begins *Shabbat*.

Candle lighting is the most evocative of all Jewish rituals. Children who watched mothers and grandmothers *bench licht* (Yiddish for "blessing the light") carry the image with them for the rest of their lives. Remembering her mother's *Shabbat* ritual at the turn of the century, Bella Chagall wrote:

> "With a match in her hand she lights one candle after another. All the seven candles begin to quiver. The flames blaze into Mother's face. As though an enchantment were falling upon her, she lowers her eyes. Slowly, three times in succession, she encircles the candles with both her arms; she seems to be taking them into her heart. And with the candles her weekday worries seem to melt away.
>
> "She blesses the candles. She whispers quiet benedictions through her fingers and they add heat to the flames. Mother's hands over the candles shine like the tablets of the decalogue over the holy ark.
>
> "I push closer to her. I want to get behind her blessing hands myself. I seek her face. I want to look into her eyes. They are concealed behind her spread-out fingers."[13]

According to Jewish law, candles are lit not at dark but at sunset—technically, no later than 18 minutes before sunset. (Candle-lighting times are listed on Jewish calendars and in Jewish newspapers.) Among liberal Jews, the common practice is to light candles when the whole household is gathered at the table for dinner.

The candles are lit before the blessing is recited, either silently or aloud. There is a custom of circling the candles with hands and arms

---

"We will sing," said Rabbi Nachman of Bratslav, "And God on high will understand us."

after lighting them, and then covering the eyes while the blessing is repeated. This practice can feel awkward or artificial to people who have never tried it or seen it done. If these gestures make you feel too self-conscious to get into a *Shabbat*-like mood, they defeat the purpose. Some people simply take a moment to take and release a very deep breath before lighting candles and reciting the blessing.

בָּרוּךְ אַתָּה, יְיָ אֱלֹהֵינוּ, מֶלֶךְ הָעוֹלָם, אֲשֶׁר קִדְּשָׁנוּ בְּמִצְוֹתָיו וְצִוָּנוּ לְהַדְלִיק נֵר שֶׁל שַׁבָּת.

Baruch ata Adonai Eloheynu Melech Ha-olam asher kid'shanu be-mitzvotav vitzivanu l'hadlik ner shel Shabbat.

Holy One of Blessing, Your Presence Fills Creation, Making us holy with your Commandments and calling us to light the lights of *Shabbat*.[14]

At least two candles are lit, symbolizing the great dualities of life: female and male, light and darkness, etc. The rabbis declared that the two candles stand for the two forms of the commandment to "remember" and "observe" *Shabbat*.[15] Although two is the minimum, there is no maximum. Bella Chagall's mother lit seven candles because she added a flame for each of her five children. Among some Sephardic Jews, candles are lit for family members who have died.[16] If guests are present at candlelighting, they can be invited to light candles for their families as well. A great blaze of candles is very festive.

According to tradition, the *mitzvah* of lighting candles is assigned to women, though it is incumbent on men in their absence. Whereas some women prefer to reserve this custom to themselves, there is a wide range of practice on this count. In many homes, all women and girls light a pair of candles, though in some families, the honor rotates and includes everyone regardless of gender.

Candlelighting is a wonderful moment for children. In many families, blowing out the *Shabbat* match is a special treat. A gift of small candlesticks on a birthday or Hannukah confers a new, more grown-up Jewish status on a child; the first time he or she uses them can be a family event. (Long fireplace matches are a good idea, and fun too.)

Generally, the candles are the short, white, and kosher (no animal fat) tapers sold for Sabbath use in Jewish stores and many supermarkets. Some people substitute colored or rainbow candles for a special occasion *Shabbat,* such as a child's birthday.

The only regulation regarding candlesticks or other ritual objects for *Shabbat* is the rabbinic principal of *hiddur mitzvah,* which states that when a physical object is needed to fulfill a commandment, it should be beautiful. Candlesticks handed down from one generation to the next are especially precious, but any object reserved only for *Shabbat* use quickly becomes a family treasure. Judaica shops tend to offer a large selection of candlesticks, but for something that already has the patina of age and experience, a second-hand store or antique shop may yield an heirloom.

After the candles are lit, someone or everyone says *Shabbat Shalom* ("Sabbath peace") or *Gut Shabbes* (Yiddish for "a good Sabbath"). In some families, everyone exchanges kisses.

BLESSINGS FOR CHILDREN

The Bible records several parental blessings, which are echoed in the custom of blessing children on Friday. There are three traditional blessings: First, the blessing for sons refers to Joseph's sons, Ephraim and Menashe, whose mother, Osenath, was an Egyptian-born noblewoman. The Midrash says that these two were singled out for praise because they held fast to their Jewish identity. Second, the blessing for daughters names the matriarchs: Sarah, whose response to adversity was laughter; Rebecca, the model of hospitality, and Rachel and Leah, who personify sisterhood in the most difficult circumstances. Lastly, there is what is known as the priestly blessing.

Some parents add or substitute a more personal message for each child—praise for something that happened during the week, or just a whispered, "I love you."

For boys:

יְשִׂמְךָ אֱלֹהִים כְּאֶפְרַיִם וְכִמְנַשֶּׁה.

Y'simcha Elohim k'Efrayim v'chi'M'nashe.

May God make you as Ephraim and Menasheh.

For girls:

יְשִׂמֵךְ אֱלֹהִים כְּשָׂרָה, רִבְקָה, רָחֵל וְלֵאָה.

Y'simeych Elohim k'Sara, Rivka, Rachel, v'Leah.

Make God make you as Sarah, Rebecca, Rachel and Leah.

Blessing the Children

May you be as Ephraim and Menashe
   of whom we know nothing
   but their names
   and that they were Jews.
And may you be as all Jews
   whose names are lost
   as witnesses to God's care,
   love, and presence.
Remember them in your words,
   and live Menschlich lives
   as they lived Menschlich lives.

May you be as Sarah, Rivka, Rachel and Leah,
   whose names and deeds
   are our inheritance;
   who bore us, raised us,
   guided and taught us
   that a touch
   is a touch of Holiness,
   and a laugh is prophecy;
   that all that is ours,
   is theirs;
   that neither Man or Woman alone
   lights the sparks of Life,
   but only both together,
   generating light and warmth
   and singular humanity.

Danny Siegel, © 1983 [17]

For both (the priestly blessing):

יְבָרֶכְךָ יְיָ וְיִשְׁמְרֶךָ. יָאֵר יְיָ פָּנָיו אֵלֶיךָ וִיחֻנֶּךָּ. יִשָּׂא יְיָ פָּנָיו אֵלֶיךָ, וְיָשֵׂם לְךָ שָׁלוֹם.

Y'varech-ch'cha Adonai v'yish-ma-recha
Ya'er Adonai panav eylecha vichuneka
Yisa Adonai panav eylecha v'yasem l'cha shalom.

May Adonai bless you and keep you
May Adonai shine The Countenance upon you and be gracious to
  you,
May Adonai favor you and grant you peace.

BLESSINGS FOR HUSBAND AND WIFE

Eshet chayil, "a woman of valor," is the phrase that begins a set of the
verses from the book of Proverbs, traditionally recited by husbands to
wives on Friday night. *Eshet chayil* is a long list of praises for a good
woman's virtues, including generosity, industry, business acumen,
beauty, wisdom, cheerfulness, and loving kindness.

In some households, the tradition of reciting or singing these verses
is abbreviated; a husband will simply look into his wife's eyes and say,
"eshet chayil," a kind of short-hand acknowledgement of appreciation
and love. Often, this traditional gesture is made reciprocal, as each
spouse simply takes a moment to kiss and say "I love you." Any such
act makes it very difficult to allow left-over quarrels to compromise the
peace and harmony of *Shabbat.*[18]

BLESSINGS FOR WINE (KIDDUSH)

The word *kiddush* comes from the Hebrew *kadosh,* which means "holy."
the term refers to all blessings made over wine, and there is a special

---

Rabbi Hanina wrote, He who prays on the eve of the Sabbath and recites the
verses that begin, "and the heaven and the earth were finished," the scriptures
speak of him as though he been a partner in creation with the Holy One.

Talmud: Shabbat 119b

kiddush on Friday night. The one-line core of the blessing is always the same, however:

בָּרוּךְ אַתָּה, יְיָ אֱלֹהֵינוּ, מֶלֶךְ הָעוֹלָם, בּוֹרֵא פְּרִי הַגָּפֶן.

Baruch ata Adonai Eloheynu Melech Ha-olam boray p'ree hagafen.

Holy One of Blessing, Your Presence fills Creation forming the fruit of the vine.

On Friday night, this blessing is sandwiched between two longer passages. The first, from the Torah, recounts the creation of the world. The second is a blessing that recalls three of the great *Shabbat* themes: the creation, the exodus from Egypt, and the sanctity of the Sabbath.

וַיְהִי עֶרֶב וַיְהִי בֹקֶר

יוֹם הַשִּׁשִּׁי. וַיְכֻלּוּ הַשָּׁמַיִם וְהָאָרֶץ וְכָל צְבָאָם. וַיְכַל אֱלֹהִים בַּיּוֹם הַשְּׁבִיעִי מְלַאכְתּוֹ אֲשֶׁר עָשָׂה, וַיִּשְׁבֹּת בַּיּוֹם הַשְּׁבִיעִי מִכָּל מְלַאכְתּוֹ אֲשֶׁר עָשָׂה. וַיְבָרֶךְ אֱלֹהִים אֶת יוֹם הַשְּׁבִיעִי וַיְקַדֵּשׁ אוֹתוֹ, כִּי בוֹ שָׁבַת מִכָּל מְלַאכְתּוֹ אֲשֶׁר בָּרָא אֱלֹהִים לַעֲשׂוֹת.

Vayehi erev vayehi voker yom hashishi. Vayechulu hashamayim veha'aretz vechol tzeva'am vayechal Elohim bayom hashevi'i melachto asher asa, vayishbot bayom hashevi'i mikol melachto asher asa. Vaye-varech Elohim et yom hashevi'i vayikadesh oto, ki vo shavat mikol me-lachto asher bara Elohim la'asot.

There was evening and there was morning the sixth day. And the heavens and the earth and all that they contain were completed. And on the seventh day God completed the work that God had made. And God rested on the seventh day from all the work that God had made. And God blessed the seventh day and made it holy, because on it God rested from all the work that God created and made.[19]

בָּרוּךְ אַתָּה, יְיָ אֱלֹהֵינוּ, מֶלֶךְ הָעוֹלָם, בּוֹרֵא פְּרִי הַגָּפֶן.
בָּרוּךְ אַתָּה, יְיָ אֱלֹהֵינוּ, מֶלֶךְ הָעוֹלָם, אֲשֶׁר קִדְּשָׁנוּ בְּמִצְוֹתָיו וְרָצָה בָנוּ, וְשַׁבַּת קָדְשׁוֹ בְּאַהֲבָה וּבְרָצוֹן הִנְחִילָנוּ, זִכָּרוֹן לְמַעֲשֵׂה בְרֵאשִׁית. כִּי הוּא יוֹם תְּחִלָּה לְמִקְרָאֵי קֹדֶשׁ, זֵכֶר לִיצִיאַת מִצְרָיִם. כִּי בָנוּ בָחַרְתָּ וְאוֹתָנוּ קִדַּשְׁתָּ מִכָּל הָעַמִּים, וְשַׁבַּת קָדְשְׁךָ בְּאַהֲבָה וּבְרָצוֹן הִנְחַלְתָּנוּ. בָּרוּךְ אַתָּה, יְיָ, מְקַדֵּשׁ הַשַּׁבָּת.

Baruch ata Adonai Eloheynu Melech Ha-olam boray p'ree hagafen.

Baruch ata Adonai Eloheynu Melech Ha-olam asher kid'shanu be-mitzvotav v'ratza vanu, veShabbat kodsho be'ahava uveratzon hinchi-lanu, zikaron lema'asay vereishit; ki hu yom techila lemikra'ay kodesh, zecher litziyat mitzrayim; ki vanu vacharta ve'otanu kidashta mikol ha'amim veShabbat kodshecha be'ahava uveratzon hinchaltanu. Baruch ata Adonai mekadesh haShabbat.

Holy One of Blessing, Your Presence fills Creation, forming the fruit of the vine.

Holy One of Blessing, Your Presence fills Creation, You have made us holy with Your commandments and delighted in us. In love You have favored us with the gift of Your holy *Shabbat,* a heritage that recalls the work of creation. It is the first day among holy days, reminding us of our going out from Egypt. You gave us Your holy *Shabbat* as a treasure to grace all our generations. Holy One of Blessing, You make *Shabbat* holy.

There are many customs for saying *kiddush.* Some families simply do the *"boray p'ree hagafen"* part of the prayer in unison. Others sing the entire *kiddush* aloud in Hebrew. In some households, one person reads the longer passages in English and only the core blessing is recited in Hebrew.

In some families, everyone stands for *kiddush;* elsewhere, everyone sits. Some make the blessing over a single cup, which is then passed or poured into other cups. Elsewhere, everyone drinks from his or her own glass.

It is also traditional to hold the cup in a way that demonstrates that this wine is not simply for drinking or even toasting. According to the *Zohar,* a medieval book of mystical Bible interpretation, the glass is held in the palm of the right hand with the fingers facing upward and curled around the base to represent a five-petaled rose, an ancient symbol of perfection and of longing for God. Any glass can be used for *kiddush,* but it is considered preferable to use a special glass or goblet to fulfill the precept of *hiddur mitzvah,* or beautifying the commandment.

Most people who grew up with a Friday night *Shabbat* home ritual, associate *kiddush* with the thick, sweet red wines of Mogen David and

Manischewitz. People who choose kosher wine today, however, have a wide selection of drier vintages. Although Jewish law calls for kosher wine, many Jews consider all wines acceptable. (For an explanation of kosher wine and food, see the chapter "What Jews Eat.") Some parents substitute watered wine or grape juice, reserved for *Shabbat*, for children. *Kiddush* cups are common gifts for *bar* and *bat mitzvah* celebrants, but a special cup for *Shabbat* also makes a wonderful present for a much younger child.

BLESSING OVER HAND WASHING

Some Jews perform a symbolic hand-washing just prior to saying the blessing over *challah*, which begins the meal. Hand-washing recalls the purification ceremonies of the ancient Temple, and so the table symbolizes the altar.

Whereas any glass or cup can be used, two-handled cups or lavers are made especially for this purpose, some of which bear the accompanying blessing:

בָּרוּךְ אַתָּה, יְיָ אֱלֹהֵינוּ, מֶלֶךְ הָעוֹלָם, אֲשֶׁר קִדְּשָׁנוּ בְּמִצְוֹתָיו וְצִוָּנוּ עַל נְטִילַת יָדַיִם.

Baruch ata Adonai Eloheynu Melech Ha-olam asher kid'shanu bemitz-votav vitzivanu al netilat yadayim.

Holy One of Blessing, Your Presence Fills Creation
Making us holy with Your commandments and calling us to wash our hands.

BLESSING FOR CHALLAH

In many languages, the word "bread" is synonymous with "food." A blessing for bread is thus a blessing over food, sustenance, life. Jews make a blessing called *motzi* ("brings") over *challah*, a word that comes from a biblical reference to a sacrificial Temple offering of dough.[20] According to tradition, *challah* is any bread prepared for the purpose of making a *motzi*, a process that requires breaking off and burning a small piece of dough and reciting a blessing. Today, *challah* generally refers to a braided egg-rich loaf with a soft, almost cake-like texture. It is available in Jewish bakeries, and happens to be one of the easiest yeast

breads to bake at home. Good recipes abound and children love braid-
ing the dough.

בָּרוּךְ אַתָּה, יְיָ אֱלֹהֵינוּ, מֶלֶךְ הָעוֹלָם, הַמּוֹצִיא לֶחֶם מִן־הָאָרֶץ:

*Baruch ata Adonai Eloheynu Melech Ha-olam hamotzi lechem min ha-
aretz.*

Holy One of Blessing, Your Presence Fills Creation, bringing forth
bread from the earth.

It is traditional to have two loaves on the table, recalling the double
portion of manna the Israelites gathered on the sixth day, so they would
not have to collect food on *Shabbat.* The double portion of bread also
symbolizes bounty. Some families use a small *challah* roll to symbolize
a second loaf. The bread is often covered with an embroidered or woven
cloth that, like special *challah* plates and knives, add to the beauty of
the *Shabbat* table.

There are many customs for saying the blessing. Some hold two
loaves together. Some sprinkle the bread with salt, a traditional reminder of tears and of the destruction of the Temple. Because metal is
considered a reminder of war, some people keep sharp knives off the
table. This is why in some households no knife is put to the *challah* at
all; it is ripped apart by hand instead.

EATING THE MEAL

The act of eating the Friday night meal, and all three meals commanded
for *Shabbat,* is considered a *mitzvah* and a blessing. The idea of anyone
going hungry on *Shabbat* seems terribly contradictory to the spirit of the
day, which is why there are so many stories about feeding beggars and
bringing strangers home on the Sabbath. Judaism has always been
respectful of the fact that basic needs must be satisfied first, and that
holiness and hunger are, in some fundamental sense, mutually exclu-
sive. As the Talmud says, "Without food there is no Torah." [21]

FOCUSED CONVERSATION

Conversation at the *Shabbat* table is for relaxing, checking in, and catch-
ing up. In some families, this idea is formalized. People take turns

talking about the important events of the previous week; news, accomplishments, and especially things studied or learned.

Conversation about Jewish topics of all sorts is very appropriate: from the weekly Torah portion to the news from Israel. It is said, "If three have eaten at the table and speak words of Torah, it is as if they have eaten from the table of God."[22]

BLESSINGS AFTER THE MEAL (BIRKAT HAMAZON)

The *birkat hamazon* (blessings for food) is a series of blessings and prayers set to a series of wonderful melodies, filled with thanks to and praise for God and full of messianic references. Praying the *birkat hamazon* is also called *benching*, the Yiddish word for blessing, and is found in most daily prayerbooks or *siddurim*. On *Shabbat*, *birkat hamazon* begins with Psalm 126:

When God brought Israel back to Zion
We were as in a dream
Our mouths were filled with laughter,
Our tongues with joyous song.

Then it was said among the nations
"God has done great things for them."
God had truly done great things for us,
and we were filled with joy.

O God, bring back your scattered children
like streams in the desert.

When the world was created, God made everything a little bit incomplete. Rather than making bread grow right out of the earth, God made wheat grow so that we might bake it into bread. In this way, we could become partners in completing the work of creation.

Midrash

They who sow in tears shall reap in joy.
Though we weep when planting
we shall sing with joy
as we return home
at harvest time.

The following is the first paragraph of *birkat hamazon*, which is
sometimes used as an abbreviated version of the longer blessing.

Holy One of Blessing, Your Presence fills creation, You nourish
the world with goodness and sustain it with grace, loving kindness
and mercy. You provide food for every living thing because You are
merciful. Because of Your great goodness the earth yields its fruit.
For Your sake we pray that we shall always have enough to eat, for
You sustain and strengthen all that lives and provide food for the
life that You created. Holy One of Blessing, You nourish all that
lives.[23]

GOING TO SYNAGOGUE

The cycle of Shabbat services begins on Friday evening with *Kabbalat
Shabbat* (welcoming or receiving the Sabbath). *Kabbalat Shabbat* was
developed by a group of Jewish mystics who lived in Safed, Palestine.
Although there are variations on the Friday evening service, virtually
all of them contain some version of *"L'cha Dodi,"* a poem set to music
from that 16th century community. Today, in many congregations
when the final stanza is sung, everyone rises to face the door to symbolically welcome to Sabbath bride.

In some congregations, the Friday night service is the biggest and
best-attended of the week. In others, the crowds come for *Shabbat*
morning services. Some synagogues include a congregational candle
lighting and *kiddush* on Friday night and some share *challah* as well.
The rabbi, or whoever leads the service, may give a sermon.

Friday night services are often followed by an *oneg Shabbat* ("joy of
the Sabbath"), a communal celebration that encourages touching base
with old friends, meeting people, sharing food, and enjoying the spirit
of the Sabbath.

For those who do not attend Friday night services, the evening is spent relaxing. After the meal, clean-up tends to be kept to a minimum, although with company and conversation, *Shabbat* can even transform dishwashing from a chore into a pleasure.

Sitting by the candles to *shmooz,* read, or study from a Jewish text (the week's Torah portion is traditional) is considered a *mitzvah,* especially because the candles are lit not merely for decoration, but for use. Some people take this time to read poetry, listen to music, sit outside and watch the night sky, read special stories to their children, or make ''Shabbat Shalom'' phone calls.

MAKING LOVE

The imagery of marriage abounds in Jewish texts; God and the people Israel are like groom and bride and the Torah their *ketubah,* or marriage contract. *Shabbat* is often described as a royal bride. The Kabbalists imagined God's unity to have been shattered by the expulsion of humanity from Eden. The feminine side of God, which is called *shechinah,* would wander the earth in exile until the redemption of the world was complete. On *Shabbat,* however, God's two halves are reconciled and united in an act of love.

In Yiddish literature of the late 19th and early 20th century, there is a keen sense that on Friday night, husbands and wives look at each other with different eyes. On a purely practical level, the men and women of the *shtetl* and ghetto looked their best. And the quarrels and conflicts of the week were put aside to abide by the Sabbath's mandate of peace. But another reason for all the smiling was the rather public secret that Friday night was the time for sex. Indeed, Jewish folklore held that *erev Shabbat* was the most auspicious time for conceiving a child.

Y'did Nefesh, a traditional song for Friday night, makes the connection between spiritual and physical union quite explicit:

Draw me to You with the breath of love,
Swiftly shall I come to stand within your radiance
That I may attain that sweetest of all intimacies.

My soul aches to receive your love
Only by the tenderness of Your light can she be healed
Engage my soul that she may taste your ecstasy.[24]

Shabbat Morning

With the morning, the focus shifts from family to community, from home to synagogue. For some, Saturday morning services are a weekly event, whereas others attend only rarely or, on special occasions, such as a *bar* or *bat mitzvah*, which means, literally, "son or daughter of the commandment," and is a rite of passage for 13-year-old boys and girls.

For those unfamiliar with Hebrew and synagogue customs, *Shabbat* morning services can seem daunting. The best way to explore and enjoy them is to try and relax. No one is there to judge you. No one will know that this is either your first time ever inside a temple or your first time in decades. Some of the most important elements of *Shabbat* are available for newcomers as well as regulars; the sight of a community of people gathered together, the music and voices, the absence of anything to *do,* and the opportunity to sit still and simply *be.*

What follows is a general outline of Sabbath worship services. Whereas variety is the hallmark of liberal observance, the essential elements that appear here are as close to "standard" as possible.

SABBATH MORNING SERVICES *(SHACHARIT)*

Commonly, there are five sections in the Sabbath morning service. The first two—morning blessings, hymns and psalms—are introductory. *Shacharit* proper begins with a call to worship *(barchu)* and continues with the *Shema* and its blessings and the standing prayer (called *Amida* or *Tefila*). This is followed by Torah reading.

The Torah, which is also called the five books of Moses or the Pentateuch, consists of the first five books of the Hebrew Bible: Genesis, Exodus, Leviticus, Numbers, and Deuteronomy. The Torah is divided into 54 sections, each of which is called a *parasha* or *sedra,* which are read, in order, in an annual cycle.

Every portion is further divided into seven parts, each of which is called an *aliyah.* On Monday and Thursday morning, and Saturday afternoon, when the Torah is also read, only one *aliyah* will be read. On *Shabbat* morning, however, all seven are read or chanted. Special blessings are recited before and after each section is read. It is a special honor, also called an *aliyah,* to be called up to read from the Torah and/or to say these blessings.

The Torah is read from a scroll, and reading it requires training and skill, especially if the words are chanted to the traditional melody. There is often a designated Torah reader called a *Baal Kriyah* (or *Baal Korey*), which means "master of the reading." A *bar* or *bat mitzvah* spends months learning to read just a few verses, but even a skilled reader reviews the weekly portion before attempting it at services.

The Torah reading varies from one congregation to the next. In some synagogues, the entire portion is chanted in Hebrew, whereas in others only a few sections will be read. Some congregations do some or all the Torah portion in English. And some have adopted the old Palestinian custom of a triennial or three-year cycle for Torah reading, so only a third of each *parasha* is read every week.

The Torah reading is the emotional and intellectual center of the service. But despite the ceremony surrounding the scroll itself, the text is not venerated. The Torah is read for communal study and as a challenge to discover new levels of meaning in its stories, characters, and ideas. Rabbis often base a sermon on the portion being read, and in some synagogues the rabbi or a congregant will lead a discussion of it. Torah study sessions like these can branch out from theology into politics and psychology as well.

In some congregations, the Torah service includes a *haftarah* reading. *Haftarah*, which means "conclusion" or "completion," refers to selections from the biblical books of the Prophets, which are arranged in readings that correspond to Torah portions. This part of the service probably dates from the second century B.C.E., when the Syrian Greeks prohibited reading from the Torah, and Jews substituted a selection from the Prophets that contained themes reminiscent of the forbidden *parasha*.

After the Torah portion has been read, there are concluding prayers and usually a familiar hymn. Some congregations have an additional service called *Musaf*.

CHILDREN AT SERVICES

Taking children to *Shabbat* morning services can be wonderful or awful, depending both on parents' attitudes and synagogue policy. Some parents feel that attending services is an important part of their children's Jewish education; they feel that just being in the synagogue, hearing the sounds of worship and seeing adults engaged in prayer, is vital. To keep very young children occupied, some parents bring a *Shabbat* backpack filled with quiet playthings (books, crayons, puzzles, etc.) to the synagogue. These toys are reserved for *Shabbat* use and are frequently replenished with new goodies and surprises.

However, other parents believe that worship services are basically an adult activity and that forcing children to sit for hours will do nothing but make them hate Judaism. They either arrange for a sitter, or take turns coming to services.

Actually, both of these approaches can be accommodated by good synagogue programming for children. Such activities include special services for school-aged children, *Shabbat*-centered arts and crafts projects and singing for little ones, and even childcare for babies. Sometimes, children join their parents at the end of the service for a final song. Some synagogues plan family services that feature singing, movement, and even puppet shows and plays to tell the story in the Torah portion. Most congregations are very supportive of parents who want to help organize such activities, if they don't already exist.

For people who do not wish to or cannot attend *Shabbat* services, ways to continue Sabbath observance through the morning include reading the Torah portion at home, singing favorite songs from the service, praying on their own, going for a walk, reading Jewish books, meditating, or any other essentially restful, Sabbath-like activity.

Shabbat Afternoon

The first order of business after services is lunch, the second official meal for *Shabbat*. (Traditionally, breakfast does not count as one of the three Sabbath meals.) The *kiddush* over wine at this meal is called "the great *kiddush*" (*kiddush rabbah*). (According to legend, the fancy name was supposed to compensate for the more impressive Friday night *kiddush*.) The second loaf of *challah* from the Friday night meal is often eaten at lunch.

The "great *kiddush*" and the blessing for bread (*motzi*) are often said in the synagogue after services, with everyone gathered around a table of wine (or spirits) and *challah*. If there is a *bar* or *bat mitzvah* celebration, the blessings may precede and kick off the *simcha,* which literally means "joy" and which is also the name for a Jewish party.

In general, however, most people have lunch at home, which is where they spend the remainder of Shabbat. It is always a *mitzvah* to invite guests home on *Shabbat,* especially those who might not otherwise have a warm, friendly place to eat. Encouraging children to invite friends over to eat and play helps make *Shabbat* special, and gives them the chance to extend their own hospitality.

Although lunch is seldom as elaborate as Friday night's meal, the noon meal is often festive or in some way different from weekday lunches. The whole notion of *Shabbat* rest discourages fancy cooking in favor of leftovers, casseroles prepared in advance, or a selection of salads and sandwich fixings. But in some families, Saturday means lunch *rabbah* (the great lunch) because it always features chocolate pudding. Shabbat can be a day of rest from saying "no" to children's insatiable passion for junk food. In some households, Shabbat is reserved for otherwise forbidden treats.

A whole culinary history could be written about *Shabbat* lunch. In order to fulfill the *mitzvah* of eating a full meal without lighting fires or doing any real cooking, hearty casseroles were kept warm either at the back of the family stove or in a community oven. In Eastern Europe, lunch was *cholent,* a heavy meat stew. In Morocco, the midday Shabbat meal was *dafina,* a concoction of chickpeas, potatoes, wheat, and meat, warmed all night in Arab bakery ovens. In Iraq, lunch was *tbeet,* a pot filled with rice and stuffed chicken, on top of which eggs were baked for breakfast.

After lunch, the afternoon stretches lazily on. The goal for *Shabbat* afternoon is to achieve the same level of relaxation one feels on the last afternoon of a two-week vacation: sad to leave but also refreshed. However, because many people find it difficult to face hours of uninterrupted leisure—especially at a time when the rest of the world is busy doing errands and cleaning out the garage—it can be helpful to make specific plans.

Traditional *Shabbat* afternoon activities include napping, visiting the sick, and walking without a particular destination in mind. Some people reserve these hours for activities and pastimes such as bicycle riding, swimming, writing letters, baking cookies, puttering in the garden, reading poetry, sitting still and really listening to music, and going on nature walks. *Shabbat* is a wonderful time for spouses to talk, and for parents and children to play. And the more an activity is saved only for *Shabbat*, the more *Shabbat*-like it becomes.

Perhaps the most-time honored *Shabbat* afternoon activity is Torah study. Some people meet weekly with family members or a group of friends to discuss the week's Torah section, a project that requires no knowledge of Hebrew or academic background in Judaism. The first five books of the Bible have been studied for more than 2,000 years, in part for the sheer pleasure of trying to comprehend its meanings. There are no correct or ultimate answers; there are simply new levels of understanding.

One way to proceed is by reading the week's portion out loud. This not only lifts the activity out of the weekday practice of reading for information, it also means that no one will have failed to do the "homework."

Nor does a *Shabbat* study circle have to be limited to the Bible. Indeed, the phrase "studying Torah" is traditionally applied to *all* Jewish learning, which includes the Hebrew language, a Jewish novel, a book of history or commentary, or even last Sunday's editorial about Israeli politics. The traditional caveat is that sad topics are avoided to preserve the joy of *Shabbat*.

SHABBAT ENDS (HAVDALAH)

According to the Talmud, *Shabbat* ends when three stars are visible in the sky. On overcast evenings, *Shabbat* is over when a blue thread is

a rest of love freely given
a rest of truth and sincerity
a rest in peace and tranquility, in quiet and safety
a perfect rest in which You find favor.

from the Shabbat Mincha Service

indistinguishable from a white thread held at arm's length. In other words, it should be dark.

Yet, there is almost no limit to how late *havdalah* can begin. The ritual that ends the Sabbath, *havdalah*, (which means "separation" or "division") dates back to Talmudic times. It is a brief, enchanting ceremony that recalls the intimate power of the Friday night home ritual, though far more melancholy because it marks *Shabbat*'s passing. Some congregations hold *havdalah* services, but this is, by and large, a home celebration. It consists of four blessings: over wine, over fragrant spices, over fire, and over distinctions.

The lighting of a candle announces the end of the Sabbath, during which making fire is prohibited. The candle used for *havdalah* has at least two wicks because the blessing refers to the "lights of the fire." *Havdalah* candles, which are available in Judaica shops, are often multicolored and contain several braided wicks.

Although the candle is lit first, the first blessing is not over fire, but over a full-to-the-brim cup of wine. The cup is raised and the blessing recited, but it is not drunk at this time:

בָּרוּךְ אַתָּה, יְיָ אֱלֹהֵינוּ, מֶלֶךְ הָעוֹלָם, בּוֹרֵא פְּרִי הַגָּפֶן.

Baruch ata Adonai Eloheynu Melech Ha-olam boray p'ree hagafen.

Holy One of Blessing, Your Presence Fills Creation, forming the fruit of the vine.

Next comes the blessing over spices. The sense of smell has been put to religious use since ancient times, and incense was used in the Temple in Jerusalem. There are a number of explanations for the presence of spices at *havdalah*. According to one legend, during *Shabbat* people are given an additional soul and when the Sabbath ends and this soul departs, the spices revive us, lest we faint. The sweetness of the spices symbolizes both the sweetness of paradise and also the wish for a sweet week to come.

בָּרוּךְ אַתָּה, יְיָ אֱלֹהֵינוּ, מֶלֶךְ הָעוֹלָם, בּוֹרֵא מִינֵי בְשָׂמִים.

Baruch ata Adonai Eloheynu Melech Ha-olam boray minai b'samim.

Holy One of Blessing, Your Presence Fills Creation making fragrant spices.

After this blessing is recited, something fragrant is passed around for everyone to sniff and enjoy. Flowers or freshly cut fruit can be used. Most Jews who celebrate *havdalah*, however, own a spicebox filled with cloves and other spices. The oldest spiceboxes date from 16th century Germany, when they were often made in the shape of towers or turrets. Today, spice boxes come in all shapes and sizes, made out of everything from tin to wood to porcelain. They can be purchased in Judaica shops, and often come as part of *havdalah* sets that include a candle-holder, *kiddush* cup, and tray.

Next comes the blessing over the fire of the candle, which has been burning.

בָּרוּךְ אַתָּה, יְיָ אֱלֹהֵינוּ, מֶלֶךְ הָעוֹלָם, בּוֹרֵא מְאוֹרֵי הָאֵשׁ.

Baruch ata Adonai Eloheynu Melech Ha-olam boray m'oray ha'eysh.

Holy One of Blessing, Your Presence Fills Creation forming the lights of fire.

The rabbis reasoned that because God started the first week with light, it is fitting to begin every week with a prayer of thanks for light. Because all Jewish blessings require some form of action, it is traditional to hold the hands up in order to feel the warmth of the flame, and to use the light to distinguish between the nails and fingers. This custom probably derives from folk beliefs that fingernails revealed omens of the future. However, because there was great rabbinic opposition to such forms of divination, the rabbis devised alternative interpretations. According to one of these, Adam and Eve were covered by a protective shell before their expulsion from Eden, so looking at fingernails recalls paradise.

Finally, there is the *havdalah* blessing itself, which thanks God for creation and for the distinctions that differentiate the universe into the place we inhabit and sanctify.

בָּרוּךְ אַתָּה, יְיָ אֱלֹהֵינוּ, מֶלֶךְ הָעוֹלָם, הַמַּבְדִּיל בֵּין קֹדֶשׁ לְחֹל, בֵּין אוֹר לְחֹשֶׁךְ,
בֵּין יִשְׂרָאֵל לָעַמִּים בֵּין יוֹם הַשְּׁבִיעִי לְשֵׁשֶׁת יְמֵי הַמַּעֲשֶׂה. בָּרוּךְ אַתָּה, יְיָ הַמַּבְדִּיל
בֵּין קֹדֶשׁ לְחֹל.

Baruch ata Adonai Eloheynu Melech Ha-olam hamavdil bayn kodesh l'chol, bayn or l'choshech, bayn Yisrael l'amim, bayn yom hashvi-i le-shayshet y'may hama'aseh. Baruch ata Adonai hamavdil bayn kodesh l'chol.

Holy One of Blessing, Your Presence Fills Creation You separate the holy from the not-yet-holy, light from darkness, Israel from the other peoples, *Shabbat* from the six other days. Holy One of Blessing, You separate the holy from the not-yet-holy.

After this blessing the wine is drunk. Before anyone drinks, however, some is spilled into a plate or tray. This gesture symbolizes sadness and loss; as *Shabbat* ends, so ends its glimpse of redemption, of a world made whole. *Havdalah* expresses a longing for a never-ending *Shabbat*, which for Jews is expressed in the image of the messiah. The prophet Elijah *(Eliyahu)* is the legendary harbinger of the messiah and, because according to Talmudic legend Elijah will come after *havdalah*, it is traditional to sing *"Eliyahu Hanavi."*

Eliyahu Hanavi
Eliyahu Hatishbi
Eliyahu, Eliyahu
Eliyahu ha-Giladi

Bimheira v'yameinu
yavo eilenu
Im Mashiach ben David
Im Mashiach ben David.

Elijah the prophet
Elijah the Tishbite
Elijah from Gilad

Come to us soon
in our days
with Messiah
child of David.

Some people begin *havdalah* with this song, and others conclude with it by lowering the burning candle into the wine while singing, timing it so that the light sizzles out with the very last word.

Russian Jews, who used schnapps instead of wine for *havdalah*, set fire to the liquor, and the smoke was thought to represent departing *Shabbat* angels. Hasidic Jews dip their fingers into the wine and touch their pockets and foreheads as invocations for a successful, wise, and sweet week.

Havdalah is a treat for kids. The ceremony is dramatic, and short enough to hold their attention, and full of ways for them to participate with all their senses. Children can be given most if not all the honors of touching, carrying, and passing the ritual objects. Indeed, it is traditional for a child to hold the candle up during the ceremony.

At the conclusion of *havdalah*, everyone says ''*Shavua tov.*'' ''A good week.'' In some families, everyone kisses or takes a moment to make a wish for the coming week. ''*Shavua tov*'' is also the name of a very simple, well-known song:

> A good week
> A week of peace
> May gladness reign
> And joy increase . . .

AFTER SHABBAT

With *havdalah* over, a new week begins and a different spirit prevails almost immediately. For those who use *Shabbat* as an escape from the 20th century (avoiding the use of electricity, phones, and so on), there is an eruption of light and sound as things are switched on again. Some people make a little ritual of cleaning and setting aside their *Shabbat* candlesticks and other ritual objects until next week. Some immediately make phone calls to invite guests for the following Friday night.

Another way to prolong the feeling of *Shabbat* in the new week is to have a party called a *Melavah Malkah*, which means literally ''escorting the queen.'' This time is sometimes used to celebrate life cycle events; for instance, Sunday weddings are often kicked off by *havdalah*, marking the separation between single and married life. Similarly, a Saturday evening party after a *bar* or *bat mitzvah* concludes a full day of celebration.

Shabbat versus Soccer

Few recipes come out looking like the illustration in the cookbook. After all, those dishes were not only prepared by a professional chef, they were also arranged for the camera by someone called a food stylist. In real life, the same dish may taste great, but it always looks messier.

The same goes for *Shabbat*. In spite of plans and good intentions, kids will balk about coming to the table on Friday night, and your spouse will be late or unable to get home at all. Or Friday night will be exactly as you want it but Saturday is just another work day for everyone. And, of course, the kids want to play soccer on Saturday morning along with the rest of their friends—Jews as well as non-Jews.

The *Shabbat*-versus-soccer question is not a big issue in families with a longstanding commitment to observing a total *Shabbat*. If the entire family spends every Saturday in synagogue, and then studies and relaxes together with other families, a whole community provides support, models and clear expectations. If, however, *Shabbat* observance is new or still developing, and part of a less supportive context, it is likely that school-aged children will challenge any new limits to their weekend activities.

In the past, the Jewish world was divided into people who observed all the laws of *Shabbat* and those who observed none of them. The choice was either/or. This is no longer the case for American Jews, who observe the Sabbath in a variety of ways. For many liberal Jews, making *Shabbat* is a goal achieved (a) sometimes, (b) partially, (c) rarely, or (d) all of the above.

Almost everyone begins at home with Friday night rituals. For some, that will remain the extent of their *Shabbat* observance. Others create a Saturday afternoon study group, or make a commitment to keeping the whole day clear for family outings. Some try to avoid all errands on Saturday but, when something important intrudes, put it off until the last minute to extend *Shabbat* as long as possible. And even on a Saturday filled with soccer, a trip to the office, and urgent errands, some families try to have everyone regroup for *havdalah* so that *Shabbat* can at least end as peacefully as it began.

Some parents worry about instituting family *Shabbat* for fear of becoming ogres who do nothing except say no to their children all day long—a position that will surely make kids resentful and rebellious. And it is true that many Jewish choices, including *Shabbat*, do impose limits that other kids may not face.

With older children, it is important to talk about the family's reasons for choosing and making *Shabbat:* Why do we go to synagogue? Why do we have to be home on Friday nights? Why do we do this stuff when even Grandma thinks it's weird? Parents need to be able to answer questions like these honestly and clearly, not simply by ending the conversation with a curt "Because I said so."

It is also important to occasionally let older children decide about *Shabbat* observance for themselves, even if you disagree with their choices. Later you can ask, "How did you feel about going to Jan's slumber party instead of staying home for *Shabbat* dinner?" Children will grow up to make their own decisions. For parents who want their children to grow up identifying themselves as Jews and cherishing their Judaism, one of the tasks of parenting is to give kids practice at making Jewish choices, and at developing Jewish priorities.

Of course, being a good parent also means making unpopular decisions about all sorts of things: from the breakfast menu to bedtime. Being a Jewish parent entails making Jewish decisions. For example, your son is invited to a friend's *bar mitzvah* on the morning of a very important soccer game. He tells you that he wants to play in the game and then go to the big party, after the *bar mitzvah* ceremony is over. If you give permission for him to go to the party and miss the religious service, you are letting him know that as far as you are concerned, Judaism is not as important as either soccer or ice cream and cake. This choice probably does not further your goals as a Jewish parent.

But, most of all, children learn from their parents' example. When adults make a heart-felt commitment to making *Shabbat*, when Jewish family rituals seem as natural and dependable as the tides and the seasons, when Jewish activities are associated with fun, then arguments about soccer games and slumber parties take their place as minor disturbances in a broader context that has been positively defined and delineated in Jewish terms.

FURTHER READING

The Sabbath: It's Meaning for Modern Man by Abraham Joshua Heschel (Farrar, Straus and Giroux, 1951) A heartfelt, evocative book about *Shabbat* by one of the 20th century's finest Jewish minds, this is the best-loved and most-quoted book on the subject. An excellent little book for study, it lends itself to being read aloud.

The Sabbath by Samuel H. Dresner, (The Burning Book Press, 1970) Another short book of essay-like chapters that focuses on *Shabbat* as the resolution for the internal and external struggles of modern life. A companion to and elaboration on Heschel's book, which is acknowledged and quoted throughout, it includes insights from a wide range of sources, from the Talmud to bestselling author Herman Wouk.

Torah with Love, a Guide for Strengthening Jewish Values within the Family by David Epstein and Suzanne Singer Stuttman (Prentice Hall Press, 1986). This book contains specific and practical suggestions for learning Torah with children.

FOR CHILDREN

Mrs. Moskowitz and the Sabbath Candlesticks by Amy Schwartz, (Jewish Publication Society, 1983.) Mrs. M. is blue about moving into a small apartment, but her mood brightens as she prepares for *Shabbat*.

Joseph Who Loved the Sabbath by Marilyn Hirsch, (Viking Penguin, 1986.) A wonderful retelling of a story from the Babylonian Talmud, about a poor man's devotion to the Sabbath. Imaginatively illustrated by Devis Grebu.

Good Deeds

When a Jewish baby is born, there is a traditional prayer that the child will grow into a life that includes Torah, *huppah,* and *ma'asim tovim.* Torah stands for learning, especially Jewish learning. *Huppah,* the wedding canopy, symbolizes love, commitment, and family. *Ma'asim tovim* means good deeds, because for Jews the doing of good is what defines a *mensch*—a human being.

Because one of Judaism's primary goals is the transformation of people into *menschen* (the plural of *mensch*), good deeds are not left to the regrettably unreliable human impulse to do good. Feeding the hungry, clothing the naked, housing the homeless; for Jews, these are not voluntary acts of charity, a word which derives from the Latin *caritas* meaning "Christian love." Jews are *commanded* through *mitzvot* to feed, clothe, and shelter those who lack the basic necessities.

The general concept of good deeds—*ma'asim tovim*—may be divided into three categories: *tzedakah, gemilut hassadim,* and *tikkun olam. Tzedakah,* the giving of money to the poor, is commonly explained as charity, although a more accurate translation is "righteous giving." *Gemilut hassadim* is usually rendered as "acts of loving kindness," and refers to the kinds of activities Americans tend to associate with volunteerism: donating time, effort, and energy to help those in need.

Tzedakah and *gemilut hassadim* are ancient Jewish concepts, discussed in the Talmud and recognized by all Jews as fundamental to Jewish observance. *Tikkun olam,* or "the repair of the world," however, is a 20th century notion (based on a 400-year old mystical story) that elevates the biblical prophets' demands for social justice to the status of a *mitzvah*. Today, *tikkun olam* is commonly defined as the religious obligation to work for peace, freedom, and justice for all people.

In fact, these three categories are arbitrary. *Tzedakah* and *tikkun olam* can be defined as expressions of *gemilut hassadim,* and the term *tzedakah* if often used to refer to all manner of good deeds. The three categories of good works are described separately in this chapter not only for the sake of organization, but also to reflect the fact that people tend to "specialize" in one or another aspect of *ma'asim tovim.* The man who volunteers at a soup kitchen every Sunday is not always someone who collects vast sums for that operation. The woman who lobbies tirelessly on behalf of Soviet Jewry is not necessarily the person who visits nursing homes.

Of course, no one is expected to do it all by him or herself. The Jewish community as a whole is considered responsible for the performance of good deeds, and is obligated to organize on behalf of the poor and the needy. The chapter "The Organizational World" in Part Three contains information about communal organizations concerned with *ma'asim tovim.*

Yet, as the Talmud states, "Though it is not your duty to complete the work, neither are you free to desist from it." [1] And because the obligation to do *tzedakah, gemilut hassadim,* and *tikkun olam* are, first and foremost, incumbent on individuals and families, this chapter contains many practical suggestions for ways of incorporating "good deeds"—*ma'asim tovim*—into everyday life.

Righteous Giving

The word *tzedakah* is related to several other Hebrew words, including *tzadik,* "righteous person," and *tzodek,* "correct." In the Bible, the word *tzedakah* generally denotes righteousness. The much-quoted passage from Deuteronomy, usually translated, "Justice, justice shall you pursue," actually calls for *"tzedek, tzedek."* [2] The Talmud is full of references, parables, and teachings on the *mitzvah* of *tzedakah* and even says, *"Tzedakah* is as important as all the other commandments put together." [3]

Giving *tzedakah* is not viewed as an expression of individual goodness or good will, but rather as a response to an obligation based on biblical imperatives and the belief that all needy humans deserve help. Whereas it has always been considered preferable to give *tzedakah* cheerfully and willingly, the important thing is the gift, not the spirit in which it is given.

This does not mean that Jewish tradition does not recognize the intrinsic value of *tzedakah* to the donor as well as to the recipient. *Tzedakah* was never considered an onerous duty or a tax; it is a privilege, a way of expressing dignity, affirming self-respect, and participating in an activity that defines a *mensch*. Doing good feels good, which is partly why Jewish law requires that even the very poor give something to those less fortunate than themselves, even if their gift comes directly from *tzedakah* given to them by someone else.[4]

The most important commentary on *tzedakah* in Jewish history was written by Rabbi Moses Maimonides in the 12th century. Known as "Maimonides' Ladder of *Tzedakah*," it lists the ways of giving in order of worthiness: from that which is given anonymously and enables another to become self-sufficient, down to that which is given only grudgingly. Maimonides was greatly concerned with sparing the poor as much embarrassment as possible. He was also quite specific about how much *tzedakah* is enough. He considered 10% of one's income an average and proper *tzedakah* budget.

Tzedakah has remained a constant feature of Jewish life throughout history. Indeed, American Jews are renowned for their generosity for support of religious and communal institutions and activities, for Israel and Soviet Jewry, and for a wide range of secular political, social, and cultural causes. For some time, though, Jewish philanthropy had

---

Rabbi Chayim of Sanz said, "The merit of charity is so great that I am happy to give to one hundred beggars even if only one might actually be needy. Some people, however, act as if they are exempt from giving to one hundred beggars in the event that one might be a fraud."

Darkai Chayim, 16th century book of moral writings

largely forgotten its Hebrew name. Today, there is renewed interest in the classical Jewish view of personal *tzedakah* as *mitzvah*.[5]

Danny Siegel, a modern master of personal *tzedakah* who is also a poet, author, and itinerant lecturer, teaches at synagogues and Jewish community centers throughout North America, enlisting *tzedakah*-doers. Under the aegis of the Ziv ("Radiance") Tzedakah Fund, Siegel has raised and distributed money in large and small amounts to individuals and agencies providing direct services with a minimum of operating costs in both America and Israel. Siegel's actions and words all make the same point: "All that needs to be done is to do it."[*]

Tzedakah does not just happen by accident. Although Jewish tradition supports spontaneous giving such as responding to beggars on the street and neighbors asking for a donation to cancer research, taking on the mitzvah of *tzedakah* means finding ways to incorporate it into the rhythms of life. Doing *tzedakah* means writing checks to charity while paying the monthly bills and teaching children about the importance of giving.

Many Jews have embraced the traditional practice of making regular donations on Jewish holidays and personal milestones. Some families put aside money for *tzedakah* before lighting *Shabbat* candles every week and on holidays. For small gifts like these, the *pushke*, which is a coin box reserved for *tzedakah* (a kind of Jewish piggy bank), has made a comeback. *Pushkes* range from works of art made of brass or silver, to blue and white aluminum cans. Making a family *pushke* can be a wonderful project, and whether the result is a glazed clay masterpiece or an old coffee can covered with children's handprints, the result will be an heirloom.

The custom of remembering the poor at moments of celebration has also been revived. In the small, tight-knit Jewish communities of the past, *tzedakah* was part of every joyful occasion; local beggars were invited to wedding feasts, and at Passover the community insured that even the poorest family could afford a proper *seder*. In that spirit, many families, synagogues, and other Jewish organizations now regularly set aside a voluntary *tzedakah* "tax." Three percent of the food costs for

---

[*] See "Further reading" at the end of this chapter for information about Siegel's books. For information about his work or to make a contribution: Ziv Tzedakah Fund, c/o Bena Siegel, 11818 Trail Ridge Drive, Potomac MD 20854.

weddings, *b'nai mitzvah*, (plural of *bar* and *bat mitzvah)* and banquets is donated to Mazon, A Jewish Response to Hunger. Mazon channels funds to soup kitchens, food pantries, and other feeding programs in the United States and around the world.*

Similarly, Jews give *tzedakah* to honor rites of passage. Some wedding invitations, *bar* and *bat mitzvah* invitations, and birth announcements request that donations be sent to a specified charity, sometimes in lieu of a gift. *Bar* and *bat mitzvah* has become a special focal point for *tzedakah*. Twelve and thirteen-year-old children are old enough to understand that the world is filled with inequities and that *tzedakah* is a way for them to make a difference. Indeed, raising money for charity and/or volunteering are part of the curriculum in most Jewish education programs.

Although the example that parents set at home is primary, people who want their children to grow up understanding that *tzedakah* is a crucial part of being Jewish also make sure that their children's formal religious school curriculum reflects the importance of this mitzvah— not only in the classroom, but also by doing projects for others.

There are many ways to make *tzedakah* a family project. Putting coins into a *pushke* every Friday night is the simplest, and it is also a way to begin talking to children about poverty and hunger and about what they can do to help. School-aged children can help decide where the *pushke* money should go, and some parents will talk candidly about the family's whole *tzedakah* budget with older children. When monthly bills are written, they open their checkbooks to show how much money is given and to whom. And in some families, children are expected to designate some portion of their allowance for *tzedakah*.

A relatively new but growing practice is the creation of *tzedakah* endowment funds for children, the interest from which is dedicated to charity. Parents or grandparents begin such funds at birth, adding to them regularly. Such an account can also be opened on the occasion of a child's *bar* or *bat mitzvah*.

Another way to make *tzedakah* part of daily life is at the supermarket. Some families allow children to pick out a can of food for donation

---

*   Mazon, A Jewish Response to Hunger, 2940 Westwood Boulevard, Suite #7, Los Angeles, CA 90064. (213) 470-7769.

to a food drive. Or you might set aside those cans at home until the collection is big enough to justify a family outing to a local food pantry. If local synagogues or the Jewish community center do not already sponsor a canned food drive, you and your children might help start one.

For adults, deciding where to send personal *tzedakah* dollars can be very difficult because there are so many worthy causes. Traditionally, *tzedakah* was allocated in concentric circles, beginning with family, the poor of the local community, and then the poor who live at a distance, especially in Israel. Although Jews have always been enjoined to help the non-Jewish poor, the primary goal of *tzedakah* was seen as helping fellow Jews who could not rely on others.

This argument remains compelling. If Jews don't support services for the Jewish elderly, the resettlement of Soviet Jews, or Jewish educational and cultural institutions, there is no reason to expect non-Jews to do so. However, many Jews also feel strongly that international and nondenominational efforts deserve their support as well.

Ultimately, deciding where to give *tzedakah* is a very personal choice. The bulk of Jewish giving is done through federations and local umbrella fund raising organizations that allocate monies to local and national Jewish agencies and also to Israel. However, some individuals and families dislike federation solicitations, and feel federation allocations are not necessarily in line with their Jewish priorities.

Whereas individual giving is the primary alternative to federation giving, there is another: the *tzedakah* collective. Sometimes organized through synagogues, sometimes simply an independent group of friends, *tzedakah* collectives give people the opportunity to participate in joint giving, but within an intimate setting where they can exercise greater control. Collective members educate themselves about various charities and clarify their own choices in the context of a community of

---

As tiny scales join to form a strong coat of mail, so little donations combine to form a large total of good.

Talmud: Baba Bathra 9b

Jews with similar values. Pooling resources gives collective members the sense that their individual contributions go further and mean more.

The question "How much is enough?" is rarely answered with Maimonides' suggested 10% figure anymore. The current consensus seems to be that a reasonable amount is between 1% and 5% of a family's gross annual income. One oft-cited rule of thumb: if the total of all charitable contributions makes no dent in your lifestyle, if you're not giving up as much as one dinner in a nice restaurant, you're probably not giving enough.

Acts of Loving Kindness

According to many Jewish sources, *gemilut hassadim* is the highest form of good works or *ma'asim tovim*. Whereas raising money and writing checks to Jewish institutions and other worthy causes is an essential *mitzvah*, there is a sense that money alone does not meet the biblical demand for righteousness. Especially in America, where it can be relatively easy to remain insulated from hunger, poverty, and pain, *gemilut hassadim* calls for personal involvement and a face-to-face encounter with real need.

Gemilut hassadim is not, strictly speaking, a *mitzvah*. Because it is a feeling, loving kindness cannot be required or commanded. But, like a *mitzvah*, loving kindness is not only about feelings, but about rolling up your sleeves, giving up an evening a week, and working for the benefit of strangers.

There are six traditional forms of *gemilut hassadim:* providing clothes for the naked, visiting the sick, comforting mourners, accompanying the dead to the grave, providing for brides, and offering hospitality to strangers. These acts are considered especially holy because, according to Midrash, God performed them for human beings by, for example, attending Eve at her wedding to Adam, comforting Isaac as he mourned for his father Abraham, and burying Moses.[6]

In the Talmud, *gemilut hassadim* is described as more spiritually powerful than *tzedakah* in three ways. First, *tzedakah* involves only money, but *gemilut hassadim* requires personal involvement. Second, *tzedakah* is given only to the poor, but *gemilut hassadim* can be done for anyone, regardless of their station in life. And third, whereas *tzedakah* can only be given to the living, *gemilut hassadim* can even extend to the dead.

The modern definition of *gemilut hassadim* extends to include activities such as feeding the hungry, helping people find jobs, visiting the elderly, teaching people to read, providing shelter for the homeless, saving animals from suffering, planting trees, lifting the spirits of the depressed, caring for orphans, and perpetuating the memory of someone who has died.

The Jewish emphasis on these kinds of efforts dovetails with the longstanding American tradition of volunteerism. Over the years, surveys have showed that almost half of all Americans do some kind of volunteer work on a weekly basis. Although Jewish volunteerism has not always matched the national average, there is evidence that this is changing. There are unprecedented numbers of shelters and soup kitchens in urban synagogues. And, increasingly, Jewish religious schools are requiring high school students to perform some kind of community service for a first-hand experience of *gemilut hassadim*.

Families can participate in *gemilut hassadim* in a number of ways. Parents who are involved in volunteer work can explain to their children exactly what they are doing and why. And though it may not be appropriate to take young children to a busy soup kitchen, there are other ways to involve kids, such as collecting outgrown and unused clothes and making a family trip to deliver them to a local shelter; baking Hannukah cookies and bringing them to a Jewish nursing home; or "adopting" an isolated Jewish elder and visiting him or her regularly.

Jewish organizations of all sorts are always in need of volunteers. So are community hospitals, nursing homes, legal aid societies, literacy programs. The list is endless, and so are opportunities for acts of loving kindness.

Repairing the World

During the 16th century, in the town of Safed in the land of Israel, Isaac Luria[7] described the creation of the world in terms that have captured the imaginations of Jews ever since:

Before creation, there was nothing but God. God was in all time and space, and God's light filled the cosmos. In order to make room for creation, God had to make some space where there was no God. So God took a deep breath to make room for the universe.

In the space from which God had withdrawn, the heavens and the earth were formed. But that meant God was nowhere in creation. So God exhaled some of God's light into the world.

But this light was too strong, too bright for the vessels that were meant to hold it, so they shattered. And the world was filled with tiny sparks of God's light.

The world is filled with these divine sparks. They are hidden, lost everywhere, and it is the responsibility of each Jew to gather some of these sparks and restore them to their place. By doing this, creation can be restored to its original, perfect state. The task of restoring or repairing the world is called *tikkun olam.*

According to a traditional reading and Luria's intent, *tikkun olam* is accomplished by performing all the *mitzvot:* from the commandments for keeping kosher and lighting *Shabbat* candles to those that mandate caring for the elderly and working for world peace. In modern times, Jews have come to understand *tikkun olam* in somewhat different terms. The repair of the world is associated with tackling problems in macrocosmic rather than interpersonal or even communal terms. *Tikkun olam* is identified with working for social justice, peace, freedom, equality, and the restoration of the environment.

This definition, however, is not an entirely modern formulation. Judaism has always blurred distinctions between religious duties and social obligations. Indeed, the Jewish notion of redemption is political in the sense that it calls not for the perfection of individual souls but for the liberation of the entire world. The prophets demanded an end to poverty, bigotry, and all forms of oppression. The words of Isaiah,

Rabbi Isaac said, "He who gives a coin to a poor man is rewarded with six blessings. But he who encourages him with friendly words is rewarded with eleven."

Talmud: Baba Bathra 9a

which are repeated at services every Yom Kippur, have never been more powerful in their insistence on action than they are today:

> Behold on the day of your fast you pursue business as usual and oppress your workers. Behold you fast only to quarrel and fight, to deal wicked blows. Such fasting will not make your voice audible on high.
>
> This is my chosen fast: to loosen all the bonds that bind men unfairly, to let the oppressed go free, to break every yoke. Share your bread with the hungry, take the homeless into your home. Clothe the naked when you see him, do not turn away from people in need. . . .
>
> If you remove from your midst the yoke of oppression, the finger of scorn, the tongue of malice, if you put yourself out for the hungry and relieve the wretched, then shall your light shine in the darkness, and your gloom shall be as noonday.[8]

For the past 200 years, Jews have been involved in virtually all organized attempts to improve human life. Sometimes, *tikkun olam* takes a specifically Jewish form, as in the work to enable Jews to leave the Soviet Union, or the search for a just and secure peace for Israel and her neighbors. However, a commitment to *tikkun olam* also requires, almost by definition, attention to many issues that are not strictly limited to Jewish interests, including the environment and ecology, nuclear disarmament and international peace, and equal protection for all, regardless of race, sex, national origin, or sexual orientation. Jews are prominent among the supporters, activists, and leaders in these and other causes.

Doing *tikkun olam* includes everything from writing letters to Congress about toxic waste to attending rallies in support of funding for public education. *Tikkun olam* means supporting candidates and voting with a self-consciously Jewish perspective. Even recycling waste paper, bottles and cans responds to the call to repair the world.

This formulation of *tikkun olam* reclaims political commitment as a specifically Jewish endeavor. And it helps erase the tendency to segregate Jewishness to those things that are done at home, or in a synagogue, or among other Jews. In a sense, *tikkun olam* demands that Jews act as Jews in every arena of life.

FURTHER READING

Gym Shoes and Irises (Personalized Tzedakah), 1982; *Gym Shoes and Irises (Book Two)*, 1987; *Munbaz II and Other Mitzvah Heroes*, 1988 (The Town House Press) by Danny Siegel. These books contain a feast of information and inspiration related to *tzedakah:* essays, practical guides to doing, quotations from the Talmud, and more. For information and to order copies: The Town House Press, 28 Midway Road, Spring Valley, NY 10977.

The Prophets, An Introduction, Volumes I and II by Abraham J. Heschel. (Harper & Row, 1962.) A treatment of the biblical prophets that is both historical and inspirational.

FOR CHILDREN

My Special Friend, by Floreva G. Cohen (Jewish Board of Education, Inc., 1986). Illustrated with black and white photographs, a book about the relationship between two boys, both members of the same congregation, one of whom has Down's syndrome.

The People of the Library

Jews are often called the "people of the book," and for good reason. The legacy of universal literacy—for women and men, for poor and rich —has set Jews apart from their neighbors throughout history.

It would be more accurate, however, to refer to Jews as "the people of the library." First of all, "The Book," the Jewish Bible, is itself a library, a collection of books. Furthermore, this one book has become the foundation and cornerstone of a 3,000-year-old tradition of intellectual inquiry, writing, and publishing.

But the basic texts of Judaism includes more than the Bible. "Jewish literacy" requires some familiarity with some of the classical sources as well: Torah, Talmud, Midrash, Kabbalah, *siddur*. The first part of this chapter contains brief introductions to these texts.

The second part is devoted to the Jewish home library. The presence of books, especially books dealing with Jewish subjects, is a hallmark of virtually all Jewish homes. Reading, study, discussion, and writing are part of the social as well as intellectual glue that has kept Judaism and the Jewish people alive. The secret ingredient of this glue, taught to children by their parents, is the pleasure of study for its own sake, which in Hebrew is called *Torah lishma*. The list of titles in this section is in no way definitive; rather it is only suggestive of the range of topics available to interested readers.

Jewish Texts: Some Definitions

BIBLE

There is no Hebrew word for bible. The English word probably comes from the Greek *biblia,* meaning "books" and reflecting the fact that the Bible is itself an anthology. When Jews talk about the Bible (as in this book), the reference is shorthand for the "Jewish Bible" or "Hebrew Bible." The Jewish Bible is called the "Old Testament" by Christians, who believe that Jesus announced a new covenant between God and humanity in the "New Testament."

The Hebrew term for the Bible is *tanakh,* which is an acronym for the three Hebrew letters that correspond to its three major divisions: *T*orah, the five books of Moses, or Pentateuch; *N*evi'im, Prophets; and *K*etuvim, Writings.

Arguments about the authorship of the Bible cut right to the heart of religious belief. Traditionalists attribute the writing of the Torah to Moses, Psalm 92 to Adam, and Song of Songs to King Solomon. Modern biblical scholars tend to disagree with these attributions and generally agree that the Bible, as we know it, was codified sometime during the first or second century C.E.

The Hebrew Bible or *tanakh* can be further broken down as such:

TORAH: THE FIVE BOOKS OF MOSES
Genesis
Exodus
Leviticus
Numbers
Deuteronomy

PROPHETS: NEVI'IM
Joshua
Judges
I Samuel
II Samuel
I Kings
II Kings
Isaiah

Jeremiah

Ezekiel

The 12 minor prophets

Hosea

Joel

Amos

Obadaiah

Jonah

Micah

Nahum

Habakkuk

Zephania

Haggai

Zakariah

Malachi

WRITINGS: KETUVIM

Psalms

Proverbs

Job

Song of Songs

Ruth

Lamentations

Ecclesiastes

Esther

Daniel

Ezra

Nehemiah

I Chronicles

II Chronicles

TORAH

Torah has many meanings. "The Torah," also called the Pentateuch and the five books of Moses, consists of the first five volumes of the Bible: Genesis, Exodus, Leviticus, Numbers, and Deuteronomy. "The Torah" also refers to the scroll on which this part of the Bible is written.

But "Torah" itself, without the article, refers to much broader concepts. "Torah" can be used to mean revelation: God's word as understood by human beings. To further complicate things, Torah can also refer to all Jewish study, all of Jewish literature.[1]

TALMUD

The *Talmud* (Hebrew for "study") is an encyclopedia of commentaries on Jewish law, and of commentaries on commentaries on Jewish law. Written in Hebrew and Aramaic, the *lingua franca* of the Near East, the Talmud comprises two major sections called *Mishna* and *Gemara*.

According to tradition, Moses received two forms of revelation on Mount Sinai; written and oral. The written law, the Torah, was much shorter and less specific than the oral law, which was transmitted through the generations, first from Moses to Joshua, then to the elders of the Hebrew people, to the prophets, and on through successive leaders until it reached the men who were, in effect, the earliest rabbis. These scholars of the first and second century C.E. began putting the Oral Law into writing in what came to be called the *Mishna*.

The Mishna (Hebrew for "recitation" or "recapitulation"), completed by third century C.E., was an attempt to put the commands contained in the written Torah into practical terms. Its authors sought to convey the idea that the laws found in the Bible did not just apply to their original contexts, but embraced all aspects of life throughout time. The six sections of the Mishna are called Orders, which are further divided into 63 smaller sections called *tractates*. The Mishna deals with holiday observances, family life, agriculture, the rituals of the Temple, and much more.

The most famous section of the Mishna is the tractate known as *Avot,* or "fathers," which contains many famous proverbs, axioms and sayings, such as, "If I am not for myself, who will be for me? If I am not for myself alone, what am I? And if not now, when?"[2] This tractate has long been published on its own as a book entitled *Pirke Avot,* usually translated as "Ethics of the Fathers."

Over succeeding generations, the study of Mishna inspired a literature of explanation and commentary, which became an object of study in its own right. This body of writing was called *Gemara,* Aramaic for "study." The Gemara, which is an unstructured, almost stream-of-consciousness transcript of discussions, arguments and stories, examines a broad range of questions from daily life. Sometimes the sublime and the ridiculous share a single paragraph:

> Who is to be considered truly wealthy?
> In the opinion of Rabbi Meir: He who derives peace of mind from his wealth.
> Rabbi Tarfon says: He who has a hundred vineyards, a hundred fields, and a hundred workers working in them.
> Rabbi Akiva says: He who has a spouse who does exquisite deeds.
> Rabbi Yossi says: He who has a bathroom near his dining room table.[3]

MIDRASH

Midrash, which means "search," or "investigation," refers not to a book but to an entire genre of biblical commentary that employs storytelling as its primary technique. Using every kind of imaginative and literary device, midrash embroiders upon the biblical text. Explaining midrash virtually requires metaphoric language. Midrash has been described as something "between commentary and fantasy . . . that sprouts up in the spaces between the consecrated words of Scripture."[4] If the compressed images of the Bible are like photographs, a midrash is the story about what happened before and after the flash went off.

There are several collection of *midrashim* (plural of *midrash*), most them produced between 400 and 1200 C.E. One of the most famous of these is *Midrash Rabbah*, "the Great Midrash." From one line in Genesis that says, "And God said, Let us make man," the *Midrash Rabbah* continues:

> When the Holy One came to create the first man, the angels took sides. Mercy said, "Let him be created, for he will be merciful." But Truth said, "Do not let him not be created because he will lie." Righteousness said,

Who is wise? One who learns from all men.
Who is wealthy? One who is happy with his portion.
Who is mighty? One who subdues his passions.
Who is honored? One who honors all creation.

Pirke Avot 4:1

"Let him be created for he will do righteous deeds." But Peace said, "Do not let him be created because he is full of strife."

The Holy One took Truth and flung him to earth, and the angels argued with God, and asked God to raise truth up again from the earth.

While the angels were arguing, The Holy One, created man. And then God said to the angels, "Why do you argue? Man is already made."[5]

CODES

The whole of Jewish law is called *halachah*, probably from the verb for "going." *Halachah* is often used to refer to the laws and rules that govern and inform Jewish life. The Talmud is not a set of laws but a discussion of the law. To find out "what the law says," people turn not to the Talmud but to the codes, which are practical, accessible guides to action based on the debates in the Talmud.

The two great codes are the *Mishna Torah*, written by Moses Maimonides, the great 12th century Mediterranean rabbi and philosopher, and the *Shulchan Aruch*, ("The Prepared Table") by Joseph Karo, a 16th century rabbi who lived in the town of Safed, Palestine. Maimonides and Karo based their guides on careful reading of Talmud, consideration of contemporary rabbis' written decisions (called responsa literature), and the Jewish practice of their times. These books remain cornerstones of *halachic* discussion and debate, which continues unabated today.

KABBALAH

The rationalist tradition in Jewish thought has been so dominant that many Jews remain unaware of the long tradition—the counter-history —of Jewish mysticism called *Kabbalah*. Kabbalah includes several books of biblical commentary, including *Sefer Yetzirah* (Book of Creation) and the *Bahir* (Brilliance.) The most influential of all mystical texts, however, is the *Zohar* (Splendor). Typified by evocative, lyrical language and concepts, the *Zohar* was a commentary on the Torah, probably written by the Spanish rabbi Moses de Leon (1230–1305).

SIDDUR

The daily book of prayer, used both in the synagogue and at home, is called the *siddur* (from the Hebrew root for "order"). The prayerbook used for festivals and the high holidays is called the *machzor*, from the Hebrew root for "cycle."

Prayerbooks have been the most commonly owned of all Jewish

books. Over time, the content and order of the prayerbook has evolved and changed. Modern prayer books tend to contain readings that reflect Jewish history and theology from many periods, including our own.

Creating a Jewish Home Library

No two Jewish homes have identical Jewish libraries. People select books as idiosyncratically as they choose art for the walls and food for the table. Book collections reflect the character, curiosity, and impulses of their owners. But given the fact that the world of Jewish literature is so vast and potentially confusing, a short, annotated list of books on subjects of general interest is provided here. Many more suggestions for further reading appear at the end of chapters throughout *Living a Jewish Life*.

Some of the titles listed here and in bibliographies throughout the book may not be readily available at general interest bookstores, though most can be ordered. Stores that specialize in Jewish books will stock most of the titles that appear in *Living a Jewish Life* and can probably order any of the others. Also, see the mail-order listing at the end of this chapter.

Most of the titles are available in paperback, and some may be out of print. Aficionados of Jewish books keep an eye on the Judaica sections of second-hand bookstores. And in our multi-media age, most Jewish home libraries contain more than books; periodicals, records, and videotapes are also important resources.

BIBLE

The Jewish Publication Society (JPS), one of the largest publishers of Jewish books in America, produces an accurate, readable translation of the Bible, available in either one or three volumes. *The Jerusalem Bible,*

Holy One of Blessing Your Presence Fills Creation, You make us holy with Your commandments and call us to occupy ourselves with words of Torah.
The blessing recited before Jewish study

published by Koren Publishers of Jerusalem, contains very accurate Hebrew and English versions in a single volume, although the English is not as readable as the JPS version.[6]

Congregation: Contemporary Writers Read the Jewish Bible, edited by David Rosenberg (Harcourt Brace Jovanovich, 1987) is a collection of essays about the books of the Bible by poets, novelists, humorists, editors, and literary critics.

TORAH

As a rule, Jews read the first five books of the bible in conjunction with some form of commentary. For close study of the Torah as it is read in its weekly portions during services, people use what is called a *chumash*. A chumash (from the Hebrew word for "five") includes both Hebrew and English versions of each week's portion, the weekly *haftarah* sections (readings from the Prophets), and English commentaries and notes.

The Soncino Publishing Company publishes two *chumashim* (plural of *chumash*), both of which feature classical commentaries from the Talmud: *The Soncino Chumash* (edited by The Rev. Dr. A. Cohen) and the *Hertz Chumash* (edited by Rabbi J. H. Hertz, 1935). The more recent *The Torah: A Modern Commentary*, edited by Rabbi Gunther Plaut (Union of American Hebrew Congregations, 1981), uses the Jewish Publication Society translation of the text, and is organized more for study than for synagogue use. The recently published *JPS Torah Commentary* is a five-volume chumash, with much larger Hebrew type, an excellent English translation, and excellent commentaries.

TALMUD

There are several good anthologies of the Talmud. *Everyman's Talmud* by Adin Steinsaltz (Bantam Books, 1976) is a brief and lucid introduction to Talmud. The Mishna is available in English in several editions of one or two volumes. The section of Mishna known as *Pirke Avot* is available in many versions, including some with explanatory notes and commentaries.

For more serious students there is *The Talmud: The Steinsaltz Edition* (Random House, 1989), which provides English readers with unprecedented access to the original text, by one of the 20th century's most erudite and prolific Jewish scholars.

OTHER CLASSIC SOURCES

The best single volume introduction to the classic Jewish texts is *Back to the Sources* by Barry Holtz (Summit Books, 1984). This volume contains eight essays written by leading experts on the major Jewish texts, including the Bible, Talmud, Midrash, Hasidic writings, and the prayerbook. Holtz's introductory essay is an elegant and succinct treatment of why people continue to read the classical sources of Judaism.

Nahum Glazter's *Hammer on the Rock* (Schocken, 1962) is a classic collection of Midrash. *Zohar, The Book of Enlightenment*, translated by Daniel Chanan Matt (Paulist Press, 1983), contains selections from the classic book of Jewish mystical commentary.

GENERAL REFERENCE

For quick, dictionary-style definitions of terms, dates, and significant historical figures, several single-volume encyclopedias of Judaism are available. One of the most comprehensive is *The Encyclopedia of Judaism*, edited by Geoffrey Wigoder (Macmillan Publishing Co., 1989).

However, there is nothing like *The Encyclopedia Judaica* (Keter Publishing Co., 1972). The "EJ," as it is known, is the *Britanica* of Judaism, and there is little it does not cover. A sixteen-volume work, it includes contributions by some 1,800 writers with substantial bibliographies after most entries.[7]

The Jewish Catalog, Vols. I, II, and III by Richard Seigel, Michael Strassfeld, and Sharon Strassfeld (Jewish Publication Society, 1973, 1976 and 1980) are paperback volumes full of Jewish information in a do-it-yourself format. All three volumes of *The Jewish Catalog* assume that readers are Hebrew-literate and somewhat familiar with Jewish law and observance.

A Guide to Jewish Religious Practice by Isaac Klein (Jewish Theological Society of America, 1979) is the standard reference book of *halachah* published by the Conservative movement; this is where you go to look up the law on just about anything.

The Joy of Yiddish by Leo Rosten, (McGraw-Hill, 1968) is more than just a funny dictionary of English, Yiddish, and "Yinglish" words; it is useful to people exploring and discovering *Yiddishkeit*—Jewishness.

The Book of Jewish Books by Ruth S. Frank and William Wollheim (Harper & Row, 1986) is a "reader's guide to Judaism" that contains well-organized and concise descriptions of hundreds of books.

Mixed Blessings by Paul Cowan with Rachel Cowan (Doubleday, 1987) is an intelligent overview of the challenges of interfaith couples based on interviews and workshops and also on the experience of the authors.

HISTORY

Books about specific periods of Jewish history abound. The following three books provide a broad overview.

Great Ages and Ideas of the Jewish People, edited by Leo Schwarz (Modern Library/Random House, 1956), divides Jewish history into six periods: Biblical, Hellenistic, Talmudic, Judeo-Islamic, European, and Modern.

Jewish People, Jewish Thought: The Jewish Experience in History by Robert M. Seltzer (Macmillan, 1980) is a survey of Jewish thought, beginning with the ancients and running through the 20th century, including a discussion of the modern movements of Judaism.

A History of the Jewish People, edited by H.H. Ben-Sasson (Dvir Publishing House, 1969), is a definitive volume of 1,000 pages that covers all Jewish history up to the modern period.

THE HOLOCAUST

Interest in the Holocaust continues to generate dozens of titles every year. *The War Against The Jews* by Lucy Dawidowicz (Holt, Rinehart & Winston, 1975) is an intense, dramatic, and exhaustively researched historical anthology of the holocaust. Fiction and memoirs provide some of the most powerful commentaries on those years: for example, *Night* by Elie Wiesel, *Survival in Auschwitz* by Primo Levi, *The Last of the Just* by Andre Schwarz-Bart.

ISRAEL

There are new books almost monthly on events and life in Israel, including a lively and diverse literature. The following books offer some background.

The Zionist Idea, edited by Arthur Hertzberg (Doubleday, 1959), is a collection of essays that provides an intellectual history of Zionism, by people who, in the 19th and 20th centuries, developed the idea that the

Jews should return to the land of Israel. It also contains brief biographies of the leaders of the early movement.

The Israelis: Founders and Sons by Amos Elon (Penguin, 1971) is a sociological description of the differences between the generation of idealists who founded the state of Israel and their *sabra* (native-born) children.

In The Land of Israel by Amos Oz (Harcourt, Brace & Jovanovich, 1983) is a series of interviews conducted by the well-known Israeli novelist. The cross-section of Israeli and Palestinian opinion expose the problems confronting the Middle East.

PHILOSOPHY

God in Search of Man: A Philosophy of Judaism by Abraham Joshua Heschel (Farrar, Straus and Giroux, 1955) is a contemporary attempt to describe the relationship between human beings and God.

A Maimonides Reader by Isador Twersky (Behrman House, 1972) is a good introduction to one of Judaism's great scholarly minds.

After Auschwitz by Richard Rubenstein (Macmillan, 1966) articulates a radical post-Holocaust Jewish theology.

SPIRITUALITY

The Way of Man According to the Teachings of Hasidism by Martin Buber (Citadel Press, 1950) is a modern interpretation of six Hasidic tales that explain some of Judaism's basic tenets.

Major Trends in Jewish Mysticism by Gershom Scholem (Schocken Books, 1941) is an historical consideration of the mystical "counterhistory" that includes Kabbalah and Hasidism.

River of Light: Spirituality, Judaism and the Evolution of Consciousness by Lawrence Kushner (Jewish Lights Publishing, 1990) is a modern introduction to midrashic thinking.

WOMEN

The impact of feminism on Judaism has been profound, which is evidenced in modern fiction as well as the following nonfiction resources. *Jewish and Female: A Guide and Sourcebook for Today's Jewish Woman* by Susan Wiedman Schneider (Simon & Schuster, 1984) is a kaleidoscopic view of the issues facing Jewish women today, from theology to birth control.

On Being a Jewish Feminist by Susannah Heschel (Schocken, 1983) is a collection of essays about the dialectic between Judaism and feminism.

The Jewish Women's Studies Guide, second edition, complied by Sue Levi Elwell (Biblio Press, 1987), is a comprehensive collection of syllabi and bibliographies and a valuable research and study tool.

CHILDREN

As the books listed here demonstrate, Jewish children's literature is flourishing in every category, from board books for pre-readers to mysteries for young adults. Suggestions for children's books are also included at the end of many chapters.

Watch the Stars Come Out by Riki Levenson (Dutton, 1985) is a story in which Grandma tells the story of immigrating to America at the turn of the century (4 and up). *Joshua's Dream* by Sheila Segal (UAHC, 1984) is the story of Zionism for children (5 and up). *The Mystery of the Coins* by Chaya Burstein (UAHC, 1988) is a mystery that contains clues from 3,400 years of Jewish history (10 and up).

A Young Reader's Encyclopedia of Jewish History by Ilana Shamir and Dr. Shlomo Shavit (Viking Kestrel, 1987) is a vividly illustrated single-volume resource (12 and up). *Fast, Clean, and Cheap (or everything the Jewish teacher and parent needs to know about art)* by Simon Kops (Torah Aura Productions, 1989) is full of Jewish arts and crafts projects. *Elijah's Violin and other Jewish Fairy Tales* by Howard Schwartz (Harper & Row, 1983) is a collection of tales filled with princesses, magic birds, and enchanted forests (Children of all ages).

For young adult readers, *The Book of Miracles: A Young Person's Guide to Jewish Spiritual Awareness* by Rabbi Lawrence Kushner (UAHC, 1987) is a simple but subtle introduction to big ideas: "For parents to read to their children, for children to read to their parents." And *Tell Us Your Secret* by Barbara Cohen (Bantam Books, 1988), is a mystery that deals with the discomforts and rewards of pluralism and the lingering pain of the Holocaust.

PERIODICALS

Magazines, newspapers, and newsletters are also part of the Jewish home library. In addition to the local or regional Jewish newspaper, which can keep you abreast of the activities, organizations, and arguments going on in your own backyard, there are several Jewish publications dealing with national and international issues. The publications listed include most of the best-known general interest magazines for laypeople. For browsing, try synagogue libraries, which generally subscribe to several.

Commentary Magazine
165 East 56th Street
New York, NY 10022-9977

A publication of the American Jewish Congress, *Commentary* is a conservative review of U.S., Israeli, and global politics.

Hadassah Magazine
50 West 38th Street
New York, NY 10019

The membership publication of *Hadassah*, the Women's Zionist Organization of America, mostly features articles on aspects of life in Israel.

The Jerusalem Post International Edition
Subscriptions Department
P.O. Box 282
Brewster, NY 10509

Published in Jerusalem, this English-language weekly features extensive coverage of Israel and the Middle East.

Lilith
250 West 57th Street
Suite 2432
New York, NY 10107

A quarterly journal of Jewish feminism.

Moment Magazine
P.O. Box 922
Farmingdale, NY 11737-0001

Readable, topical articles on current events, politics (American and Israeli), and religious issues.

New Menorah
P'nai Or
6723 Emlen Street
Philadelphia, PA 19119

A quarterly "Journal of Jewish Renewal" published by P'nai Or Religious Fellowship, the new-age, neo-Hasidic group founded by Zalman Schachter-Shalomi in the 1960s.

Sh'ma: A Journal of Jewish Responsibility
P.O. Box 567
Port Washington, NY 11050

Sh'ma's short articles, clustered around a different topic each issue, create a sense of lively discussion.

Shofar
43 Northcote Drive
Melville, NY 11747

A bimonthly for school-aged children: recipes, holidays, and current affairs.

Tikkun
P.O. Box 6406
Syracuse, NY 13217

A bimonthly Jewish "critique of politics, culture and society," *Tikkun* features long, heady essays of a progressive-left bent.

Movement Publications: The following magazines are published by different branches of the liberal Jewish community. They are automatically sent to members of their affiliated synagogues.

Conservative Judaism
c/o Jewish Theological Seminary
3080 Broadway
New York, NY 10027

The Reconstructionist
c/o Reconstructionist Rabbinical College
Church Road and Greenwood Avenue
Wyncote, PA 19095

Reform Judaism
838 Fifth Avenue
New York, NY 10021

Ordering Jewish Books
(And Other Resources) by Mail

If your community lacks a good Jewish bookstore or if you enjoy shopping by mail, the following publishers and distributors will send information, lists, and/or catalogs on request:

Alden Films
P.O. Box 449
Carlsburg, NJ 08510
(Jewish films for rental, many available on video)

Alternatives in Religious Education
3945 Oneida Street
Denver, CO 80237

Jason Aronson, Inc.
230 Livingston Street
Northvale, NJ 07647

Anti-Defamation League of B'nai B'rith
823 United Nations Plaza
New York, NY 10017

Biblio Press
27 West 20th Street, Room 1001
New York, NY 10011
(Books by and about Jewish women)

B'nai B'rith Book Club
P.O. Box 410
Beech Creek, CA 16822

Behrman House
235 Watchung Avenue
West Orange, NJ 07052

Davka Corporation
845 N. Michigan Avenue
Chicago, IL 60061
(Computer software)

The Jewish Book Club
P.O. Box 944
Northvale, NJ 07647-0944

JEWISH LIGHTS Publishing
P.O. Box 276
S. Woodstock, VT 05071

Jewish Publication Society
1930 Chestnut Street
Philadelphia, PA 19301-4599

Jonathan David Co.
68-22 Eliot Avenue
Middle Village, NY 11379

Kar-Ben Publishing
6800 Tildenwood Lane
Rockville, MA 20852
(Children's books)

Ma'Ayan Books
P.O. Box 3197
Framingham, MA 01701

Sifriyon-B'nai Brith
P.O. Box 410
Beech Creek, PA 16822

Tara Publications
29 Derby Avenue
Cedarhurst, NY 11516
(Jewish Music)

Torah Aura Productions
4423 Fruitland Avenue
Los Angeles, CA 90058
(Creative educational resources)

Union of American Hebrew Congregations
Publications Department
838 Fifth Avenue
New York, NY 10021
(Reform movement)

United Synagogues of America Publications
3080 Broadway
New York, NY 10025
(Conservative movement)

What Jews Eat

The philosopher Martin Buber described Judaism as a system for living without distinctions between the secular and the spiritual. He wrote, "Basically the holy in our world is what is open to God, as the profane is what is closed off from Him . . . hallowing is the event of opening out. . . ."[1] *Kashrut,* the system of rules and laws regulating what Jews eat and how Jews prepare food, can be understood as a way of hallowing the very mundane act of eating, as a way of "opening out" to God with every meal.

For over 2,000 years, *kashrut* has been a defining element of Jewish life; it is part of the cultural glue that kept Jewish communities interdependent and united, and also a constant affirmation of Jewish differentness in even the most fundamental areas of life. Because the laws of *kashrut* so clearly set Jews apart, food often became a focus of anti-Semitism. There are countless stories about Jews being forced to eat pork—or dying rather than comply.[2]

Even today, *kashrut* is a kind of litmus test. Orthodox Jews consider *kashrut* an essential and nonnegiotiable aspect of Jewish identity and observance. But most American Jews do not observe the laws of *kashrut;* they do not "keep kosher." There are many reasons why *kashrut* is so widely ignored; for one thing, unlike many other *mitzvot, kashrut* does not reward the doer with a sense of peace or the satisfaction of having done something constructive or helpful to others.

Yet, there is increasing interest in the dietary laws among liberal Jews. In general, there is a nondefensive willingness to re-examine and learn from traditional observances. Furthermore, because many people are making major dietary changes for reasons of health, fitness, and even in response to political and ecological concerns, the notion that eating also has a spiritual dimension no longer seems alien or strange.*

What's Kosher, What's Not

The laws of *kashsrut* divide all edibles into two categories: *kosher* and *trafe*. The word *kosher* means "fit" or "proper." *Trafe,* which comes from the Hebrew for "torn" or "damaged," designates things that are unfit or improper to eat.

Kashrut posits two essential dualities. In addition to the basic distinction between kosher and *trafe* is an equally important division of kosher foods into three categories: dairy *(milchig),* meat *(flayshig),* and neutral *(pareve.) Kashrut* demands a complete separation of dairy and meat. *Pareve* foods, which include all fruits, vegetables, and many fish and eggs, can be prepared and eaten with either dairy or meat products.

The primary source for the dietary laws is the Torah, which lists the animals, birds, fish, and insects that may and may not be consumed by the people of Israel.[3] However, the laws that regulate food preparation were laid out in the Talmud and subsequent codes of law. For example, the biblical injunction against boiling a baby goat in its mother's milk[4] was elaborated by the rabbis into the total separation of milk and meat that calls for different sets of dishes, utensils, and eventually even dishwasher racks. Although the laws of *kashrut* are very detailed, food presents too many specific issues for any written code to address them all, which is why one of the major tasks assigned to rabbis through history has been to answer questions about *kashrut*.

The fundamental categories of *kashrut* are:

FRUITS AND VEGETABLES
(from the ground)

Everything that grows is both kosher and *pareve*. Every kind of plant, herb, weed, grain, tree, shrub, moss, fungi, fern, and bush is kosher. Every fruit, flower, vegetable, seed, root, and nut is permitted.

---

* Of course, Judaism is not unique for having religious dietary laws. Almost all of India —containing 20 percent of the world's population—eat no meat whatsoever, and many do not touch eggs or milk either. Islam forbids all alcohol and pork.

FISH

Any fish that has both fins and scales is kosher. This encompasses a great many varieties, including (but not limited to) anchovies, bluefish, carp, flounder, grouper, halibut, lake trout, mackerel, perch, rainbow trout, salmon, tuna, whitefish, and yellowtail. Kosher fish are also pareve, and can be served with either dairy or meat.

Nonkosher fish include shellfish (crustaceans such as crab, lobster, mussels, and shrimp), eels, porpoise, shark, whale, and all other sea mammals. Frog, turtle and octopus are also *trafe*.

MEAT

All animals that both chew a cud *and* have a split hoof are kosher. This includes antelope, buffalo, cattle, deer, eland, hart, gazelle, goat, moose, sheep, and yak. Trafe animals include camels, donkeys, pigs, horses, and rodents.

However, for meat to be considered kosher, even permitted animals must be ritually slaughtered according to the laws of *sh'chitah* by a butcher called a *shochet*, a person who is conversant with the relevant religious teachings and has the required hands-on skill. Furthermore, because meat may have no trace of blood on it, after ritual slaughter and inspection it is soaked in water, salted, and soaked again.

FOWL

Most domestic birds are kosher, including chicken, turkey, duck, and geese. Domesticated pigeon, dove, and song birds are also permitted. Fowl are considered meat, and must be slaughtered, inspected, soaked and salted as already described.

Wild birds and birds of prey are forbidden. *Trafe* birds include eagle, heron, ostrich, owl, pelican, swan and vulture. Eggs from nonkosher birds are prohibited. Eggs from kosher birds are kosher and *pareve,* however, a single spot of blood renders an egg *trafe*.

DAIRY PRODUCTS

All dairy products are permitted.[5]

WINE AND LIQUOR

"Kosher wine" is a designation given to wine made under rabbinical supervision, with the intent of being used for *kiddush*. However, many Jews treat all wine as kosher.[6]

Kosher wine is no longer limited to the sticky sweet vintages of Manischewitz and Mogen David. Today, the variety of kosher wine is staggering and includes pricey bottles from France as well as from Israel and the United States. Because it is considered a *mitzvah* to support Israel and products made by Jews in general, many people make a point of buying kosher wine, especially if they plan to make a blessing over it.

All beer, grain, and fruit liquors are kosher and *pareve*. Some cream liquors are dairy.

HI-TECH TRAFE

Food in America often contains the likes of BHT, MSG, mono- and diglycerides, food colorings, preservatives, and growth hormones. Although none of these things are technically *trafe*, some Jews do consider them as such. Because Judaism places great value on protecting health, careful reading of labels and the avoidance of potentially harmful additives and ingredients can be seen as a religious act as well as prudent shopping.

The Meaning of *Kashrut*

The most common assumption is that *kashrut* was implemented to protect health and life. Whereas rationales based on health have been offered for centuries, there is little evidence to support the argument that God wants Jews to forego spaghetti carbonara because ham mixed with cream causes bodily harm.[7] Jews who keep strictly kosher have managed to clog their arteries with chicken fat while assiduously avoiding bacon grease.

Actually, the health argument has been widely dismissed since the time of the Talmud. Rabbis have always "explained" *kashrut* as something Jews do because God demands it in the Torah. The act of obeying the commandment—of performing the *mitzvah*—is its own reward. However, because rabbinic Judaism also encourages Jews to discern God's intent in the Torah and to find personal meaning and fulfillment in the laws, *kashrut* has been given many interpretations.

Perhaps the most compelling explanation is the idea, restated in modern times by Martin Buber, that *kashrut* hallows the everyday. The intent of *kashrut* is not to deny the body's needs or pleasures, but to turn a natural function into a holy act.

According to another ancient line of thought, *kashrut* has been interpreted as a way of instilling reverence for all life, especially animal life. There is evidence that boiling a goat in its mother's milk was a pagan ritual that the Hebrews rejected, perhaps simply as a way of distinguishing themselves from their neighbors. But the injunctions against boiling or slaughtering a baby goat in front of its mother have long been interpreted as ways of preventing cruelty to animals. The biblical mandate not to "cause pain to any living creature" *(tsa'ar ba'alei chayim)* has been cited as an explanation for the rules of ritual slaughter and as the justification for Jewish vegetarianism.

According to many interpreters, God's original plan did not include meat-eating at all. The description of Eden includes a completely herbivorous and vegetarian world: "I give you every seed-bearing plant that is upon the earth, and every tree that has seed-bearing fruit, they shall be yours for food."[8] It is only in the story of Noah that humanity was given permission to eat meat, and then as a concession to the debased state of the species. Later in the Bible, Isaiah's vision of a redeemed world is entirely vegetarian. ("And the lion shall eat straw like the ox.")[9]

To the rabbis who wrote the Talmud, it seemed clear that because only God could give life, only God was permitted to take it. Although they were disturbed by any killing, even for food, the fact remained that most people ate meat. Thus, they instituted the elaborate laws regarding animal slaughter, which reinforced the idea that Jews kill only by divine sanction. Specific prayers were prescribed, and quick, relatively pain-free (for the era) methods were mandated. Jews were thus effectively prevented from hunting.

Choosing *Kashrut*

For people who grew up in kosher homes, there is nothing strange or difficult about using two sets of dishes, buying meat from kosher butchers, or foregoing cheeseburgers. *Kashrut* is as normal as apple pie. Kosher food is comfort food. But for those who have no family or gustatory memories of special meals and special recipes, *kashrut* may seem restrictive, daunting, or just irrelevant.

Jews rarely take on a *mitzvah* like *kashrut* simply because God comands it, or even because, "That's the way I was raised." The reasons given by some liberal Jews who keep kosher include: It is something that connects me to countless generations of Jews; it helps remind me and my children that we are Jews at all times; it is part of the overall discipline of being Jewish, which is a discipline I choose to practice. But for many Jews who keep kosher, the decision does not lend itself to rational explanation; it just feels right, they say. It just feels good.

Although *kashrut* may be a system for cultivating a holier approach to life, it is not always easy. It entails a certain amount of self-denial that will be far more difficult for meat-and-potatoes people than folks who prefer fish and salad for dinner. Choosing to keep kosher can be a difficult decision on many levels. For one thing, it is not easy to explain to others. Keeping kosher means embracing a basically non-Western system of self-discipline that runs counter to American culture, which encourages consumerism and instant gratification. It means making a very fundamental and emotionally loaded distinction between yourself and others: one that includes not only non-Jews, but also Jews who do not keep kosher and Jews who keep kosher differently from you.

Moreover, any major change in eating habits can be a deeply unsettling experience. Unlike animals, human beings do not simply eat to sustain life. For people, eating, like sex, is not simply a physical act. Eating is arguably life's first sensual pleasure, and the table is an important setting for social as well as physical sustenance. Furthermore, food places us in historical, ethnic, and economic contexts, even when it expresses idiosyncrasies and individuality.

And yet, *kashrut* continues to be a way of life for many Jews. The following list describes the various ways that people keep kosher, arranged in levels of increasing complexity and challenge.

BIBLICAL KOSHER

Basically, this means avoiding all animals and fish prohibited in the Torah. At the Chinese restaurant, it means passing up the spring rolls unless you determine they contain no shrimp or pork. Some people also read labels in order to avoid foods prepared with lard and other non-kosher meat products.

BIBLICAL KOSHER PLUS
SEPARATION OF MEAT AND MILK

As above, plus not mixing meat and milk at the same meal. This means not cooking chicken breasts in butter, or ordering meats served with cream sauces at restaurants.

KOSHER MEAT

This represents a quantum leap. Fresh meat is purchased only at a kosher butcher shop, and buying frozen meat must display a *hechsher*, a symbol of rabbinic supervision. Restaurant dining means vegetarian or *pareve* meals.

FURTHER SEPARATION OF MEAT AND MILK

At home, this entails two separate sets of dishes, cutlery, and pots and pans. Some people institute a waiting period (one to six hours) after eating meat before dairy is served. (Traditionally, there is no waiting period for serving meat after eating dairy products.)

RABBINIC SUPERVISION

Some Jews will only eat prepared foods that have been produced under rabbinic supervision and bear a *hechsher*. This reflects concern not only about kosher ingredients, but also about the status of the utensils and environment in which food is prepared. In order to maintain this level of *kashrut*, some people limit dining out to kosher restaurants and to the homes of others who keep kosher. However, some people who are quite strict at home will eat vegetarian meals in nonkosher restaurants and homes.

VEGETARIANISM

Some Jews give up meat altogether. In addition to the biblical and religious justifications for this practice, there are also political, ecological, and ethical rationales for Jewish vegetarianism as well. Given that meat is such a resource-intensive food and that so many other sources of high-quality protein are now available, a vegetarian lifestyle can be seen as a modern fulfillment of the goals of *kashrut* and of Judaism; living a holier life and helping to repair the world.[10]

Vegetarianism simplifies *kashrut* because it does away with the need to find kosher meat and issues around mixing meat and dairy. Restaurant meals are dairy or *pareve*.

A NOTE ON DINING OUT

Most liberal Jews who keep kosher eat at nonkosher restaurants and in nonkosher homes. Practice varies from individual to individual, from family to family. Some who are kosher at home will eat only vegetarian meals at other people's homes and at restaurants, whereas others make a fairly complete separation between what goes on at home and what they do in public (that is, there may be nothing but kosher meat in the freezer, but at McDonald's, the family has cheeseburgers.) Whereas this apparent double standard disturbs some people, those who practice different levels of *kashrut* at home and on the road see their choices as a way of making a distinction between what goes on inside a Jewish home and what happens in the rest of the world.

KASHRUT AND CHILDREN

The idea of turning into "*kashrut* cops" repels some people from considering any observance of Jewish dietary laws. However, children raised in kosher homes do not necessarily feel deprived. If home cooking is kosher cooking, the idea of drinking milk with a roast beef sandwich will seem as foreign and unappetizing as roasted bugs (which also happen to be *trafe*). Reading labels can be made into a game, and so can keeping meat and milk dishes separate.

It is, of course, far more difficult for an older child to understand a decision to suddenly outlaw cheeseburgers on the backyard grill if she's been eating them for as long as she can remember. Transitions should be slow, methodical, and fully explained. As in every other aspect of observance, if parents' commitment to *kashrut* is genuine, their attitude positive, and their approach flexible and open, children will learn by example.

A Kosher Home

Traditionally, a kosher home is one in which only kosher meat is pre-pared and eaten and where the separation of dairy and meat products requires separate dishes, cutlery, pots, pans, and cooking utensils. Some observant families even own two sets of dish towels, dish rags, sponges, pot holders, and cutting boards. (Glassware is exempt from this division and may be used on all occasions.)

However, because there are so many styles and levels of *kashrut* today, everyday decisions about how to keep a kosher home also vary. Some families that do not cook or eat meat and milk at the same meal use a single set of dishes and utensils. Others keep dishes and utensils strictly separated, but use the same clean-up gear for all meals. However it is defined, a kosher home is one in which family members respect, understand, and follow the same rules.

People who choose to keep kosher usually do it in a series of incre-mental steps rather than one leap. *Kashering*—making kosher—a home is a big step. Rabbis and friends who keep kosher are a good source of practical advice about the "how-tos" of setting up a kosher home.

MISTAKES

There is an old story about a great rabbi who arrives in a strange town where he is invited to spend the night in the mayor's home. As the mayor escorts the sage to his house, he boasts, "Rabbi, you should know that we adhere to the highest standards of *kashrut*. No one has ever made a mistake in my house." to which the rabbi replied, "Well then, I couldn't possibly eat in your house."

No matter how *kashrut* is defined or observed, mistakes will happen: a dairy pot gets used for reheating chicken soup; halfway through the soup that the waitress promised was strictly vegetarian, you discover a big chunk of beef. Ever realistic about human foibles, Jewish law is very explicit about how to correct errors. According to *halachah*, certain things that are *"trafed"* are boiled, others buried in the ground, and still others thrown away. Liberal Jews often correct errors by washing the offending item, and trying not to make the same mistake again.

The bottom line on accidents is that they do not invalidate anything. It has been suggested that the way people handle mistakes says a great deal about their understanding of *kashrut* as a *mitzvah*. Screaming at a spouse or a child over mixing up the spoons seems way out of line with a discipline intended to keep you in touch with holiness. However, if mix-ups are an everyday occurrence and *kashrut* is the source of tension, it might be time to reexamine why and how you are keeping kosher.

SHOPPING KOSHER

Shopping for kosher food is not difficult. Regular supermarkets and specialty shops can supply virtually everything except perhaps meat. (Supermarkets with substantial Jewish customers often stock frozen kosher meats.) Most cities of any size support at least one kosher butcher. People living in smaller communities either shop by mail or commute to larger Jewish centers to buy meat.

Shopping kosher, however, does require a fair amount of label reading. First you must see that products are free of lard (rendered, non-kosher animal fat). Foods designated "kosher" are thus sought not only by Jews, but also by Moslems and vegetarians who want to avoid pork or meat products. Another reason for reading labels is to determine whether a product contains any milk products, which would make it incompatible with a kosher meat meal.

When buying packaged and prepared food, some people only buy foods that bear a symbol called a *hechsher,* which is a validation that the product is kosher and prepared under rabbinical supervision. *Hechshers* appear on a wide variety of products, from cheeses to cake mixes to canned fish. The FDA permits use of the ® (for kosher) wherever there is rabbinic superivison. There are other *hechshers* as well, granted by regional or local rabbinic boards. Some of the better-known symbols include:

Union of Orthodox Jewish Congregations, NY

Organized Kashrut, Brooklyn, NY

Rabbi J. H. Ralberg, NY, NY

Kosher Supervision Service, Hackensack, NJ

(K.V.H.) Kashrut Commission of the Vaad Horabanim (Rabbinical Council) of New England, Boston, MA

KOSHER COOKING

"Vesti da Turco e mangia da Ebreo." This ancient Italian adage advises "dress like a Turk and eat like a Jew." [11] Given the reputation of Jewish food in America, that seems a rather startling statement.

Although there are glorious exceptions, Jewish-American cooking is associated with cholesterol-laden, heartburn-producing, over-cooked, over-salted, and bland meals. The tendency toward starchy, heavy food is probably the heritage of Central and Eastern European grandparents, whose lives included heavy manual work in cold climates.

Actually, Jewish culinary history is rich and diverse, reflecting the fact that Jews have lived all over the world. Sephardic Jews have an entirely different culinary heritage and vocabulary, which includes dates, raisins, leeks, plum sauces, exotic spices, and various fish preparations. The modern Israeli love affair with the ground chickpea patties called *felafel* have made the dish a staple among Jewish Americans as well. [12] All of this culinary richness was accomplished in spite of the constraint of *kashrut*. Jewish cooks have found ways to prove the Talmudic dictum that every forbidden food, even ham, has an exact, kosher taste equivalent. [13]

Hundreds of Jewish and kosher cookbooks have been published, and these are an especially good source for special holiday menus and recipes. However, there is virtually no cookbook (except maybe *The Wonderful World of Pork*) that is useless to the kosher cook. Cuisines based on oil rather than butter—that is, Italian, Middle Eastern, and most Asian culinary traditions—are full of wonderful ideas for kosher cooking. Of course, all vegetarian cookbooks are cover-to-cover resources.

It is also easy to adapt and change recipes to conform to *kashrut*, or fit into a meat or dairy menu. For example, in many cases using non-dairy margarine instead of butter will not affect the flavor of a dish. And meat-based soups can become *pareve* with the substitution of vegetable stock for beef or chicken bouillon.

KOSHER FOR PASSOVER

Kashrut takes on a whole new set of issues during the holiday of Passover when, in memory of the exodus from Egypt, Jews eat no leavened foods. In order to keep "kosher for Passover," all food must be absolutely free of any leavening agent, such as yeast. Thus all breads are forbidden, as is beer.

However, the prohibition against leaven extends not only to things made with yeast but any foodstuff likely to ferment, which includes everything made with flour, including pastas and most cereals. These restrictions put many constraints on cooking. In baking, for example, potato starch and matzo meal are substituted for flour. Passover cookbooks are a big help in planning interesting leaven-free meals. And all manner of prepared food may be purchased with a "Kosher for Passover" *hechsher*, which means the product was prepared in a leaven-free as well as kosher environment. (See "Passover" in Part Four)

As in all things, Jews observe Passover *kashrut* in a wide variety of ways. Keeping kosher for Passover traditionally requires an intensive house cleaning to free the house of even a trace of leavening, or *hametz*. Because the prohibition is so complete, some people observe Passover by using dishes, pots and pans, utensils and cutlery that have never touched *hametz*. At Passover, many families that do not keep kosher at all will, nevertheless, clean the house of *hametz* and avoid bread and all foods made with flour.

KOSHER ETIQUETTE

In general, people are fairly respectful and accommodating of dietary needs and restrictions. The best way to avoid giving offense (or being offended) regarding *kashrut* is to discuss observance in advance of sitting down at the table, especially because guests and hosts may not be aware of each other's practice.

A kosher-observant guest invited to dinner in a nonkosher home for dinner should volunteer information about what he or she can and cannot eat. Likewise, kosher-observant hosts can help by tactfully explaining "the rules" to their guests who offer to bring food or drink. At Passover in particular, when levels of *kashrut* often change, it is a good idea to be especially careful. A basket of fruit or "kosher for Passover" candy are among the safest edible "hostess gifts."

The most important rule of thumb is always, "When in doubt, ask." If everyone is relaxed and tolerant enough, questions can lead to an interesting conversation about the hows and whys of *kashrut*.

FURTHER READING

"Kashrut: How Do We Eat?" by Sheila Weinberg, *The Jewish Family Book* by Sharon Strassfeld and Kathy Green (Bantam Books, 1981). This essay presents a coherent and timely discussion of how *kashrut* can express modern concerns regarding food, health, ecology, family, and spirituality.

The Jewish Dietary Laws by Samuel H. Dresner (The Burning Bush Press, NY 1959). This much-cited essay explains *kashrut* in terms of Judaism's impulse to sanctify everyday life.

How to Run a Traditional Jewish Household by Blu Greenberg (Simon & Schuster, 1983). Greenberg's chapter on *kashrut* is a guide for the Orthodox homemaker that also includes personal anecdotes about keeping kosher even while traveling in the Soviet Union, and a heart-felt appreciation for a life-long commitment to this *mitzvah*.

Classic Cuisine of the Italian Jews by Edda Servi Machlin, (Dodd, Mead & Co, 1981). This cookbook is fascinating for two reasons: it contains a history and memoir of the Jewish community of Pitigliano, a medieval village in Tuscany in which Jews have lived since the 14th century and it includes dozens of unfamiliar and spectacular recipes, including one for *prosciutto* (a delicate Italian ham) made out of goose leg.

Judaism and Vegetarianism by Richard H. Schwartz, PhD. (Micah Publications, 1988). A source book that provides a biblical justification for vegetarianism and deals with issues such as compassion for animals, feeding the hungry, and ecology. It also includes a bibliography, a list of Jewish vegetarian groups and activities, short biographies of famous Jewish vegetarians, and, of course, recipes.

Other books devoted to this topic may be purchased from Micah Publications, 255 Humphrey St., Marblehead, MA 01945.

Traveling Jewish

If making Jewish choices happens only at home or in a synagogue, then traveling on business or for pleasure means leaving Judaism behind along with the cat and the television set. But when Jewishness is an authentic part of self and life, it does not get shelved when the newspaper delivery is suspended.

Traveling Jewish can be a special delight; an opportunity for learning about the world, about Judaism, and about one's self in many unique ways. Celebrating Shabbat in a hotel room can be a way of calming down and of finding peace and balance during an otherwise dreadful business trip. Attending services at an ancient synagogue or visiting the Jewish cemetery in a distant European or Asian city can utterly change your perception of an entire culture. Giving money to a begging child in a poverty-stricken land can move you to reconsider your budget for *tzedakah*.

Jewish choices on the road take two forms; the first of which involves recreating personal Jewish routines. Lighting candles and saying blessings in a vacation cottage by the sea or in a tent on a mountainside can become a treasured memory. Packing and shopping for a vacation *Shabbat* focuses the trip in a particular way. (Most Judaica stores sell traveling candle holders, *kiddush* cups, and *hannukiot* that fold up to eminently packable proportions.)

Jews who keep kosher find it relatively easy to maintain their practice on the road. Airplanes and ocean liners generally offer kosher as well as vegetarian and low-salt alternatives for travelers. Kosher meals are available in the most unlikely places, such as the Air Lanka flight from Colombo, Sri Lanka to Bangkok, Thailand.

Although there are kosher cruises and kosher resorts in the Caribbean and in Mexico as well as in the Catskill Mountains, people have managed kosher trips to the Orient, Africa, and the Soviet Union, simply by eating vegetarian. In cities and countries where there are Jewish communities, seeking out kosher restaurants can lead to very special travel experiences and a sense of belonging to a global family.

Traveling Jewish also means seeking out new Jewish experiences. This means finding a Jewish neighborhood, eating in a kosher restaurant, or visiting the local Jewish museum. Obviously, traveling abroad offers the most fascinating opportunities for Jewish exploration. Once you have seen all the landmarks that every tourist visits, there is the opportunity to make a far more personal connection with a foreign culture. Attending a service in Rome or New Delhi, and hearing the Hebrew and the melodies, can make you feel at home where you felt alien and cut off only moments before. If you find yourself very far from home during a Jewish holiday, there is also the opportunity to explore local customs. Imagine Hannukah in Hong Kong, Passover in Paris, or Sukkot in Singapore. But even on business trips in North America, attending services at a synagogue near the hotel can forever alter your feelings about trips to Cleveland, Houston, or Toronto.

There are countless stories about unexpectedly warm welcomes for total strangers simply because they identified themselves as Jews. Travelers have been invited to people's homes, given tours of the city, and the like. Of course, not all Jews are hospitable or effusive, and it would be naive to expect to be treated like a long lost sibling just because you are in what seems an exotically non-Jewish place. In cosmopolitan

---

May it be Your will, Adonai, God of our parents, to lead us in peace and guide our steps in safety, so that we arrive at our destination alive, happy, and in peace. Deliver us from enemies and danger along the way. May we find favor, kindness and compassion in Your eyes and in the eyes of all we meet. Hear our prayers, for You are a God Who listens to prayers. Holy One of Blessing, hear our prayer.

The traditional traveler's prayer,
recited by the mezuzah at the door before a voyage.

cities such as Hong Kong, for example, Jewish travelers are not a curiosity, and the local Jews have their own lives to live.

FURTHER READING

The Jewish Traveler, edited by Alan M. Tigay, (Doubleday, 1987). A collection of articles originally published in *Hadassah Magazine*. Each piece outlines Jewish history, demographics and places to see and visit in 48 cities throughout the world, including London, Nairobi, San Francisco, Rio de Janeiro, and Tel Aviv.

The Jewish Travel Guide, published by *The Jewish Chronicle-London*, a British newspaper, is an annual travel guide which contains the names of synagogues and Jewish schools, kosher restaurants and kosher food stores, and local Jewish organizations in hundreds of cities and countries all over the world. The guide is arranged by country, and provides Jewish contacts in both well-traveled and out-of-the-way places.

Community

According to a Yiddish proverb, "The best synagogue is the heart." To have meaning, Judaism must be rooted in personal reflection and choice. Many people have attributed Judaism's survival to its focus on the family, the home of the heart. The private aspects of Jewish life are the most accessible, the easiest to understand, and perhaps the most fulfilling.

But there is a necessary counterpoint to Judaism's emphasis on hearth and home. "Do not separate yourself from the community," says the Talmud.[1] In other words, Judaism's vitality does not reside solely within individuals. It also depends on the energy and momentum generated by groups of people working together in all kinds of settings: synagogues, schools, charitable agencies, cultural activities, social clubs, and political groups.

In a sense, the organized Jewish community exists to support individual Jews in their decision to live as Jews. Because no one can make Jewish choices alone. Lighting candles every Friday night, reading sophisticated Jewish books, celebrating the holidays at home with family, and never eating shrimp again may all be deeply meaningful, but there is a limit to a totally insular, personal Judaism. There is a limit to how much anyone can learn without teachers or other students to challenge their assumptions. There is a limit to how fully anyone can explore a Jewish commitment without exercising it in a public forum. One rabbi suggests that although it is possible to stay personally inspired and faithful to Jewish goals for several years, at some point energy is bound to ebb and inspiration wane. Exhaustion and a sense of defeat can set in.[2]

Another Yiddish proverb says, "Life is with people." Jewish life is most fully experienced in the company of other Jews. Especially in the absence of extended family, which is the norm for many Americans, the Jewish community can create a larger human context for all aspects of life, an indispensable source of identity, growth, recognition, and support, especially at times of transition. Births are greeted with resounding congratulations; illness and deaths are surrounded by healing concern.

The dialectic between public and private, personal and communal, is an obvious benefit to individuals. But it is also necessary for the survival of Judaism. Individuals can not educate rabbis, cantors, and Jewish teachers. Nor can individuals provide for the needs of all the Jewish elderly, or advocate for Jews who are persecuted or attacked. These functions, and many others, require both financial support and group effort by a community that cares about the continuation of its culture, faith, ideas, and dreams.

Continuity is, in fact, one of Judaism's most compelling demands. The Talmud tells the tale of a man named Honi, who one day saw an old man planting a carob tree. Honi asked, "How long will it take for that tree to bear fruit?" The old man replied, "Seventy years." "But you are already old; you will never live that long," said Honi. "I know," said the man, "but my parents and grandparents planted fruit trees for me, so I am planting fruit trees for my children and my grand-children."[3]

As long as there have been Jews, there have been Jewish communal groups. At first these were called tribes, and membership was all-inclusive, automatic, and permanent. Today, membership is more voluntary. Becoming a part of the community requires phone calls, filling out application forms, writing checks; in other words you make an effort and then a choice. Plugging into a community means making connections with other people. Joining a synagogue, attending a lecture or class, volunteering to serve on a committee, organizing a discussion group; any and all of these are opportunities to connect, make friends, learn, and put down roots.

Of course, all human contact entails friction, and Jews are a notoriously contentious bunch. There is no marriage without quarrels. But as with marriage, most subscribers agree the benefits far outnumber the aggravations. Fortunately, the American Jewish community is large and diverse, with countless places and ways to fit in. And, in the great Jewish tradition of dissent, if you do not like what you find you can always start your own.

The goal of the third section of this book is to make it easier to join forces with the Jewish community, to help you find a niche where your Jewish journey can be encouraged, challenged, and enriched. The first chapter, "Synagogues," talks about shopping for a congregation, a place of learning, prayer, and community. "The Organizational World" is an annotated introduction to some of the major religious, philanthropic, social welfare, educational, and advocacy groups and agencies of the Jewish community. And in "A Nation of Students," the traditional concept of a lifetime of joyful study is put into its modern context, from preschool to adult study groups.

The doors to the Jewish community are wide open. Browsers are welcome.

Synagogues

A synagogue is a *Beit K'nesset,* a house of gathering or assembly. A place to find lifelong friends, a place where teenagers forge Jewish identities over pizza, and where families go to laugh at the annual Purim play and to organize canned food drives for the hungry.

A synagogue is a *Beit Midrash,* a house of study and a house of stories. It is a place with classrooms and a library, and teachers and students of all ages. A place of argument and enlightenment.

A synagogue is a *Beit Tefilah,* a house of prayer. A place to say words of praise that are older than memory, a place to sing about the birth of a child, a place to sit in sorrow, and a place to search for peace.

Judaism purposefully mixes and confuses these categories: community, prayer, and learning. Among Jews, prayer services require the presence of the community, represented by a quorum of ten called a *minyan.* The study of Jewish texts is considered a form of prayer.

People go to synagogues to meet the need for human contact, spiritual fulfillment, and intellectual stimulation. People rarely find precisely what they are looking for in synagogues, in part because their criteria are impossibly high, and in part because synagogues rarely live up to their own goals. Still, over the course of their lifetimes, most American Jews belong to a synagogue. Finding a synagogue that feels like a communal and spiritual home is not always easy. This chapter offers suggestions about how to explore what liberal Jewish congregations have to offer.

History

The first building associated with Jewish worship was built in Jerusalem by King Solomon during the 10th century B.C.E. The complicated rituals described in the book of Leviticus—burning incense, animal sacrifices and all—took place in this temple, *The* Temple. The ancient Israelites traveled from all over the land for the festivals and holidays celebrated there and only there.

This centralized form of worship, performed by the priestly castes of Kohanes and Levites, was interrupted in 586 B.C.E when the Babylonians conquered Jerusalem and took the Jews into captivity. Scholars do not agree about the precise beginnings of what we would recognize as synagogues, but groups of Jews probably began meeting for the purpose of prayer and Torah study during the Babylonian captivity.

When the Babylonians were defeated by the Persians in the sixth century B.C.E., the Jews were permitted to return to Jerusalem and public readings of the Torah on *Shabbat,* Mondays, and Thursdays began. By the time of the destruction of the Second Temple by the Romans in 70 C.E., synagogues and regular patterns of worship were part of Jewish life, both in and outside of Israel.

By the second century of the Common Era, the synagogue was so much a fact of Jewish life that it was incumbent on any community that could muster a *minyan*—ten adult Jews—to build one. Synagogues were eventually built everywhere—Alexandria and Rome, Worms and Barcelona, Singapore and New Delhi—with architecture that reflected the styles of their time and host cultures. There are Byzantine, Romanesque, Gothic, Renaissance, Baroque, and Moorish synagogues. In Kai Feng, China, one was built after the pattern of the region's Taoist temples.

An individual who prays alone must hope that the time of prayer is an acceptable one; for the prayer of a congregation there is never an unpropitious time.
Midrash; Deuteronomy Rabbah 2:12

Actually, "synagogue" is not a Hebrew word. The term appeared in the Christian Bible as the Greek translation of the term *beit k'nesset*, meaning "house of assembly." Until the 18th century, Jews used the word "temple" only to refer to the Temple of Jerusalem, which would, according to tradition, be rebuilt by divine command. But the Reform movement (described below) rejected the notion of a rebuilt Temple and reclaimed the word as a synonym for synagogue. *Shul*, the Yiddish word for synagogue, comes from the German *Shule*, or "school." *Shul* was once used solely in reference to Orthodox congregations, but the word is now increasingly used to refer to liberal Jewish synagogues as well.

The Movements

Although there is a tendency to romanticize the Jewish past as a period of unanimity and universal piety, sectarianism has permeated Jewish history from the ancient days of the Pharisees and the Sadducees. But the Enlightenment introduced a whole new dimension to the divisions within the Jewish world. The subsequent political emancipation, which unlocked the ghettos and opened the great universities of Europe, permitted Jews to step outside their ethnic identity and act as individuals. For the first time, Jews had the option of becoming citizens of the wider world without having to convert to Christianity.

In response to this revolution in consciousness, the precursors of the modern Jewish movement—Reform, Conservative, and Orthodox—made their debuts. Despite their differences, all three schools of thought faced the same challenge: reconciling the traditions and beliefs of Judaism with modern intellectual and political realities. Out of that dilemma, liberal Judaism—the process of reconsidering and wrestling with tradition, and then self-consciously choosing how to be Jewish—was born.

American liberal Judaism may be divided into three major denominations or movements: Reform, Conservative, and Reconstructionist. Each of these has a central organization with which most individual congregations are affiliated. Each movement trains educators and rabbis, and publishes books, magazines, and teaching materials. The Reform and Conservative movements also train cantors and sponsor national youth groups.*

Although the three movements differ in their approach to theology and practice, all ordain women as rabbis, engage in interfaith and intermovement dialogues, and actively support the state of Israel. Although there are differences, the three also share the basic assumption that Jewish law, *halachah,* is an historical collection of human responses to the divine.

Despite formal divisions and even heated arguments among the movements, the hallmark of liberal Judaism is its diversity. Because every congregation is autonomous, official movement statements or position papers do not necessarily describe all affiliated synagogues. Indeed, movement affiliation may describe little more than the rabbi's alma mater, and even that is changing because some congregations now hire rabbis trained in the seminaries of other movements.

Diversity is most apparent in worship practice. In one Reconstructionist or Reform synagogue, for example, prayer shawls and head coverings may be the rule, and the service equally divided between English and Hebrew. Meanwhile, in another congregation of the same denomination down the street, there may be no head coverings and a virtually all-English worship service. Services at Conservative synagogues tend to be more consistent but, again, there are significant variations.

Programmatically, congregations have unique strengths and weaknesses. Some synagogues "specialize" in social action programs, some focus on education programs, whereas others devote a great deal of attention to worship and spirituality. The only way to find out what is going on inside any particular *shul* is to walk through its doors.

REFORM

The Reform movement was the first organized attempt at a systematic liberal Jewish theory and practice. Although it began in early 19th century Germany, the Reform movement matured and flourished in the United States in German-Jewish immigrant communities, and now numbers approximately 300,000 affiliated families in some 840 congregations.[1]

---

* All organizations mentioned in this chapter are listed with their addresses in "The Organizational World."

The early Reform movement was characterized by rationalist philosophy and a "light unto the nations" theology that saw the Jews as special heirs to the biblical prophetic tradition of social justice. Reform instituted many radical changes in synagogue observance, including the use of vernacular languages, musical instruments, and mixed seating for men and women. Reform leaders eased restrictions on Sabbath activities and rejected the dietary laws, in some measure as an effort to attract Jews who were abandoning Judaism altogether. Classical Reform Judaism was often charged with being assimilationist and more concerned with Christian approval than with Judaism's integrity. However, the Reform movement began an era of Jewish political and social activism that helped redefine Judaism's place in the world. Reform Judaism has changed a great deal since its beginnings, and continues to evolve. Many Reform Jews are re-evaluating and finding new meaning in practices, symbols, and rituals once dismissed by the movement.

Reform Judaism affirms the ability of every Jew to choose, on the basis of study and experimentation, the observances and rituals that bring him or her closer to God. *Halachah* or Jewish law serves as a resource, but does not determine these choices. For Reform Jews, the Talmud and its subsequent elaborations are part of Judaism's evolving insights as to how individuals and communities make God available in their lives.

CONSERVATIVE

Conservative Judaism, which also had its roots in early 19th century Germany, was formulated in early 20th century in the United States where it now estimates a membership of 250,000 families affiliated through some 825 synagogues.[2] It was conceived as a middle ground between Reform, which was viewed with alarm as having gone too far, and traditionalists, who were seen as unrealistic in their rejection of modern opportunities and insights.

Whereas Conservative Judaism shares with Reform the idea that Jewish law is historical and therefore changing, it supports a commitment to the workings of the law. According to the Conservative view, although the law itself changes in response to social, economic, and political realities, individuals are nonetheless expected and encouraged to conform to certain classical behaviors, such as keeping kosher, Sabbath and holiday observance, and daily prayer. The authority of these behaviors and of the laws contained in the Torah and later commentaries derives from the belief that these were inspired by God.

Although Conservative Judaism counts certain ritual behaviors as necessary and even mandatory, the range of practice among Conservative Jews is extremely varied. Indeed, the religious practice of many Conservative Jews does not differ from that of many Reform and Reconstructionist Jews, whereas others who belong to Conservative congregations embrace a lifestyle essentially indistinguishable from that of many Orthodox Jews.

Conservative Judaism does respond to important changes in modern life. For example, the ban on *Shabbat* driving was lifted to enable suburban Jews to get to their synagogues. However, the tension of trying to hold the middle ground led to a rift within the movement in the 1980s, when the Conservative seminary began to ordain women as rabbis.

RECONSTRUCTIONIST

The Reconstructionist movement, the smallest of these three, began as Mordecai Kaplan's vision of a new direction for Conservative Judaism. A longtime faculty member of the Conservative rabbinical seminary, Kaplan was eventually convinced by his students to lend his support to the founding of the Reconstructionist Rabbinical College in Philadelphia. The seminary, which opened in 1968, trains leaders for the synagogues and *havurot* (or fellowships, described below) that were formed in response to Kaplan's teachings.

Kaplan conceived of Judaism not simply as a religion but as an evolving, changing civilization with a religious basis. Kaplan believed that Jews in every generation had an obligation to keep Judaism alive through the process of reconstructing it, reinterpreting ancient rituals and practices and discovering new meanings in them. The 70 or so Reconstructionist congregations in the US today tend to be small and feature lay participation and creativity in ritual and worship.[3] According to Reconstructionism, the rabbi is not an authority but a facilitator and resource who teaches and guides congregants in their own process of creating Jewish community. Kaplan's ideas have had a great impact on many Reform and Conservative Jews.

ALTERNATIVES

In addition to the three formal branches of liberal Judaism, there is a network of alternative Jewish institutions that fulfill the functions of synagogues for their members. Generally, these groups do not hire rabbis, though some do pay a teacher, rabbi, or "guide." Nor do they own buildings, though some have grown into synagogues, complete with mortgages. But as a rule, alternative synagogues are antiorganizational organizations, self-governing groups in which members are responsible for every aspect of communal life: from running worship services to teaching to balancing the books. These groups require more of a commitment of time and work from their members and usually do not offer the full range of synagogue "services," such as a religious school. However, they can provide a kind of intimate, hands-on Judaism, a fact that has led large congregations to foster small groups within their membership.

Most of these small independent groups call themselves either *havurot* or *minyanim*. Although there is no technical difference between them, they tend to have somewhat different focuses. The word *havurah* comes from the Hebrew *haver* or "friend," and is usually translated as "fellowship." As autonomous groups, each *havurah* chooses its own activities and sets its own calendar of events, services, and meetings. Because they often concentrate on home- and family-based celebrations, members sometimes describe *havurot* as their extended families. A *havurah* might meet to break the Yom Kippur fast, build a communal *sukkah* and eat in it, enjoy a Hannukah party, or celebrate a Passover *seder* together. Some *havurot* schedule regular book discussions, and some attend Jewish cultural events, such as plays and films, as a group.

The National Havurah Committee (NHC) counts some 120 *havurot* on its mailing list, but, given the independence of these groups, no one really knows how many there are in North America. The NHC runs regional workshops and annual retreats, and provides technical assistance to new groups.

A *minyan* is the name of a quorum of ten adult Jews traditionally required for certain prayers to be said and for a full worship service to be held. The term is also applied to a service, as in "going to a *minyan*."

Although groups called *minyanim* run many of the same kind of family and holiday-focused activities as *havurot,* they tend to be more prayer-focused and somewhat more traditional. *Minyanim,* often formed to permit women's full participation in public worship, tend to use more Hebrew in ritual observances and prayer services. Their members also tend to be more observant of dietary laws and Sabbath restrictions.

The warmth and intimacy that typifies these small groups has inspired many synagogues to encourage members to form *havurot* and *minyanim* within the congregation. Synagogue-based groups are just as varied as the independents: some meet for study or family-centered holiday observance, and some hold alternative services in synagogue classrooms. Synagogue-based *havurot* and *minyanim* also function as extended families for their members, and are a way of knitting a large congregation closer together.

In addition to *havurot* and *minyanim,* there are several "New Age" Jewish groups around the country, which combine an emphasis on Jewish mysticism with insights from Eastern religious thought, holistic healing, feminism, self-realization, vegetarianism, and a commitment to progressive politics. Some are quite large and well-established, such as the Aquarian Minyan in Berkeley, California, and the *P'nai Or* (Faces of Light) Religious Fellowship, based in Philadelphia with affiliates in other cities. Founded by Rabbi Zalman Schachter-Shalomi, *P'nai Or* runs workshops and retreats that often feature meditation, story telling, and dance.

Joining a Synagogue

Because the criteria for what makes a "good" synagogue are so personal, selecting a synagogue is rarely a simple or straightforward process. Expectations may be vague or confused. Past experiences may create anxiety. Of course, many Jews join a synagogue strictly on the basis of geography, becoming members of congregations closest to them without even considering the choice they are making. But increasingly people are looking around before they make a commitment. Whereas it may seem a little crass to talk about "shopping" for a spiritual home, it's far less mechanical than selecting a synagogue only because it saves on commuting. This chapter contains many possible questions to ask while shopping for a synagogue that suits you and your family.

To begin the process, ask people who already belong to a congregation whether they are satisfied with their affiliation and what they like about their synagogue. If personal recommendations do not help, the phone book lists synagogues in the Yellow Pages, and local, regional, or national offices of the three movements can provide for listings of their affiliates. Some cities have a Jewish directory assistance-type service as well.

In general, it is not a good idea to go synagogue shopping during the high holidays. Rosh Hashanah and Yom Kippur services are not representative of what goes on the rest of the year, and the rabbi and staff will probably be extremely busy and not as free to schedule meetings with prospective members.

A good first step is to attend a regular *Shabbat* service. Call the synagogue office and find out when services are held. The call can be anonymous, or you can say that you are thinking of joining the synagogue, in which case you may be referred to the rabbi. Or a membership committee person may call you back, to tell you something about the congregation and to offer brochures, a copy of the temple newsletter, or membership materials. Some congregations hold regular open house sessions for prospective members, and some are closed to new members. Occasionally, potential members are invited for Shabbat dinner, and then attend services with members of the congregation.

On a first visit to any synagogue, it can be helpful to remember that few people feel altogether comfortable their first time anywhere. Customs vary from one congregation to the next, so newcomers always feel somewhat awkward, especially when everyone else seems to know all the words to all the songs. Try to relax. Hum along with the melodies.

Look around at the faces in the sanctuary. Is a wide range of ages represented? Are single people evident? Are there children around and/or is there special programming for them? Do you see people you would like to meet?

Regarding the service: Is the amount of Hebrew used intimidating or inadequate for you? Are supplemental readings meaningful? Who leads the service? Are lay people helping or does the rabbi (and/or cantor) do it all? Are people smiling? Do they seem engrossed in the prayers or are they dozing?

Do you like the way the music is used in the service? Does the cantor perform or do people sing along? If the rabbi gives a sermon, does it challenge or bore you? Does he or she seem to have a rapport with the congregants? As the service progressed, did you get more relaxed, or more tense?

In addition to your reaction to the synagogue, consider the synagogue's reaction to you. It is not unfair to expect people to say hello or offer the traditional greeting *"Shabbat Shalom."*

Unless your first impression is totally negative, go a second time, and a third. Are you starting to strike up conversations with people? Has the rabbi greeted you? If your first visit is on a Friday night, remember that the congregants who attend Saturday morning services may be an altogether different group of people. It might be worthwhile to attend a whole *Shabbat*'s worth of services as well as a lecture or adult education class. Explore the range of programs the synagogue offers to see how and where you might fit in. Ask yourself whether this particular *shul* can meet your needs and those of your family, not only now but in five or ten years as well.

There are many more questions to ask about a prospective congregation: Does the schedule of adult education classes or lectures appeal to you? Does the synagogue ever run retreats? How good is the religious school for children? (See "Elementary Education" in the chapter "A Nation of Students") Is there a synagogue youth group? Does the synagogue stress family education and family programming? Are there special events on the holidays where children and parents participate together? Does the synagogue help organize and foster *havurot*, small groups that function as extended families within the larger community? Does the temple have special programs for elders? Is there a nursery school? A women's group?

Does the congregation participate in local interfaith programs? Is

---

If a house was built just as a house, and then afterward it was dedicated as a synagogue, it is considered a synagogue. However, it is not considered holy until people have prayed in it.

Shulchan Aruch, Orach Chaim 153:8

there an active social action committee, and what are its priorities? How does the synagogue relate to its interfaith families and to their children? If this question is relevant to you, it should be asked immediately. Although many synagogues welcome non-Jews as full members of the congregation, some limit the participation of non-Jewish spouses and children of non-Jewish mothers.

THE RABBI

Some small congregations may have only a part-time rabbi and some function without one altogether. Large congregations may have several on staff. But regardless of size or affiliation, most synagogues are closely identified with their rabbis and people often select or reject a synagogue on the basis of its leader.

The rabbi's job description is almost dizzying. Congregational rabbis are "spiritual leaders" who teach and preach. They officiate at religious ceremonies and rituals. They make hospital rounds. They are family, marriage, and spiritual counselors. They act as representatives of the Jewish community at interfaith meetings and secular events. Some rabbis function as business administrators of their congregations and as principals of their religious schools.

Not surprisingly, few rabbis are good at all these tasks. A superb pastoral counselor may be a mediocre preacher; an inspired leader of prayer may be a terrible administrator. Despite the improbability of finding one human being who can excel at everything, most people bring impossible expectations to their relationship with the rabbi, who is inevitably cast in a parental role as well.

In the past few decades, there has been slow movement away from the model of the authoritarian rabbi: the one with all the answers, the one who personifies Judaism to his or her congregation. In much the same way that the physician's role as the ultimate, unquestioned medical authority has been challenged by more sophisticated patient-consumers, laypeople are taking more responsibility for their own Jewish lives. This is actually less a break from tradition than an acknowledgment of the rabbi's true status; not priest, but teacher. But in spite of the move toward greater lay participation, rabbis still shape their synagogues in fundamental ways. The rabbi generally sets the tone of worship services, leads in policy decisions regarding Sabbath observance within the synagogue, and provides leadership in his or her own areas of interest and strength.

Before joining a congregation, it is a good idea to schedule a private meeting with the rabbi, but preferably not during the late summer or early autumn, when rabbis are preparing for the high holidays and the beginning of the school year. In synagogues where there is a senior rabbi and a junior or associate rabbi, try to speak with both. Although you may have more contact with the associate rabbi, the senior rabbi sets the tone for the congregation. (Besides, junior rabbis often leave to get their own pulpits after two or three years.)

Go to the meeting with the rabbi prepared to answer some questions. You will probably be asked about your Jewish background and what you and your family want from the congregation. It is also a good idea to prepare a few questions of your own, for example: What makes this congregation unique? What do you do best here? In the rabbi's opinion, what are the congregation's failings? What needs to be improved? What is expected from congregants and how important is lay participation?

Although parents may have many questions about religious education, synagogues can place too much emphasis on children. This approach, which one rabbi has dubbed "pediatric Judaism," tends to revolve around children's programming and assumes that adults have virtually no interest in their own Jewish lives. Thus it might be a good idea to ask: How can this synagogue help *me* grow as a Jew?

Finally, before meeting with a rabbi, it is also useful to examine your own feelings about the rabbinate. Many Jews harbor negative childhood memories of *the rabbi,* and are therefore intimidated, suspicious and even hostile toward anyone with the title. Interviewing a rabbi is not unlike a first meeting with a physician or a therapist; someone with whom you are going to have an intimate but professional relationship. It is best to try and leave expectations and old grudges at home.

OTHER STAFF

It may also be worthwhile to meet with the synagogue's other professional staff, in particular, the cantor and, if applicable, the director of education or religious school principal.

THE CANTOR

The job of the cantor is to lead the congregation in prayer and song. The title of cantor (in Hebrew *hazzan, hazzanit* for female cantors) is given to people trained in liturgical music. The Reform and Conservative movements both run cantorial schools, which operate as graduate programs in Jewish liturgical music. Cantors frequently lead services and officiate at funerals in the absence of a rabbi, and are usually licensed by the state to perform weddings.

Cantors have very different approaches to their musical and congregational roles. Some perform and are listened to whereas others invite the congregation to sing along. Some cantors lead services quite often, and in some synagogues they are put in charge of *bar* and *bat mitzvah* preparation. There are congregations where the cantor teaches in the religious school, or is its principal.

THE DIRECTOR OF EDUCATION

If the synagogue runs a religious school, the director of education or principal and school committee chair will set educational policy. Meet with them if you plan to enroll a child in the congregational school. Like cantors, directors of education may be a major force in the congregation, shaping programs for adults as well as children, and generally contributing to the educational and spiritual life of the community. Indeed, directors of education, like cantors, often function as associate rabbis.

MEMBERSHIP

There are as many ways to belong to a congregation as there are reasons to join. Some people see synagogue membership as a necessary evil, like life insurance. They pay their dues against future needs (for a *bar* or *bat mitzvah*, wedding, or funeral) or as a way of insuring children's Jewish identity. Their monthly checks are the total extent of their commitment.

If, however, you join a synagogue with hopes of exploring your own spirituality, or expanding your sense of community, or delving into Jewish thought, signing the membership form is just the beginning. The next step is finding a niche. Attending services and classes are among the best ways to explore possibilities and to begin feeling like someone who belongs.

Synagogues are complex organizations, and it is a good idea to know how they function. Although there are enormous variations, most are governed by a volunteer elected board of directors. In some congregations, prestige is attached to officer-holders, with leadership positions going to people who support the institution with substantial financial gifts. Elsewhere, people rise through the ranks of committees and become community leaders solely as a result of commitment and ability.

Like most nonprofit organizations, committees charged with various aspects of communal life do most of the work. Joining a committee is one way to get immersed in synagogue life, lore, feuds, and politics. Synagogue committees may include: *membership*, which recruits and meets with new members; *finance*, which may prepare budgets or raise money; *ritual/worship*, which helps plan religious services and works closely with the rabbi and cantor; *adult education*, which plans courses, lectures, and events such as weekend retreats; *school*, which oversees the school and may be broken down in various ways (preschool, high school, family education, youth group, etc.); *social action*, which is involved with issues of social and political concern, ranging from helping resettle Soviet Jews to providing sanctuary for Central American refugees to running soup kitchens and shelters for the homeless; *tzedakah*, or charitable works, which may run educational, action, and fundraising activities; *chevra kadisha* (literally, holy society), which helps members cope with death, burial and mourning; etc. The list can go on and on: *Israel, social, music, interfaith, Soviet Jews, library*. . . .

Obviously, all these activities require financial support. Synagogues operate like businesses, with fixed expenses for mortgage, staff, utilities, and movement dues, which support seminaries, youth programs, and summer camps. Most synagogue expenses are met by annual membership dues, which can range from less than one hundred to several thousand dollars. Some congregations have sliding scales, others charge a fixed amount, which may be reduced or waived by special arrangement. No synagogue turns people away because of inability to pay dues, but each congregation handles financial need in its own way—some with more sensitivity than others. In addition to dues, there may be other financial expectations of members, such as pledges to a building fund, school fees, and charges for attending adult education courses and lectures.

Perhaps the oldest joke in the long history of Jewish humor is the one about the Jew who was stranded on a desert island. When a ship happens across him years later, his rescuers find three huts. "Why three?" he is asked. "I live in one," he says, "The other two are synagogues." "Why on earth would you need two synagogues?" asks the rescue party. "One I pray in. The other I wouldn't be caught dead in."

No two Jews can agree on much of anything—especially when it comes to religious practice. Many large, venerable synagogues began as a renegade splinter group from another even more venerable congregation. If there is no synagogue that provides you with reasonable levels of comfort and fulfillment, you can always begin your own congregation or *havurah*.

Starting a synagogue or *havurah* means focusing your religious and communal goals, usually in agreement with several other families. It also requires a huge investment of time, money, and work. But creating an authentic communal spiritual home is its own priceless reward.

FURTHER READING

Explaining Reform Judaism by Eugene B. Borowitz and Naomi Patz (Behrman House, 1985)

Conservative Judaism: Our Ancestors to our Descenders by Elliot Dorff (United Synagogue of America, 1977)

Exploring Judaism: A Reconstructionist Approach by Rebecca Alpert and Jacob Stab (Reconstructionist Press, 1985)

The movements publish magazines and other literature about their views, positions, and programs. Write to the national movement offices for a list of publications. The addresses appear in "The Organizational World."

The Organizational World

Nothing demonstrates the vitality of Jewish life so well as its array of organizations, agencies, federations, committees, associations, and councils. The alphabet soup of the Jewish organizational world represents every conceivable area of Jewish concern, and provides leadership and assistance at every level, from feeding the Jewish elderly in America to supporting various strategies for peace in the Middle East.

Jews, and thus organized Jewish communal life, have been in North America since the earliest days of its colonization. Initially, communal groups focused on basic needs: providing for kosher meat, buying land for cemeteries, building synagogues and schools, and so forth. But, as each new wave of Jewish immigration expanded the needs of the community, the organizational mandate expanded also.

For a time, many social and cultural needs were met by *landsmanschaften,* or associations comprised of people from the same town in the old country. These groups pooled their resources to provide such services as death benefits for widows and orphans. Hebrew Free Loan societies were established to make low-cost credit available for immigrants. And the traditional Jewish commitment to *tzedakah,* "righteous giving," supported thousands of small relief efforts and individual projects. Continuing the traditions of Eastern Europe, Jews saw to it that poor members of their community could, for example, buy the appropriate food for Passover.

Communal efforts became larger and more sophisticated in the 19th century, when Jewish communities built hospitals and supported a growing social work network. And as the Jewish community grew and diversified, the need for a more integrated, centralized way to raise and allocate funds became increasingly apparent. By the beginning of this century, the "federations" became a force in American Jewish life.

Federations began as loose associations of community service groups and agencies that pooled fund raising efforts to avoid competition and to enhance effectiveness. Today, Jewish federations (which have different names in different cities) support a vast array of programs, which can be divided into three broad categories: social service (Jewish Big Brother/Big Sister, family and children's agencies, services for the elderly, etc.), education (support for local schools, vocational counseling, etc.), and self-defense (typified by the Anti-Defamation League). The federations also send vast sums to Israel.

Federations are the primary fund-raising bodies for local Jewish communities, and they are famous for their successful solicitations. But Jewish federations are much more than funding conduits. Indeed, they tend to be the most powerful Jewish leadership bodies in most cities, assessing and planning for the needs of the community, setting programmatic goals and directions. In addition to their fund-raising role, federations also sponsor many "young leadership" study and issue-oriented groups. And while they employ professional administrators, federations depend on volunteers to do the nitty-gritty work of fund raising and staffing committees.

Almost all Jewish organizations depend on volunteer efforts as well as financial support from members of the community. Volunteer opportunities are virtually unlimited, from serving juice to children in synagogue preschool classrooms to participating on the committees that make important decisions about the future of American Jewry. Every organization represents a doorway into Jewish communal life and to a sense of belonging and of making a difference.

To find out how to get involved, or to learn how to obtain services,

The longest road in the world is the one that leads from your pocket.

Yiddish proverb

several large cities now have Jewish information services, a kind of Jewish "directory assistance." But because virtually every Jewish organization is, at least theoretically, connected with all other Jewish groups, referrals may be obtained from almost any Jewish agency or Jewish professional.

The national and international Jewish scene is fluid, ever-changing, and potentially confusing. Organizations are constantly in the process of redefining themselves and even splitting in response to changing realities. For example, the Jewish National Fund, which began in 1901 to buy land for Jewish settlement in Palestine, now supports land development and the forestation of Israel. B'nai B'rith, which began as a fraternal and social group for German Jews, has grown to become an international organization with a presence in 48 countries. In 1989, B'nai B'rith's women's division split off to form an independent organization. New organizations are established in response to needs that are perceived as being unmet by existing groups; the American Jewish World Service was incorporated in 1985 to provide a Jewish presence in the area of international assistance to developing nations. A great many Jewish groups are multipurpose, with overlapping mandates; most feature some Israel-related component.

The list published below covers only a fraction of the large number of national and international organizations in existence. This collection is included only to suggest how individuals, synagogues, and local agencies fit into the bigger picture, and no slight to unlisted organizations is intended. Most of the groups listed will, upon request, send brochures and other published materials. For a complete directory of Jewish groups in North America, consult *The American Jewish Yearbook*, which is published by the Jewish Publication Service and the American Jewish Committee and available in Jewish libraries and synagogues.

Movement Organizations

REFORM

Union of American Hebrew Congregations (UAHC)
838 Fifth Avenue
New York, NY 10021
The congregational body of the Reform movement and the place to write for information about local congregations, programming, and movement literature.

Hebrew Union College-Jewish Institute of Religion (HUC-JIR)
3101 Clifton Avenue
Cincinnati, OH 45220
The rabbinical seminary of the Reform movement. With campuses in Cincinnati, New York, Los Angeles, and Jerusalem, HUC trains rabbis, cantors, and educators, and also runs other programs.

Central Conference of American Rabbis (CCAR)
20 E. 40th Street
New York, NY 10016
The professional organization of Reform rabbis.

CONSERVATIVE

United Synagogue of America (USA)
155 Fifth Avenue
New York, NY 10010
The congregational body of the Conservative movement and the place to write for information about local congregations, programming, and movement literature.

Jewish Theological Seminary (JTS)
3080 Broadway
New York, NY 10027
The rabbinical seminary of the Conservative movement, JTS also runs a cantorial program, and undergraduate and graduate programs in Judaica. The University of Judaism in Los Angeles is a JTS-affiliated center for undergraduate and graduate study.

Rabbinical Assembly (RA)
3080 Broadway
New York, NY 10027
The professional association of Conservative rabbis.

RECONSTRUCTIONIST

Federation of Reconstructionist Congregations and Havurot (FRCH)
Greenwood Avenue and Church Road
Wyncote PA 19095

Reconstructionist Rabbinical College (RRC)
Greenwood Avenue and Church Road
Wyncote PA 19095
The rabbinical seminary of the Reconstructionist movement.

Reconstructionist Rabbinic Association (RRA)
Greenwood Avenue and Church Road
Wyncote PA 19095
A professional association for graduates of RRC and other rabbis who identify with Reconstructionism.

ALTERNATIVES

The National Havurah Committee
c/o Havurah of South Florida
9315 SW 61 Court
Miami, FL 33156

Society for Humanistic Judaism
28611 W. Twelve Mile Road
Farmington Hill, MI 48018
A nontheological organization of congregations and groups for those who value a secular Jewish identity.

INTER-DENOMINATIONAL

The movements do talk to one another under these auspices, among others.

National Jewish Center for Learning and Leadership (CLAL)
421 Seventh Avenue
New York, NY 10001
A leadership education program that seeks to bridge the gaps among Reform, Conservative, Reconstructionist, and Orthodox Jews.

Synagogue Council of America
327 Lexington Avenue
New York, NY 10016
The coordinating body of national Conservative, Reform and Orthodox rabbinical and synagogue organizations.

EDUCATION AND YOUTH

American Zionist Youth Foundation
515 Park Avenue
New York, NY 10022
Israel-related programming for Jewish youth, including tours of Israel.

B'nai B'rith Hillel Foundations, Inc.
1640 Rhode Island Avenue, NW
Washington, DC 20036
The national body that sponsors cultural, religious, educational and social programs at colleges and universities.

B'nai B'rith Youth Organization (BBYO)
1640 Rhode Island Avenue, NW
Washington, DC 20036
A national network of independent and inter-denominational high school youth groups.

Coalition for Advancement in Jewish Education (CAJE)
261 W. 35th Street
Floor 12A
New York, NY 10001
Founded in 1976, an inter-denominational organization of educators committed to excellence and innovation in Jewish curricula.

Hashachar (formerly Young Judea)
50 W 58th Street
New York, NY 10019
Sponsored by Hadassah (see below), a national Zionist youth group program, with summer camps and other activities in Israel.

Hashomer Hatzair
The Socialist Zionist Youth Movement
150 Fifth Avenue, Suite 911
New York, NY 10011
This group stresses the notion of Zionism as the national liberation of the Jewish people and promotes the kibbutz (collective farm) movement.

Habonim
27 W. 20th Street
New York, NY 10011
The youth movement of the United Kibbutz movement, Habonim runs high school and college programs in Israel as well as summer camps in North America, modeled on Israeli kibbutz life.

Jewish Education Service of North America (JESNA)
730 Broadway
New York, NY 10003
An interdenominational coordinating and consulting agency for education and community organizations. JESNA licenses Jewish educators and disseminates Jewish educational materials, including films and speakers.

National Ramah Commission
c/o JTS
3080 Broadway
New York, NY 10027
The Conservative movement's association of summer camps.

North American Federation of Temple Youth (NFTY)
838 Fifth Avenue
New York, NY 10021
The Reform movement's high school youth program, based in individual synagogues and organized into regions throughout the US and Canada.

United Synagogue Youth (USY)
155 Fifth Avenue
New York, NY 10010
The Conservative movement's youth program, based in individual synagogues.

Service Organizations

Federations, which have different names in different cities, support the bulk of local Jewish social service organizations, some of which also receive funding from non-Jewish sources, such as the United Way. There are scores of independent Jewish organizations that support medical research, hospitals, and services for Jews and non-Jews who are deaf, blind, retarded, or suffer from cancer and other diseases. The groups listed here are national bodies that serve local service organizations.

Association of Jewish Family and Children's Agencies
P.O. Box 248
Kendall Park, NJ 08824-0248
This is the umbrella organization for community-based Jewish family and children's agencies, which provide counseling services and other kinds of programs for people of all ages. The Association can help people find services in their communities.

Council of Jewish Federations, Inc.
730 Broadway
New York, NY 10003
The umbrella organization for 300 local federations, the Council provides technical assistance for planning, public relations and fund raising.

The JCC Association
15 E. 26th Street
New York, NY 10010
The JCC Association is the organization of Jewish community centers, YMHAs and YWHAs (Young Men's/Young Women's Hebrew Associations), and camps. It provides services to Jewish military families and Jewish veterans, and also has a lending library of films, videos, and recordings.

National Council of Jewish Women
15 E 26th Street
New York, NY 10010
NCJW supports projects with particular emphasis on women's issues, children and youth, aging, and special education programs in Israel.

North American Association of Jewish Homes and
Housing for the Aging
2525 Centerville Road
Dallas, TX 75228
This group represents and supports housing for Jewish elders and acts as an information clearinghouse.

INTERNATIONAL PROJECTS

American Jewish Joint Distribution Committee
711 Third Avenue
New York, NY 10017
"The Joint" organizes and finances rescue, relief, and rehabilitation programs to Jews in 30 countries, especially Israel.

American Jewish World Service
1290 Avenue of the Americas 11th floor
New York, NY 10104
AJWS provides medical and agricultural assistance, primarily to countries in Africa, Asia, and Latin America.

American ORT Federation Inc.
(Organization for Rehabilitation through Training)
817 Broadway
New York, NY 10003
Supports vocational training in 30 nations, especially Israel.

HIAS, INC. (Hebrew Immigrant Aid Society)
200 Park Avenue, South
New York, NY 10003
Begun 1880 to aid the settlement of Jewish immigrants in the United States, HIAS now assists the resettlement of Jews in the US and Israel and helps refugees around the world.

National Conference of Soviet Jewry
10 E 40th Street, Suite 907
New York, NY 10016
&
Union of Councils for Soviet Jews
1411 K. Street, NW, Suite 402
Washington, DC 20005
Both organizations run a variety of programs on behalf of Soviet Jews.

North American Conference on Ethiopian Jewry
165 E. 56th Street
New York, NY 10022
&
American Association for Ethiopian Jews
2789 Oak Street
Highland Park, IL 60035
Both groups provide information about assistance to Ethiopian Jews.

COMMUNITY RELATIONS

This catch-all category is used to describe groups that describe, define, and advocate for Jewish interests in the Jewish community and in secular forums. Some of the groups listed here are large and multipurpose, others are smaller and more focused. As a group, they represent a wide range of political viewpoints.

American Jewish Committee
165 E. 56th Street
New York, NY 10022
Founded in 1906, a multipurpose organization committed to preserving the rights of Jews around the world, fostering Jewish life in the US and Israel, and supporting interfaith relations. The AJC publishes Commentary *magazine.*

American Jewish Congress
15 E. 84th Street
New York, NY 10028
Among its primary concerns the Congress lists civil rights, religious freedom, and the continued separation of church and state in the United States.

Anti-Defamation League of B'nia B'rith (ADL)
823 United Nations Plaza
New York, NY 10017
Through education, lobbying and interfaith programs, the ADL combats anti-Semitism and other forms of bigotry.

B'nai B'rith International
164 Rhode Island Avenue, NW
Washington, DC 20036
A large organization begun in 1843, B'nai B'rith programs include community service, public affairs programming, adult and youth education, and support for Israel and Soviet Jewry.

Jewish Fund for Justice
1334 G Street, NW Suite 601
Washington, DC 20005
A grant-making organization that works with other religious and ethnic groups to combat poverty in the United States.

New Jewish Agenda
64 Fulton Street #1100
New York, NY 10038
"Agenda" runs forums and conferences and is concerned with disarmament and peace issues, Arab-Jewish reconciliation, feminism, economic justice, and gay and lesbian rights.

World Jewish Congress
1 Park Avenue, Suite 418
New York, NY 10016
With members in 70 countries, WJC often represents Jewish interests at the United Nations and other international forums.

CULTURAL AND SOCIAL

There are dozens of organizations that support individual Jewish museums, libraries, art groups, and archives. Those listed here have a broader mandate.

American Jewish Historical Society
2 Thornton Road
Waltham, MA 02154
Collects and displays material on the history of Jews in America.

American Sephardi Federation
8 W. 40th Street, Suite 1601
New York, NY 10018
Supports Sephardic religious and cultural activities.

Jewish Publication Society
1930 Chestnut Street
Philadelphia, PA 19103
Since 1888, the premier publisher of Jewish books for adults and children.

National Yiddish Book Center
P.O. Box 969, East Street School
Amherst, MA 01003
Collects and distributes out-of-print and used Yiddish books.

Simon Wiesenthal Center
9760 W. Pico Blvd
Los Angeles, CA 9760
The Center runs a museum and a library, and sponsors educational projects dedicated to keeping alive the memory of the Holocaust and its victims.

Workmen's Circle
45 E 33rd Street
New York, NY 10016
A secular Jewish organization founded in 1900, it supports Yiddish culture in the US and Israel.

World Congress of Gay and Lesbian Jewish Organizations
PO Box 18961
Washington, DC 20036
Founded in 1980, this organization provides information about local gay and lesbian Jewish groups and about regional and international conferences.

YIVO Institute for Jewish Research
1048 Fifth Avenue
New York, NY 10028
YIVO, which has one of the world's great Yiddish archives, was founded in Europe before World War II. It supports research on the social history of the largely destroyed Eastern European Jewish community.

ISRAEL

The relationship between the Jewish people and the land of Israel dates back to the biblical promise that Abraham's progeny would inherit the land, a dream that was kept alive in Jewish literature and liturgy for centuries. In fact, Jews have lived in the land of Israel since the exodus from Egypt. However, the vast majority lived in the Diaspora and except for a brief time during the Hasmonean period, Jews did not have political control over the land from the time of the Babylonian destruction of Jerusalem in 586 B.C.E. until the founding of the state of Israel in 1948.

For some Jews today, the idea of Zionism is unrelated to Jewish ritual or observance; indeed, for some Zionists, Judaism is a nationalist movement. For other Jews, Zionism expresses a religious mandate. In the most general terms, however, a Zionist is someone who supports the state of Israel.

The connection between the American Jewish community and Israel is both passionate and practical. The 1989 *American Jewish Yearbook* listed 77 North American organizations whose sole mission was helping Israel, a number that does not reflect the many other groups that also send money and programmatic support to Israel. Between 45% and 50% of the money raised by local Jewish federations goes to support programs in Israel. Americans also send funds directly to political parties and peace groups, to social service agencies, universities, and cultural institutions in Israel. The groups listed here tend to have a broad focus on Israeli life and society.

American Israel Public Affairs Committee (AIPAC)
500 N. Capital Street, NW
Washington, DC 20001
A registered lobby that meets with members of Congress on legislation that affects Israel.

American Red Magan David for Israel
888 Seventh Avenue
New York, NY 10016
Provides support for Israeli first aid and ambulance services.

Association of Reform Zionists of America (ARZA)
838 Fifth Avenue
New York, NY 10021
A Reform movement organization that supports religious pluralism in Israel, and the strengthening of the Israeli Reform movement.

Hadassah, the Women's Zionist Organization of America
50 W 58th Street
New York, NY 10019
Hadassah sponsors Zionist youth programs and supports various programs in Israel, especially the Hadassah-Hebrew University Medical Center.

Jewish National Fund of America
42 E 9th Street
New York, NY 10021
The fund-raising organization for forestation and land reclamation in Israel.

The Movement to Reaffirm Conservative Zionism (MERCAZ)
155 5th Avenue
New York, NY 10010
The Zionist action organization of the Conservative movement.

New Israel Fund
111 W 40 Street
New York, NY 10018
NIF supports the efforts of Israelis seeking social justice and funds projects seeking to protect and strengthen the democratic process in Israel, women's rights, and Arab-Jewish cooperation.

The United Jewish Appeal, Inc. (UJA)
99 Park Avenue
New York, NY 10016
The UJA raises money for humanitarian purposes, mostly in Israel. Its funds come mainly through local federations and its work in Israel is carried out by the Jewish Agency.

World Zionist Organization—American Section
515 Park Avenue
New York, NY 10022
Supports and promotes immigration to Israel.

Zionist Organization of America (ZOA)
4 E. 34th Street
New York, NY 10016
Runs programs in Israel and fosters Jewish unity through Zionism.

A Nation of Students

Study may be the only undisputed and shared value upon which all Jews, regardless of affiliation or belief, can agree. Indeed, study is seen as its own reward and considered one of life's great pleasures.

Historically, Jewish learning was valued above wealth or fame, and community standing was based on academic erudition. Having a scholar in the family was such a source of pride that, in the days of arranged marriages, promising students were preferred even over wealthy young men as matches for daughters. Knowledge of Torah and Talmud was considered a virtue second to none. Well, almost none. The Talmud says, "An animal is better than a sage without sensitivity to people's feelings." [1]

The sweetness of learning is a common theme in traditional writings: "Anyone who teaches Torah in public and does not make the words as pleasant as honey from the honeycomb for those who are listening, it were better that he not teach the words at all." [2] On the first day of school in some Eastern European communities, children were given sweet cakes in the shapes of the Hebrew letters.

But study was not considered a virtue for children only. Education was considered a lifelong obligation and joy for Jews of every status. A common Yiddish greeting is, *"Zog mir ein possock,"* "Tell me a verse," or "Teach me something." In the Torah, the Israelites were challenged to become a "nation of priests." The Jews became a nation of students.

For the past century, the Jewish passion for learning has been applied to secular studies with well-known and impressive results. Today, Jews tend to be very demanding consumers of secular education: seeking out and paying for the best schools, the most innovative curriculum, and the finest teachers. However, similarly high standards have not always been applied to Jewish education.

Unfortunately, many adults see Jewish learning as an obligation and a chore. This attitude often stems from memories of Jewish schooling that were less than inspiring, and sometimes downright awful. Too often, religious school is treated as an unpleasant but necessary rite of passage; an inoculation against assimilation that is momentarily painful but good for you in the long run. And for most people, Jewish education ends after *bar* or *bat mitzvah*.

But these low expectations are starting to change. Jewish educators have improved curricula and teaching methods, and parents are demanding excellence in Jewish schooling.

Of course, there are many ways to define excellence or success in education. For the purposes of this chapter, successful Jewish education is defined as the process that teaches skills, concepts, vocabulary, curiosity, and, above all, sets in motion a lifetime of Jewish study. However, it must be noted that, although schools can go a long way in achieving this goal, no institution can succeed in the absence of Jewish interest and commitment at home.

Most schools welcome interest and input from parents. Thus, if the Jewish education offered in your synagogue or in your city is not up to your standards, it is possible to join a committee and make changes. Alternately, if you do not find a course, school, or staff that meets your needs or standards, hiring a teacher or even starting your own school are options that people exercise all the time.

This chapter outlines the range of cradle-to-retirement opportunities for learning that are available in most Jewish communities, and suggests ways to explore them. One good place to start might be the local Bureau of Jewish Education (BJE), which can provide listings and other kinds of information. (To find the BJE, call any synagogue or Jewish agency.)

Daycare and Preschool

In the 1980s, the Jewish communal world began to respond to the growing needs of working parents for early childhood education programs. That demand has created a whole new world of Jewish daycare centers, preschools, and summer day camps. Increasingly, Jewish community centers, YM/YWHAs, and synagogues are providing for the youngest Jews, with everything from half-day nursery schools to full-time daycare for infants and toddlers. Jewish family daycare, offered by state-licensed Jewish providers in their own homes, is yet another option. (Finding these settings often requires a word-of-mouth connection; however, some good places to look include bulletin boards in synagogues, Jewish Community Centers, YM/YWHAs, and listings in local Jewish newspapers or weekly newspapers distributed in largely Jewish neighborhoods.) Because these programs are new and in direct competition with the best that the secular world has to offer, Jewish daycare and preschools tend to be state-of-the-art operations run by well-trained, enthusiastic early childhood professionals.

Most Jewish learning for very young children happens at home: setting the table for *Shabbat*, attending synagogue-sponsored family events, listening to the grown-ups talk about Israel, reading bedtime stories about Purim and Hannukah. However, an early education program can reinforce and supplement these family lessons.

But Jewish preschools are not where pale children sit at tables memorizing Hebrew. Most early childhood specialists today feel that formal "study" is not appropriate for preschoolers at all. The guiding philosophy is that learning is a developmental process, which means that children are encourage to learn through play.

In many ways, there is little difference between a day at a Jewish preschool and a day at a secular program, and, in fact, many Jewish preschools accept non-Jewish students. Children enrolled at Jewish preschools sing, do art projects, play outside, visit the fire station, take naps, eat snacks, and sit down to listen to stories during "circle time." What is different at Jewish early education programs is the content of the story, the name of the song, and the subject of the art project.

Jewish programming varies a great deal from one preschool setting to the next. Some incorporate only a little Jewish content: *menorahs* in December, Purim masks in March, and that's about it. But other schools encourage children to act out Friday night home rituals, or teach the Hebrew *alef-bet* along with the English alphabet.

Apart from Jewish content, the same criteria that apply to all early education programs apply to Jewish daycare and preschool: the operation should be licensed, clean, and cheerful, the ratio of staff to children should be low and at least in compliance with state law, and parental visits should be welcome at all times. Before enrolling children, parents should spend time at the center. The primary consideration in choosing daycare or a preschool is that children have a happy, safe experience. If their first memories of "school" are fond ones that include pleasant associations with things Jewish, they will have made a wonderful discovery.

Elementary Education

Parents who want to provide school-age children with a formal Jewish education have two options: full-time private day school or a part-time religious school with sessions after school and/or on weekends. With parental support and participation, either choice can result in a successful Jewish education and a positive Jewish experience.

Some criteria apply to both kinds of settings. Parents need to visit, attend classes, look at the art projects hanging on the walls, examine the textbooks and other materials in use, and talk to both other parents and to the principal or director. The special criteria that apply to Jewish education mostly concern the curriculum, which is more than just a listing of courses and books, but a philosophy of learning and an approach to Judaism. The following list includes both general and specific questions to consider when selecting a Jewish elementary school program for your child.

Are subject areas developed from year to year for continuity? Do teachers stress dialogue and discussion? Are lessons taught through

From what age should a parent begin to teach his child?
From the moment he begins to speak.
Shulchan Aruch, 16th century code of laws

lectures, worksheets, or games? Do students ever participate in plays or concerts?

How long do teachers tend to stay employed in this school? Are they offered in-service training? What is the student absentee and drop-out rate? How many students continue their Jewish education through high school?

Is there a regular music program or song leader? Is Israeli folk dancing part of the school experience? How much time is devoted to arts and crafts and other kinds of expressive arts?

What is the body of Jewish knowledge that the school hopes to teach? What kind of Jew does the school hope to "produce?" Is religious observance expected of children, and how is that expectation expressed? Is prayer a part of the classroom experience? In the more advanced grades, is a single theology or approach to *halachah* (Jewish law) taught, or are different points of view presented?

DAY SCHOOL

Nationally, full-time parochial education—dayschools—represents the fastest-growing institution of Jewish learning. There is at last one private Jewish day school in every American city with a Jewish population of more than 6,000 people.[3] Although day schools are usually associated with Orthodox Jews, many liberal schools are now well-established and proliferating. The Conservative movement sponsors a large network, many of which are named for Solomon Schechter, a founder of the Conservative movement. Reform and unaffiliated community day schools are found mostly in larger cities. It is not unusual for any day school to serve children from a diverse spectrum of the community: from Orthodox to secular Jews. Given the diversity, the information provided here is necessarily general, and, even so, probably does not take into account all possible variations.

As with other private schools, Jewish day schools vary in curricular and pedagogic approach, which can range from creative to traditional, from very competitive to noncompetitive. Every school has its strengths and weaknesses, and the principal of headmaster tends to set the tone and the agenda. Jewish day schools are typically run by rabbis with a background in education, or people who hold advanced degrees in Judaica and education.

Some schools divide the day between Judaic studies (including Hebrew language and literature, classic Jewish texts, the Jewish calendar, Jewish history, and Israel), and a full complement of secular studies (including mathematics, science, history, and English language and literature). Many day schools emphasize Hebrew, which is not only taught but used as a language of instruction. Thus there is the potential for graduates to be fluent or near-fluent Hebrew speakers and readers. Reform day schools tend to emphasize secular studies, however, secular academics tend to be excellent in all Jewish day schools.

It is probably not a good idea to select a Jewish day school strictly on the basis of its secular academic instruction and success, or only because the public schools are not an option. Jewish schools do have their religious agendas and parents should be aware that if they are ambivalent or unclear about their own Jewish identity or level of practice, they may be putting children in a difficult position. Even so, children can have a positive experience in a day school that does not exactly reflect their family's Jewish beliefs and practices.

Socially, day schools offer a totally integrated Jewish experience and a full-time immersion in unconflicted Jewish identity. Many schools begin the day with a morning prayer service. Cafeteria food is kosher. The school calendar is arranged around the Jewish calendar; obviously there are no Christmas carols and no Easter break. Nor is there any division between sports and Jewishness, or math and Jewishness. School friends will be Jewish friends, and, whereas some members of the secular faculty may be non-Jews, the majority of adult role models will be knowledgable, committed Jews.

An added advantage noted by many parents is the fact that attendance at a Jewish school means free time for kids who might otherwise be enrolled in afternoon or weekend religious school. Day school can also be a communal focus, a place where parents can meet other like-minded adults.

There are some drawbacks to the day school option: among them, expense. Whereas some schools provide scholarships, private education is costly. Also, attendance at a day school often means that parents have to arrange transportation. With school friends scattered all over town, after-school and weekend play dates often require more commuting.

Another factor to consider in choosing a day school is that many stop at the sixth, seventh, or eighth grade. The options for secondary school are then secular high school or a Jewish high school, which are fewer in number and tend to be run by and for Orthodox Jews. Both of these transitions have been successfully negotiated by a great many day school graduates, and the principal should be able to address this concern and put you in touch with parents and students who made the leap.

The local Bureau of Jewish Education can direct you to local day schools. National resources include: The Jewish Educational Service of North America, (JESNA),* which can put you in touch with the area BJE, and the Jewish Community Day School Network, an organization of independent schools. The Council for Reform Jewish Day Schools is an independent organization connected to, but not formally affiliated with, the Reform movement. They can be reached through the national Union of American Hebrew Congregations office. The Solomon Schechter Day School Association (located at the United Synagogue of American offices) can be helpful in locating the nearest affiliated school, or in starting a new school.

RELIGIOUS SCHOOL

The majority of Jewish parents choose a supplementary program for Jewish learning, offered after school or on weekends. Hebrew schools or religious schools are usually run by synagogues. The exceptions include unaffiliated programs started by groups of parents, sometimes associated with universities. Also, the Workmen's Circle runs secular programs that stress Yiddish rather than Hebrew.

It is extremely difficult to generalize about religious schools because they vary in almost every way, beginning with their hours of instruction. Time requirements range from one to eight hours per week, with variations between grades. And despite various "official" criteria from the different movements, religious school faculties, administrations, and curricula are virtually idiosyncratic. In some synagogues, the rabbi or cantor runs the school; in others there is a paid school administrator or principal. The principal might hold a graduate degree in Jewish educa-

---

* All groups mentioned in this chapter are listed, with addresses, in "The Organizational World."

tion, and teachers might be well-trained and well-paid. However, some schools are entirely run and taught by volunteers.

Paid or volunteer, teachers may be extremely knowledgable and motivated. But because of the chronic Jewish teacher shortage, professional standards are not widely observed. And because very few religious schools can afford to hire full-time teachers, it is not unusual for the staff to include people with little or no Jewish background, or with little or no teaching experience. In other words, the range for educational quality in religious schools runs the gamut from excellent to abysmal.

Measuring the academic achievement of religious school education is difficult, in part because expectations are all over the map. Many parents expect religious schools to produce Jewish identity and Hebrew literacy in the absence of support from home. Then again, others expect very little, considering any experience to be "better than nothing."

However, it is possible to devise both demanding and reasonable goals for supplemental Jewish schooling. Some of these might include: a working Jewish vocabulary (*mitzvot, tzedakah, Shabbat, kiddush,* Torah, Maimonides, Herzl, Kristallnacht, Tel Aviv, etc.); the ability to read prayerbook Hebrew; and familiarity with the Jewish calendar of holidays and life cycle rituals. It is also reasonable to expect children graduating from religious school to know more about the Torah and the Bible than a few stories. But most important, a religious school can nurture children's natural curiosity and enthusiasm for Jewish learning within a friendly, warm, and positive environment. Although the formal curriculum is crucial, the way it feels to learn there, and be there, will ultimately determine whether religious school becomes a good or bad memory.

Many religious schools now feature special off-site programs. *Shabbat* retreat weekends are a particularly vital and invigorating teaching tool. These nights or weekends away from home with classmates and teachers are part summer camp, part spiritual retreat, and part slumber party, creating an instant Jewish community that is often the high point of the school year. The presence of retreats for school children of various ages is a sign of a lively religious school.

People choose religious school programs for several reasons. Some parents feel that a supplementary education can provide what they want for their children in terms of developing a positive Jewish identity an a sense of belonging. Indeed, religious school can introduce not only the child to new friends, but integrate the entire family into the life of the congregation. Cost is also factor, because religious schools are much less expensive than day schools and, in some synagogues, tuition is covered by dues.

There are, however, some inherent problems with even the best supplemental Jewish education. Afternoon programs put tired, restless kids into classrooms. Also, religious school is invariably in competition with other afterschool and weekend programs.

Another major dilemma for religious schools is the fact that many parents enroll their children for only a few years, in preparation for *bar* or *bat mitzvah*. Children attend classes, study with tutors and then disappear after the big day. The *bar/bat mitzvah* "mill" approach offends many people, and various religious schools and synagogues deal with this issue differently. Some congregations do not permit *bar* or *bat mitzvah* for students who have not been enrolled in the school for several years. Others will enroll students at any point, hoping that the experience at religious school will make children want to return for high school classes. One clue to the vitality of a religious school is the number of students who stay past *bar* and *bat mitzvah* and enroll in and graduate from the high school program.

However, one of the biggest problems for religious schools has less to do with students than with parents. If Mom permits virtually any other activity (skiing or shopping or cramming for a math test for *real* school) to take precedence, if Dad never sets foot in the synagogue, or if the folks do not even ask about what happened in religious school today, then a child will start to treat the whole experience as the parents do—as an afterthought. But if parents make religious school a priority and permit few absences, if they support the school by volunteering on committees and for fields trips, and if they are involved in Jewish study

The world is only maintained by the breath of school children.

Maimonides, The Mishneh Torah

themselves, then religious school can be an important part of learning how to make Jewish choices for a lifetime.

FAMILY EDUCATION

Jewish family education has become a popular title for a range of programs that involve both parents and children doing and learning together, reflecting the fact that the most important Jewish learning takes place within the family. These are commonly offered by synagogues as a supplement to religious school programs, but may also be sponsored by Jewish community centers, YW/YMHAs, and some summer camps. Activities are geared to interest children of various ages, and many include things like baking *challah*, creating a mural about Passover, learning a Hebrew song, and preparing for a Hannukah party. For families with older children, there may be fewer arts and crafts and more discussion and study.

Family education can be a relaxed, nonthreatening way for adults to start or renew their own Jewish education. Indeed, one of the goals of family education is to enable and empower parents to act as Jewish teachers for their children. Making Jewish choices as a family in a public setting also dispels the notion that Jewish activities are solely for children.

One of the most memorable kinds of family education experiences is the family retreat, which is usually a weekend spent at a conference center, camp or inn. Away from familiar contexts, chores, and usual expectations, studying and playing in an entirely Jewish context—this is time and space where all kinds of learning are possible. Family education programs and retreats take careful planning, and are usually well-attended and immensely rewarding.

There are many published resources for parents who want to enrich their families' Jewish life. See the suggestions for "further reading" at the end of most chapters in this book. The Reform and Conservative movements produce materials for just this purpose. And of course, rabbis, Jewish educators, and other parents have their own ideas and resources to share.

SPECIAL EDUCATION

The Jewish world has begun to respond to the need for special education programs for the physically and mentally challenged, as well as for those with emotional or learning problems. There are many kinds of programs for children with special needs, including *bar* and *bat mitzvah* tutoring and camping opportunities. A Jewish special education fair is held annually in New York and other cities to display materials and resources for learning disabled students.

Some resources for Jewish children with special needs exist only on city or regional levels and may not be well known. To find out what is going on in your community, start with the local Jewish family agency and the Bureau of Jewish Education. Rabbis and religious school principals may be aware of other resources within their congregations as well.

Among the better known national efforts:

> The Jewish Braille Institute of America, founded in 1931, produces braille and large print books, as well as audio cassettes recordings. The Institute's free lending library of Judaica includes books in Hebrew, English, Yiddish, and other languages. The Institute is located at 110 E. 30th St., New York, NY 10016.

> The Ramah camps run by the Conservative movement in California, Massachusetts, and Wisconsin offer the Tikvah program for children who are learning disabled or who are emotionally or mentally challenged. Tikvah, which means hope, provides opportunities for travel to Israel, and even employment at the camps as counselors. Contact Tikvah, c/o The Ramah Commission, 3080 Broadway, New York, NY 10027.

> P'tach (Parents for Torah for All Children), is a national group begun by two parents in 1979, who wanted their learning-disabled son to be able to attend a yeshiva, an Orthodox day school. The headquarters are located at 1363 49th St., Brooklyn, NY 11219.

The parent should teach the child on the level of the child's understanding.
Talmud: Pesahim 116A

High School

Full-time Jewish high schools are found in cities with a large enough Jewish population to support one large or several smaller elementary day schools. Although the majority of these are run by Orthodox Jews, their student bodies usually include students from liberal homes. Some high schools offer a dual-track program to accommodate students who did not attend an elementary Jewish day school.

Most of the information regarding elementary day schools applies to religious high school as well. On the whole, Jewish secondary schools are academically strong institutions whose graduates are accepted by the colleges and universities of their choice. And after years of full-time education, graduates are highly literate Jews. From a social standpoint, conflicts with parents about dating non-Jews, or participating in events on *Shabbat* or holidays, are comparatively rare.

However, the vast majority of Jews do not choose day school education for their teenagers. In fact, the vast majority of Jewish children in America do not continue in any institution of Jewish learning after *bar* or *bat mitzvah*. Many Jewish educators feel that this is a great shame.

High school students are ready to learn about anti-Semitism and the Holocaust. They are often eager for conversations about personal responsibility, ethics, God and spirituality, and the problem of evil in the world. Religious high school programs can address these kinds of subjects and engage teenagers with *tzedakah* or social action activities such as fund-raising for Jewish agencies, working in local soup kitchens, or volunteering at Jewish nursing homes.

Larger synagogues, consortia of congregations, and interdenominational community organizations run "Hebrew high schools," again, with many variations. Some programs are weekly, others meet more often. Some stop after eighth grade and others go through eleventh or twelfth grade, ending with a confirmation or graduation ceremony.[4]

Teenagers are savvy consumers and they will reject programs that do not challenge or excite them. Given the distractions and competing interests of adolescence, a thriving Hebrew high school indicates a good program, or at least some excellent teachers. Finally, the social aspects of Hebrew high schools are also important. Because they provide a place to meet other Jews of similar ages and interests, Jewish high school programs offer opportunities for making Jewish choices as young adults.

Youth Groups

For many adolescents, youth groups provide an independent forum for developing a Jewish identity. A youth group creates a local community of friends who may attend different high schools and would not otherwise meet. Because youth groups are part of regional and national organizations that run conferences, retreats, and summer camps, the chance to travel and meet Jewish kids from all over the city, state, and country is both a great attraction and a wonderful informal Jewish learning experience. For those who get involved, the social events, religious services, conferences, first loves, and late-night bull sessions that are the mainstay of youth grouping are a source of strong, positive, and entirely personal (rather than family-oriented) Jewish memories.

There are three large national youth organizations that operate on regional, local, and chapter levels. The North American Federation of Temple Youth or NFTY is the youth program of the Reform movement. United Synagogue Youth or USY is run by the Conservative Movement, which also sponsors a pre-high school program called Kadima. Unlike NFTY and USY chapters, which are usually run by synagogues, the B'nai B'rith Youth Organization or BBYO is sponsored by local B'nai B'rith chapters. The three organizations run all sorts of programs, including summer camps, youth leadership training programs, and tours of Israel. In general, youth grouping crosses movement lines. BBYO is interdenominational and, especially in smaller communities, it is common for kids from the Conservative synagogue (which may not have enough teens to start its own group) to join the local NFTY chapter, or vice versa.

There are also Zionist youth organizations that promote interest in and support for Israel through summer camps, year-round youth group activities, and programs in Israel. These include: Hashomer Hatzair, the Socialist Zionist Youth Movement; Hashachar and pre-high school Young Judea, which are run under the auspices of Hadassah; and Habonim, the youth movement of the United Kibbutz movement and, historically, of the Labor Zionist movement.

Synagogues that sponsor youth groups provide adult advisers, and the national organizations are run by professional staffs. However, most decisions about youth group programs, conferences, and social events are made by the members and their elected leaders. The structure of committees, offices, and boards of directors on chapter, regional, and national levels mirrors the world of adult Jewish organizations, which makes youth grouping a leadership training program. It is common for youth group *machers* (Yiddish for "big shots") to assume leadership roles in the adult Jewish community later in life.

Youth group programming varies a great deal and includes classes and seminars with rabbis and other teachers, and writing and leading creative *Shabbat* and holiday worship services. Social action projects are very popular. Although the Zionist groups are focused on Israel, all Jewish youth organizations run tours that bring thousands of Jewish-American teens to Israel every summer. Youth group tours usually include some combination of sightseeing and time spent working on a *kibbutz* or at an archaeological site. Some even arrange for American youth to do volunteer work on behalf of the disadvantaged in Israel *à la* Peace Corps. For further information, a good place to start is the Israel Program Center at the American Zionist Youth Foundation.

Summer Camp

American Jews have been sending their children to Jewish summer camps since the early 20th century. At its inception, Jewish camping was an extension of Jewish day schools, that is, a way to create a year-round Jewish learning experience while getting the kids away from the hot city. Over time, Jewish camps added the full complement of American camping experiences: softball, hiking, canoeing, swimming, arts and crafts, and so forth.

Jewish camping has grown and diversified, and parents now choose Jewish camps for a wide variety of reasons. Some simply want their children to play with other Jews, others seek a total immersion in Jewish practice for their kids. Jewish summer camps can provide the easiest and most pleasant way to learn Hebrew outside of a summer in Israel. Zionist camps sponsored by organizations like Hashachar, Habonim, and Hashomer Hatzair focus on Israel in song, dance, and language. There are camps for the religious and camps for secularists. Camps for children of all ages.

There are some camps where the only obvious Jewish element is the campers' last names; these tend to be for-profit camps run by individuals and families. However, most Jewish camps are nonprofit programs run by large organizations, such as local federations or their agencies. The Reform movement sponsors nine camps around the country. The Conservative movement runs the six Ramah camps. The following discussion of Jewish camping refers only to camps that feature Jewish programming.

The best way to select a summer camp is to start a year early and visit several. But there are many other ways to explore what different camps have to offer. The JCC Association publishes a catalog of over 100 nonprofit Jewish summer camps. Synagogues and Jewish community centers run summer camp fairs, at which representatives set up booths and talk to prospective campers and their parents. Camp directors often spend the winter months on the road recruiting campers. Some questions to ask camp directors might include: How old are the counselors and on what basis are they hired? What is the staff-to-camper ratio? Most important, how many campers return from one summer to the next?

The best source of information about Jewish camping is word of mouth. Both parents and kids should do some research, and the child's opinion deserves serious consideration, because they are the ones who literally live with this decision.

Summer camp is expensive. But if money is keeping you from sending your child to a Jewish camp, be sure to ask whether scholarships are available. Local federations may provide financial aid, and some synagogues have automatic scholarships for kids going to camps run by their movement.

Many parents—especially those who remember their own Jewish camping experiences fondly—see summer camp as an educational and Jewish priority. Jewish camping allows children to try on Jewish ideas and practices on their own. Spending time in a beautiful place where the rhythms of daily life are set according to a Jewish clock, where there are no distractions or competing pressures from the secular world, can be an important experience. Camp is a place where being Jewish is easy and fun, and where peer pressure is generally on the side of doing more rather than fewer Jewish activities. The staff—especially the high school and college-age counselors—are very special role models. Perhaps most importantly, Jewish camp memories belong wholly to the child as an individual, not as a member of a family.

College

Living away from home for the first time, being exposed to new ideas and systems of belief, college is a time when young people may feel confronted by ultimate questions about the meaning of life, good and evil, and personal responsibility. Thus, college can be a time for forging a new, more mature connection to one's religious heritage. Choosing a college or university where it is possible to continue making Jewish choices means bringing Jewish criteria to the application process.

If Jewish studies are of paramount interest to a high school senior, there are several colleges to choose from. Both the Reform and Conservative seminaries (HUC and JTS), as well as the Conservative-affiliated University of Judaism in Los Angeles, offer joint undergraduate degree programs affiliated with local secular universities. Independent colleges of Judaica that offer joint degree programs with other institutions of higher education include Hebrew College in Brookline, Massachusetts, Spertus College of Judaica in Chicago, and Gratz College in Philadelphia. Yeshiva University in New York, the oldest and largest independent Jewish university in the United States, is run under Orthodox auspices, and offers an exceptional range of undergraduate and graduate programs. At Brandeis University, the private nonsectarian school founded by the American Jewish community in 1948, undergraduates can take courses in Hebrew, Judaic Studies, and Jewish education.

Of course, not every student is going to major in Jewish Studies. Still, the opportunity for doing some Jewish study may be a consideration in selecting a college. Hundreds of private and public colleges and universities offer opportunities for Jewish classroom learning. Jewish Studies departments have proliferated over the past 20 years or so, and even schools that do not have an entire department frequently offer classes with specifically Jewish content. A look at the course catalog might reveal "The Literature of the Holocaust" listed in the English department. The religion or philosophy department may devote several courses to Jewish thought and philosophy. For more information about Jewish studies, the B'nai B'rith Hillel Foundation publishes a catalog entitled *Jewish Studies at American and Canadian Universities.*

Jewish academics are less important than Jewish social life for many students, who want information about the presence of other Jews on campus and the availability of Jewish social, cultural, and religious programs. B'nai B'rith also publishes a manual called *Jewish Life on Campus,* which lists current Jewish enrollment figures at North American schools and outlines Jewish and Israeli programming.

Although local federations sponsor and fund some campus activities, most Jewish college programming is run under the auspices of campus Hillel centers.[5] These student centers, sponsored by the B'nai B'rith Hillel Foundation, are nondenominational and fairly autonomous. Each one provides a different combination of services, depending both on the student body and the staff. Some Hillels have several full time staff members, including one or more rabbis, who tend to set the tone of the center. Hillel programs and worship services also serve Jewish faculty members and sometimes attract participation from the surrounding community.

Some Hillels run kosher kitchens and as many as four separate worship services every *Shabbat,* with different liturgies for Reform, Conservative, egalitarian-traditional, and Orthodox students. Some Hillels are renowned for their lecture series and their Israeli folk dance evenings, and most sponsor some sort of social action or community service programs. Hillel offices can also help students arrange a junior year abroad in Israel.

Adult Education

For many people, making Jewish choices begins with study of some aspect of Judaism, which is varied, complex, and rich enough to inspire several lifetimes of dedicated learning. Jewish adult education embraces history, ethics, fiction, law, spirituality, theater, music, languages, sociology, poetry, humor, film, and modern geopolitics.

On one level, all the adult Jewish student needs is access to a good bookstore or a decent Jewish library, and subscriptions to some Jewish magazines. In the absence of bookstores and libraries, there are Jewish book clubs and mail order catalogs.

However, the tradition strongly encourages communal learning. In the Talmud, Rabbi Eliezer spoke of a student who studied silently, but after three years forgot all he had learned.[6] The classroom is a cornerstone of the Jewish community, one of the *raisons d'etre* of the synagogue. And according to traditional Jewish values, there is no greater honor or pleasure than studying with a great teacher. Taking a course is one of the best ways to transform feelings of Jewish inadequacy and illiteracy into a sense of engagement, empowerment, and mastery.

Adult education opportunities are provided by all sorts of groups, including Jewish community centers, YM/YWHAs, and local chapters of national organizations. Colleges and universities sometimes offer evening courses in Judaica for part-time students or auditors. Local Jewish newspapers invariably contain advertisements and listings for lectures and courses. Upon request, organizations that sponsor adult education programs will gladly add you to their regular mailing list.

Virtually all synagogues sponsor adult education programs, the content of which is usually determined by a committee of members. Usually, the rabbi(s), cantor, and director of education will teach some courses, with others offered by members of the religious school faculty, congregants, and guest teachers and speakers.

The range of courses and lectures for the adult learner is virtually limitless and in larger communities there is almost always something for everyone: lectures by visiting scholars, weekly conversations about the Torah, college courses with demanding reading lists, weekend Sabbath retreats, beginning prayerbook Hebrew and advanced modern He-

---

If you have studied with one teacher, do not say, "It is enough," but, rather, go study with another, too.

Avot de Rabbi Natan A:3, 5th century

brew conversation, classes in basic Judaism (often geared toward but not limited to prospective converts), close readings of a mystical text, introductions to the liturgy, Talmud study, workshops for interfaith couples, holiday cooking classes, Jewish feminist study groups, film series, and panel discussions on Israeli life and politics.

Additionally, there is a long-standing tradition of Jewish "independent study." Studying with a *hevra*—a circle or fellowship of friends—can be a very satisfying forum for Jewish learning. Such groups range from monthly book discussions to weekly *Shabbat* afternoon considerations of the Torah portion, to seasonal study sessions about upcoming holidays. To find study partners, put up a sign on a synagogue or community center bulletin board, place a personal ad in the local Jewish newspaper, or ask a rabbi or other teacher if he or she knows other adults who would like to meet to discuss Jewish mysticism, Jewish child-raising issues, or whatever is on your mind.

FURTHER READING

"Learning" in *The Jewish Family Book* by Sharon Strassfeld and Kathy Green (Bantam, 1981). This section contains several articles on Jewish education written from different points of view.

The Hadassah Magazine Jewish Parenting Book edited by Roselyn Bell (Free Press, 1989). A collection of essays which first appeared in *Hadassah Magazine*, these brief but informative pieces cover a very wide range of practical parenting issues, including talking to kids about anti-Semitism, raising Jews in small towns, adolescence, and all aspects of Jewish education.

The Jewish Student's Guide to American Colleges by Lee and Lana Goldberg (Shapolsky Publishers, 1989). This guide describes Jewish opportunities at more than 75 campuses.

Observance

Rabbi Abraham Joshua Heschel wrote, "Jewish ritual may be characterized as the art of significant forms in time, as architecture of time."[1] Heschel, one of the great teachers of the twentieth century, thought of *Shabbat* as the essential expression of Judaism's "architecture of time." He referred to the Sabbaths as "our great cathedrals." Judaism provides other ritual structures, too, in the annual cycle of holidays and in the ceremonies that mark life's rites of passage.

There is another, more personal metaphor that is sometimes applied to Jewish cycles of observance. Tradition—made up of history and custom, memory and song—is like a mirror, a tool for considering life and self in the context of Judaism. Looking into it, every person may call forth something new. Not answers. Mirrors do not supply answers. Yet there is something special about a mirror that can change the way people see themselves. The source of the transforming power of this mirror is time. Possessing context, connection, and continuity, time is both why and how Jewish holidays and life cycle observances "work."

Time seems tender and almost palpable at the holidays because every celebration is a window on the past: when parents were children lighting their first Hannukah candles, when the light from the candles was the brightest light in the house, or when the Maccabees lit a lamp in a rededicated Temple. Every Hannukah distills the present, like a snapshot. Every Hannukah is a "first:" the first year the "baby" is allowed to light the candles, the first year without Grandpa.

Every time a couple meets under the *huppah,* the Jewish wedding canopy, it is as if time collapses. The details of the day—the style of the bride's dress, the music, the menu—are forgotten. Suddenly and forever it is the first wedding when, according to one legend, God braided Eve's hair. And it is the ultimate wedding, the culmination of 4,000 years of Jewish weddings.

This section of *Living a Jewish Life* offers introductions to Jewish observances, holidays, and rituals, and includes many examples of the creative ways that Jews are using the mirror of tradition today. Many books have been written about the Jewish holidays and life-cycle rituals, and for more details about each of these, consult the books listed at the end of the following chapters.

Jewish Time

The holidays are islands where people can stop to reflect on the meaning of their days, to consider the distance between who they are and who they wish to be, the distance between today and the day when the world will be what we want it to be. Like *Shabbat*, the holidays are about providing a glimpse into what life and time will be like when those wishes are realized. These islands in time are not abstract ideas, but ritual structures built of customs, prayers, food, songs, family gatherings, liturgies, and memories. They are embedded in the Jewish calendar, which expresses a particular understanding of time and eternity.

The Calendar

For nearly 2,000 years, Jews have juggled two time zones, straddled two calendars. According to the secular calendar, the date changes at midnight, the week begins on Sunday, and the year starts in the winter. According to the Hebrew calendar, the day begins at sunset, the week begins on Saturday night, and the new year is celebrated in the autumn.

The secular or Gregorian calendar is a solar calendar, based on the fact that it takes 365.25 days for the earth to circle the sun.[1] With only 365 days in a year, after four years an extra day is added to February and there is a leap year. The Hebrew calendar is both solar and lunar. The months are lunar and made up of either 29 or 30 days, which add up to a 354-day year, 11.25 days short of a solar year. The discrepancy is corrected with the occasional addition of a leap month tucked between the spring months of Adar and Nisan.

The Hebrew month begins with the new moon, when no moon is visible in the sky, so the moon is full on the 15th of every month. The names of the Hebrew months are: Tishrei, Heshvan, Kislev, Tevet, Shvat, Adar (and seven times every nineteen years, Adar II), Nisan, Iyar, Sivan, Tammuz, Av, and Elul. The calendar year changes on Rosh Hashanah, on the first day of Tishrei, when according to the traditional Jewish reckoning of time, the world was created. In the autumn of the year 2000, the Hebrew calendar will read 5761 years since the creation of the world.[2]

The Gregorian and Hebrew calendars are never quite in sync, thus the inevitable grumbling about how the Jewish holidays are never "on time"—somehow either too late or too early in relation to the secular date. But because their purposes are so different, the two calendars are rarely in conflict. The Gregorian calendar is the calendar of the work week, the school year, and the mundane needs of daily life. The Hebrew calendar has exclusively religious purposes: it is for keeping track of holidays, and is used for writing Jewish marriage contracts, and for determining the anniversary of a death. The secular calendar is a tool for keeping track of time, for managing time, unlike the Hebrew calendar, which is not used for civil purposes anywhere, not even in Israel. The secular calendar stretches endlessly into the future. The Hebrew calendar is a tool for cherishing time, and for sanctifying it. The Jewish calendar moves forward toward redemption in a dance with the past, choreographed by the holidays.

The Jewish holidays have two main sources: biblical and historical.[3] The Torah established the observance of Rosh Hashanah, Yom Kippur, Sukkot, Shmini Atzeret, Pesach (Passover), and Shavuot. They are called "holy convocations," or "a Sabbath unto the Lord," and the Torah contains specific instructions for celebrating these days and for refraining from work on them.

The Torah also assigns reason and meaning to these five holidays: Rosh Hashanah is for sounding the ram's horn and for the new year, Yom Kippur is the day for asking forgiveness, Sukkot is about the harvest, Passover is for remembering slavery and the exodus from Egypt, Shavuot is about the harvest of the first fruits.

Another group of historical holidays were developed in response to transforming events in the experience of the Jewish people: Purim reacts to the dangers of living in exile; the day of mourning called Tisha B'Av became part of the calendar after the destruction of the Temple in Jerusalem; and in the second century B.C.E., after the Maccabees fought and won the right to Jewish self-rule in the land of Israel, Hannukah became an annual celebration of rededication. The historical development of the calendar continues in modern times with the addition of Yom HaAtzmaut and Yom HaShoah, which are, respectively, Israel Independence Day and Holocaust Remembrance Day.

The historical, evolutionary nature of the Jewish calendar is also demonstrated in the way certain festivals have waned and waxed in their observance. Shmini Atzeret, for example, with its unique prayer for autumn rain, may have made spiritual sense in the context of an agricultural and Temple-oriented society. However, as the Jews became a more urban and Torah-centered people, Simchat Torah, a postbiblical observance, came to overshadow and even preempt the older holiday. For modern Jews, the Holocaust and not the destruction of the Temple has become the focus of communal grief, thus Holocaust Remembrance Day has come to eclipse Tisha B'Av as the primary observance of public mourning.

Perhaps the most confusing aspect of Jewish holiday observance is the discrepancy regarding celebrations on the second day of Rosh Hashanah, Sukkot, Passover, and Shavuot. For example, some Jews observe two *seders* and eat *matzah* for eight days, whereas others attend only one *seder* and eat bread again after seven days. The difference in practice dates back to sometime around the 4th century C.E. over doubts as to the exact date of the new moon, which is invisible. Rather than risk celebrating on the wrong date, Jews living outside of the land of Israel begin two-day observances of the holidays that required refraining from work and attending worship services. This division continues: Israeli Jews and many Reform Jews celebrate holidays based on the new moon for a single day; however, many Diaspora Jews continue with two-day observances.[4]

Making Yontif

Yontif is the Yiddish word for holiday. Literally, it means "good day" and is based in the Hebrew, *yom tov.* Hence the greeting, *"Gut yontif."* *
As with *Shabbat,* the Jewish holidays only have meaning in the doing. The operant verb for holidays is not "celebrating" or "observing," but "making." Thus, making Jewish choices about the holidays is a matter of "making *yontif.*"

Jews make *yontif* in many different ways; some are traditional, some brand new. The following chapters contain many suggestions about how to make *yontif.* However, the richness of each holiday makes it impossible to do any of them justice in an introductory book. In other words, the holiday chapters contain a smaller proportion of the entire "menu," which is why more comprehensive bibliographies are included. Books about the holidays are a mainstay of every Jewish home library, and in a sense, the holidays are the best curriculum for Jewish education because they encompass nearly every religious, cultural, and historical theme of Judaism.

Each holiday has its own mood, texture, and weight. Some of these qualties are inherent in their content and observance. Yom Kippur is somber. Purim is hilarious. Although virtually every holiday has some synagogue observance connected with it, some holidays are primarily liturgical; Rosh Hashanah is a good example, whereas others like Hannukah are essentially home-based.

In addition to their social construction, the various holidays have different qualities and different importance in every Jewish household. For example, many people consider Purim largely a children's holiday. They focus on dress-up and the kids' plays and pageants at the synagogue or in religious school. But there are adults for whom Purim is the occasion for both serious (and silly) study, not to mention the costume party of the year.

Furthermore, individual and family interest in a particular holiday sometimes wax and wane, and not only as a result of children's ages. Enthusiasm for a celebration can be sparked by any number of reasons:

---

* The Hebrew term for holiday is *chag.* The Hebrew greeting, *Chag sameach,* means "happy holiday."

a good lecture, a book or movie that speaks to the themes of the holiday, or an event in the past year. For people who have recently lost a loved one, for example, attending Yom Kippur services can feel like part of the mourning process.

The meaning and joy of the holidays is uncovered year by year in the process of making *yontif.* But perhaps the most important part of that process—the make-it-or-break it element—is preparation, or *hachanah* in Hebrew.

Hachanah includes everything from buying *matzah* for Passover to making paper chain decorations for Hannukah, from meditating on the unkind words you wish you hadn't said in preparation for Yom Kippur to reading bedtime stories about Queen Esther during the week before Purim. *Hachanah* is the difference between mechanical holidays and meaningful holidays, between enforced holidays and holidays that are genuinely fun.

Jewish tradition is replete with examples of the importance of preparing for the holidays. The entire 40 days before Yom Kippur are considered a period of spiritual preparation. And then, as soon as Yom Kippur is over, even before breaking the fast, preparations for Sukkot begin with the hammering of the first nail in a *sukkah,* the hut in which Jews celebrate the harvest festival. According to the Hasidic view, these preparations are themselves holy; by orienting secular time toward the celebration to come, *hachanah* sanctifies even the most mundane details.

Still, there is a crucial difference between preparing and celebrating, between *hachanah* and *yontif.* The point of getting ready is not merely to have delicious meals or a big party when the day finally arrives. *Hachanah* is that which enables people to have the experience of basking in life, of enjoying the present without worrying about what is left unfinished. This sense of celebration, or, rather, this taste of redemption, is the goal of all Jewish rituals, but of *Shabbat* and the Jewish holidays in particular.

The menu that follows consists of ideas, strategies, projects, and approaches for making *yontif.* This is not offerred as a "to-do" list; there is more here than any one person or any one family can reasonably undertake. This is a "can-do" list: a catalog of the ways that people explore the Jewish holidays.

GETTING ORIENTED

Buy a beautiful Hebrew calendar and hang it on the wall. Get one with plenty of room for notes and scribbling and, before hanging it, mark the week or the *Shabbat* before every holiday as a reminder to start getting ready.

Some families specialize in one particular holiday; all their friends know that the So-and-Sos really "do" Hannukah with a big party complete with dancing, a royal feast, and gifts for everyone. But others celebrate some, most, or all of the holidays with a series of parties, which can be the occasion for inviting people you've been meaning to get to know better.

Pick a primary symbol for each holiday, for instance the *hannukiah* (the eight-candle candelabra of Hannukah) or the Sukkot *etrog* (a citrus fruit imported from Israel). Learn as much as you can about it and feature it everywhere: in centerpieces on the table, in conversation, in stories, and in art projects for children.

As markers in time, the Jewish holidays can be a way to organize all kinds of memories. Pictures of ten years' worth of Passover gatherings make for a sweeping image of continuity and change. Or have a family portrait taken every year during the same holiday.

Continuity is good, but so is change. The holidays acquire more and more meaning as they are repeated consistently. The same menus, the same guests, and the same ritual objects taken out only once a year all add to the evocative power of the day. But holidays can also be opportunities for growth and innovation. Just as individuals change from one year to the next, so can their holiday observance.

FAMILY TIME

There are all kinds of families. And regardless of their size or composition, holidays create time and space for relaxing, sharing, listening, and enjoying one another. For families with children, the holidays can be formative Jewish experiences. They are times redolent of both continuity and change and special in many ways, including missing school and feeling different from the rest of the secular world.

There are many ways to enhance this experience. Taking time to talk about the holiday at the Friday night *Shabbat* table, for example, is one way to help children prepare and also to let them know that the grown-ups have begun getting ready.

Reading stories about a holiday in anticipation of its celebration is another way to prepare with kids. Older children can be encouraged to write their own story about the holiday or to participate in writing a family *midrash,* which is an imaginative tale based loosely on the events and characters associated with each holiday.

Holidays are like chapter headings in a family history. The light of holiday candles can prompt the telling of "our" stories: of Sarah's first Hannukah, when she tried to eat the candles; of the time everyone went to Grandma's house and all the presents were forgotten at home; or of favorite gifts, guests, parties, and so on.

It is a good idea to try and strike a balance between activities for children and time for adults. Arts and crafts projects may be the perfect way for pre-schoolers to get acquainted with a holiday, but that's probably not entirely fulfilling for parents. Besides, if children see that their parents are really not involved, they will learn that making *yontif* is essentially kid's stuff, that is, something to be outgrown.

SETTING THE MOOD

Decorating for the holiday—making tangible preparations—is a good way to enter into a spirit of celebration. This can include everything from buying fresh flowers for the table to making a centerpiece using holiday symbols. Children's artwork about the holiday can be featured on the refrigerator or front door.

One nice holiday project is to create special place settings. Commercial placemats are available for Passover and Hannukah, but children can make their own by covering an original drawing or painting with clear Contact paper. Likewise, you can create "dinnerware" for holidays, either by purchasing a new set of plastic tableware, by using a clear Contact paper over a paper plate or by getting a "decorate a plate" kit, which is shipped off so the original design can be permanently baked on.

Another way to set the mood is with music. Recordings of traditional and modern holiday songs abound, as well as music that reflects the diversity of Jewish culture: everything from cantorial singing to Israeli rock n' roll, from American Jewish bluegrass to modern classics, such as Leonard Bernstein's "Kaddish" or Steven Reich's "Tehillim." English/Hebrew tapes for children are a popular way to introduce Jewish vocabulary and Hebrew words to youngsters, and their parents.

EATING

The holidays are experienced with all the senses, and special dishes are associated with certain times of the year. Apples and honey *are* Rosh Hashanah. Potato pancakes *(latkes) are* Hannukah.

There are family traditions about holiday foods as well. It isn't Passover without Mom's *matzah* stuffing. Shavuot means Aunt Molly's cheesecake. It is easy to start this kind of family table tradition, simply find a dish beloved by everyone in the household and more or less reserve it for the holiday. Holidays are also a good excuse for baked treats. Making cookies, cupcakes, and candy can be a great way to involve children in holiday preparations.

Cookbooks are a way to explore the holidays from a nonintellectual perspective. Most Jewish cookbooks contain a special section on holiday food, and there are dozens of books devoted entirely to holiday recipes. For North American Jews, the vast majority of whom are of Eastern European descent, cookbooks devoted to the Jewish cuisines of Greece and Italy can be a revelation, and not just gastronomically. The fact that holiday traditions include such a breadth of flavors and aromas seem to validate the variation and experimentation in modern Jewish life.

TREATS

In order to associate the holidays with pleasantness, some people give gifts (especially to children) on major holidays. Similarly, some parents plan trips to a bookstore or a music store for a holiday-related book or tape. Eating special desserts or going out for ice cream are other ways to heighten the sweetness of a holiday.

It is traditional to wear new clothes on *Shabbat* and on the holidays. For older children and teenagers, shopping for a new Passover dress or shirt may be a good way to get into the spirit and celebration of the holiday.

STUDY

One way for adults to enter into the spirit of the holidays is to learn something new about each one. Study can take many forms, from enrolling in a course about the holiday cycle to simply reading a book or a chapter of a book about the upcoming festival. Many holidays have Torah readings and other traditional texts associated with them.

TZEDAKAH

It has long been the Jewish custom to share holiday joy by making contributions to the poor. Convening the family to decide where to send money "this season" can be a great way of focusing on the holiday. Some people make a point of sending money to organizations that have something to do with the holiday. For example, environmental causes seem an appropriate choice on Tu B'Shvat, which celebrates trees and the natural world.

GOING TO SYNAGOGUE

In addition to worship services, many synagogues offer activities pegged to most holidays: from communal candle-lighting and meals in the temple *sukkah* to *Purimshpiels* (Purim plays or pageants) to study sessions on Shavuot. Attending synagogue activities is a good way to participate in communal life and learn about the holidays at the same time.

SPIRITUAL PREPARATION

In the rush to run errands, cook, and get everything finished before a holiday begins, it is easy to forget about making oneself ready for *yontif*. For Jews, spiritual preparation has long been associated with *mikvah*, the ritual bath of purification, but this kind of preparation can be done at home too. Before lighting holiday candles, going to synagogue, or sitting down to eat, it is a good idea to make time for a leisurely bath, a solitary walk, or for reading something to shift mental gears from the hectic pace of everyday life to holiday mode.

THE YONTIF SEDER

The word "*seder*," which means "order," is most closely associated with Passover. The Passover *seder* is the order of the readings, blessings, and rituals that take place before, during, and after the ritual meal on the first and (for some) second nights of the holiday. People have also created *seders* for Tu B'Shvat, Hannukah, and Purim; they are essentially ritual menus of songs, readings, blessings, and activities surrounding a meal.

The *yontif seder* is similar to the *Shabbat seder*, which is the order of blessings, customs, and songs surrounding the Friday night meal, described in detail in the chapter on *Shabbat*. Similarly, most of the holidays described in the following chapters begin with a festival meal that includes a few blessings. The basic *yontif seder* consists of four blessings: over candles, wine *(kiddush)*, the season *(sheheheyanu)*, and bread *(motzi)*.

Candles: Festival candles mark the beginning of most holiday celebrations, just as Shabbat candles mark the beginning of the Sabbath. If a holiday begins Friday night, the blessing for the candles concludes with the words, *shel Shabbat v' yom tov*, or "the lights of *Shabbat* and the holiday."

בָּרוּךְ אַתָּה, יְיָ אֱלֹהֵינוּ, מֶלֶךְ הָעוֹלָם, אֲשֶׁר קִדְּשָׁנוּ בְּמִצְוֹתָיו, וְצִוָּנוּ לְהַדְלִיק נֵר שֶׁל (שַׁבָּת וְשֶׁל) יוֹם טוֹב.

Baruch ata Adonai Eloheynu Melech Ha-olam asher kid'shanu bemitzvotav vitzivanu l'hadlik ner shel (*Shabbat v'shel) yom tov.

You abound in Blessings, Adonai Our Lord, You make us holy with commandments, and call us to light the lights (*of *Shabbat* and) of the holiday.

Wine: The *kiddush*, or sanctification over wine, can be done in a number of ways. The full *kiddush* for holidays usually includes at least a phrase and as much as a paragraph about the specific festival, and is published in most daily prayerbooks, or *siddurim*. However, many people use the basic *kiddush* for any occasion.

בָּרוּךְ אַתָּה, יְיָ אֱלֹהֵינוּ, מֶלֶךְ הָעוֹלָם, בּוֹרֵא פְּרִי הַגָּפֶן.

Baruch ata Adonai Eloheynu Melech Ha-olam boray p'ree hagafen.

You Abound in Blessings, Adonai Our Lord, You make the fruit of the vine.

---

*   Add on Friday evening.

The Season: *Sheheheyanu* is a blessing recited on many sorts of occasions, ceremonies, and rituals. At the holidays, it acknowledges the advent of a new time in the year, and a new time in the life of the people gathered at the table.

בָּרוּךְ אַתָּה, יְיָ אֱלֹהֵינוּ, מֶלֶךְ הָעוֹלָם, שֶׁהֶחֱיָנוּ וְקִיְּמָנוּ וְהִגִּיעָנוּ לַזְּמַן הַזֶּה.

Baruch ata Adonai Eloheynu Melech Ha-olam
Sheheheyanu vikiamanu vihigianu lazman hazeh.

You Abound in Blessings, Adonai Our Lord, You have kept us alive. You have sustained us. You have brought us to this moment.

Bread: Called the *motzi*, the blessing over bread represents all the food at the meal. The *motzi* acknowledges that human beings are, ultimately, dependent upon gifts from the earth.

בָּרוּךְ אַתָּה, יְיָ אֱלֹהֵינוּ, מֶלֶךְ הָעוֹלָם, הַמּוֹצִיא לֶחֶם מִן־הָאָרֶץ:

Baruch ata Adonai Eloheynu Melech Ha-olam Hamotzi lechem min ha'aretz.

You Abound in Blessings, Adonai Our Lord, You bring forth bread from the earth.

Dinner is served.

FURTHER READING

There are dozens of books about the holidays, and many more that contain chapters about the holidays. The following titles are among the best contemporary volumes.

Seasons of Our Joy by Arthur Waskow (Bantam, 1982). The preface outlines a vision of the holiday cycle as a whole, reconciling the seasons of the sun and the seasons of the moon, the needs of individuals and the needs of the community and the world. Each chapter contains a discussion of a holiday's mood and origins, talks about traditional and nontraditional ways to prepare, and describes holiday observance. The "new approaches" sections include interesting new interpretations, often feminist. The language is poetic and informal and, although its "new age" leanings may not appeal to everyone, *Seasons of Our Joy* is well-written and can easily be read from cover to cover.

The Jewish Holidays by Michael Strassfeld (Harper & Row, 1985). This is very comprehensive guide to the holidays, containing masses of information ranging from the practical to the historical and arcane. Each chapter contains commentaries about the meaning of the holiday from historical and theological perspectives, as well as mini-essays published in the margins by five contributing scholars. An excellent resource, *The Jewish Holidays* conveys a rather traditional approach.

The Jewish Way by Irving Greenberg (Summit Books, 1988). This is not a how-to book. It contains no directions for building a *sukkah* or making Purim masks. *The Jewish Way* treats the holidays as the "master code" of Judaism, the theme of which is redemption, or the idea that the world can be perfected through human effort. According to Rabbi Greenberg, the goal of the holiday cycle is to cultivate that hope for redemption. Greenberg, a modern Orthodox rabbi, assumes a fair amount of familiarity with Herbew terms. Still, it is an excellent text for adult study.

The Jewish Festivals by Hayyim Schauss (Schocken, 1938). This venerable classic contains wonderful, brief histories of how each holiday was celebrated through the ages, from the days of Temple observance to the beginning of this century. Schauss occasionally drifts into historical fiction, setting scenes in an Eastern European neighborhood, or in the homes of Marranos, the secret Jews of Spain. However, it adds a kind of warmth, depth, and flavor that more straightforward books often lack.

When a Jew Celebrates by Harry Gersh (Behrman House, 1971). This is a popular textbook in religious schools for students in grades 5 and up, but educators often recommend it to adult readers as well. Books produced for children have the advantage of not assuming any previous knowledge, and thus explaining things simply and carefully. While Gersh is frankly didactic (*"Pesach* is not just about the past. It is about today and tomorrow, and about what Jews should be doing with their time all their lives.") his directives tend to be gentle. *When a Jew Celebrates* covers life cycle rituals as well as the Jewish holiday cycle.

HOLIDAY COOKBOOKS

The Jewish Holiday Kitchen by Joan Nathan (Schocken Books, 1988). This book is a classic.

The Sephardic Holiday Cookbook by Gilda Angel (Decalogue Books, 1986). This volume reveals that in the Mediterranean, pomegranates, not apples, are customary for Rosh Hashanah.

CHILDREN'S BOOKS

Kar-Ben Copies, Inc. publishes indestructible little "board books" for pre-readers about most of the holidays.

Happy Holiday Pop-up by Saul Scharfstein (Ktav, 1983). A one-page summary of each holiday, complete with a pop-up illustration for Rosh Hashanah, Sukkot, Hannukah, Purim, Passover, and Shavuot.

The Holiday Adventures of Achbar by Barbara Sofer (Kar-Ben Copies, Inc, 1983). Achbar the mouse lives in the home of Detective Schuster and family. For young readers.

Jewish Days and Holidays by Greer Fay Cashman (Adama Books, 1988). Cheerful, bright, and complete, the story of each holiday is told in one to three pages, with information about holiday celebrations as well. Grade 4 and up.

Choosing to be Chosen by Ellen Frankel (Ktav, 1985). The adventures of Sarah Pearl Eisenberg who manages to get into some kind of scrape on every Jewish holiday, often with her non-Jewish friend Dierdre Riley. Discussion questions follow each chapter. Grade 4-5.

Chag Sameach, A Jewish Holiday Book for Children by Patricia Shaffer (Tabor Sarah Books, 1985). Black and white photographs of families celebrating the holidays. This book is noteworthy for its depiction of multi-racial Jewish families. (See ''New Traditions'' for ordering information).

FAMILY RESOURCES

Building Jewish Life by Torah Aura Productions. This series incorporates photographs and cartoons with a clear, readable text full of information. The series includes books on: Hannukah, Passover, Purim, Rosh Hashanah and Yom Kippur, Sukkot and Simchat Torah. These volumes contain a ''For the Parent'' section in the back, with more sophisticated explanations of the symbols and rituals of the holidays for adults. Activity books are also available.

Home Start Kits (Behrman House Publishing Co.). A series of booklets on two levels for the major holidays and *Shabbat,* mailed to you in sequence. Level I is for nursery school-kindergarten. Level II is for grades 1 and 2. The booklets contain stories, blessings, songs, puzzles, and recipes. For information: Behrman House, 235 Watchung Avenue, West Orange, NY, 07052. 1-800-221-2755.

Together (Melton Research Center of the Jewish Theological Seminary of America). A series of useful booklets on the holidays and other topics (Israel, Torah, *Shabbat,* God) published by the Conservative movement. For information: Melton Research Center, 3080 Broadway, New York, NY 10027.

Rosh Hashanah and Yom Kippur

Picture people running around, sneaking up behind one another with a big ram's horn, giving it a blast, as if to say, "Wake up! It is upon us again." The liturgy of Rosh Hashanah is designed to get you to wake up and pay attention not only to who you are, but to who you have been and who you mean to be.

Yom Kippur is not eating, not drinking, not sleeping very much, not having sex, not dressing in fine clothes and looking in the mirror and seeing what you're going to look like after you've died. And the most joyous noise a Jew can hear is the sound of the *shofar* announcing the end of Yom Kippur, because it means that you have lived through the day of death and not died.

Rosh Hashana is about reverence and gratitude for life, the motherlode of all religious insight. Yom Kippur is about telling the worst truth about yourself, and getting new life from that.[1]

Rosh Hashanah (the New Year) and Yom Kippur (the Day of Atonement) are the most prayer-filled of all the Jewish holidays. The Hebrew word for prayer is *tefila,* which is a reflexive form of the verb "to judge." For Jews, prayer—especially the prayers of the Days of Awe—are best understood as a form of reflection and self-judgement.

The two holidays that begin the Jewish year are unlike virtually every other. Neither one is based on an agricultural festival or historical event. Neither one is associated with the kinds of symbols and home celebrations that make other Jewish holidays beloved of children. Instead, the Days of Awe, *yamim noraim,* are synagogue-based, liturgical, and existential. They confront every Jew with the fact of his or her own mortality, and thus with an appreciation of life. Although these holiays are not inherently "fun" the way that Sukkot, Hannukah, Purim, or Passover can be, they are deeply compelling.

Indeed, Rosh Hashanah and Yom Kippur are the only times when all American synagogues are filled to the rafters. Jews who rarely or never attend worship services find their way to the longest, most formal services of the Jewish year. The reasons for this loyalty are complex. Childhood memories and nostalgia draw many people. And some rabbis have suggested that there is a magical element to high holiday services that makes attendance seem like the renewal of an ancient Jewish life insurance policy, a hedge against death, or at least a repudiation of assimilation.

By and large, making *yontif* for the Days of Awe means attending worship services. There are many ways to prepare for these holidays and to mark their observance at home, which will be outlined here. But because of the importance of community worship, this chapter outlines holiday services, introduces some liturgical themes and key Hebrew words found in Rosh Hashanah and Yom Kippur services, and offers a few comments on the subject of prayer. However, because individual congregations make so many choices about the content and form of services, the outline below is extremely general, representing only a fraction of the menu from which rabbis and ritual committees make their selections.

PREPARATION

According to tradition, the entire Hebrew month that precedes Rosh Hashanah, Elul, is dedicated to preparing for the Days of Awe. Psalm 27 is added to daily worship services and the *shofar*, a ram's horn, is sounded every weekday morning. Special penitential prayers called *selichot*, from the Hebrew for "excuse" or "to be sorry," are recited during Elul, and on the Saturday night preceding Rosh Hashanah, many congregations hold a late-night *selichot* service. Some synagogues run adult education programs about the approaching Days of Awe during Elul.

The most common personal preparation for these holidays is the sending of New Year's cards. These greetings originated from the custom of signing letters during the month of Elul with the phrase, "May you be inscribed [in the Book of Life] for a good year." Many beautiful commercial cards are available, but some families now make their own. Children can create a design to be photocopied, or make one-of-a-kind cards for special people.

Another way to get into the spirit of the holidays is to buy a *shofar*, the horn of a ram, available in Judaica stores. A *shofar* is not a sacred object but something both children and adults can play with. A *shofar* can even be used as the family alarm clock in preparation for the holidays to come.

It is also customary to wear new clothes for Rosh Hashanah, and to get a haircut in anticipation of the new year.

Because Rosh Hashanah is associated with both the creation of the first human beings and with the creation of the world, children enjoy decorating the table (or the refrigerator door) with birthday-related projects. Children can also decorate the table and the house for the break-the-fast meal that follows the Yom Kippur fast.

Traditionally, the weeks before the Days of Awe are associated with mending relationships, apologizing, and asking for forgiveness for transgressions big and small. People call out-of-town relatives and friends. Some families make a ritual out of resolving conflicts and clearing the air of arguments big and small with a family "retreat:" at an inn for the weekend, during a quiet afternoon outing, or just by gathering to look at the family album. And some people visit the graves of family members and loved ones who have died.

STUDY

Of all the holidays, the Days of Awe seem the most intellectual. Because so much time is spent in services, it can be helpful to browse through the special holiday prayerbook or *machzor* (Hebrew for "cycle") you will be using. Getting familiar with the structure and content of the prayers can make the services more accessible and meaningful.

The *machzorim* or holiday prayerbooks commonly used in liberal congregations are: *Mahzor for Rosh Hashanah and Yom Kippur,* edited by Rabbi Jules Harlow (Rabbinical Assembly, Conservative, 1972); *Gates of Repentance* (Central Conference of American Rabbis (Reform), 1984), *The New Machzor* (Media Judaica, 1985), and *The Wings of Awe* (B'nai B'rith Hillel Foundation, 1985). Some congregations put together their own high holiday prayer book, using these and other sources.

Holiday prayerbooks contain the holiday Torah and *haftarah* portions. The Rosh Hashanah Torah readings (Genesis 21 and 22) are among the most powerful and problematic in the Torah. The first includes the story of the birth of Isaac, the casting out of Hagar and Ishmael into the desert, and their subsequent deliverance. Genesis 22 contains the test of Abraham's faith, when he is asked to sacrifice his son Isaac. This story is referred to as "the binding of Isaac," or the *akedah*.

The Haftarah portions (prophetic readings) for both the morning and afternoon Torah services on Yom Kippur are also favorite texts for study and discussion. The morning passage from Isaiah rejects piety divorced from a commitment to social justice: "Behold, on the day of your fast you pursue business as usual, and oppress your workers. . . . Such fasting will not make your voice audible on high."[2] The *haftarah* for the afternoon of Yom Kippur is the four-chapter Book of Jonah, which is available in illustrated versions for children.

TZEDAKAH

It is customary to give money to the poor during this season. Because Rosh Hashanah is a celebration of life, some make an annual blood donation before the holiday. Many make a contribution to a hunger-related charity for an amount equivalent to a day's worth of meals at Yom Kippur. During the memorial or *yizkor* service of Yom Kippur, one of the prayers pledges *tzedakah* in the memory of a loved one who has died, so some people make a point of making a donation to a charity that was particularly important to a person being remembered.

Another way of performing a *mitzvah*, a holy act, during the Days of Awe is to go to a Jewish nursing home to visit the residents and/or to assist with or attend the Rosh Hashanah and Yom Kippur services for those who cannot get to a synagogue.

CHILDREN AND SERVICES

Rosh Hashanah and Yom Kippur are days of intense prayer and reflection in the synagogue, clearly not an easy setting for children. In some congregations there is little in the way of special programming; parents keep small children quiet or leave them at home while school-age kids are expected to attend and behave during adult services. However, many synagogues provide a full menu of age-specific activities, including babysitting for toddlers, singing and organized play for pre-schoolers, and an abbreviated service for school-aged children.

Making Rosh Hashanah

AT HOME

The evening meal that begins the holiday constitutes the entire home celebration for Rosh Hashanah. Families tend to create their own holiday traditions around this dinner: menus and recipes, special table settings and decorations, or guests who return every year. Because Rosh Hashanah is often referred to as the "birthday of the world," some parents provide a birthday cake, complete with candles, for dessert.

Dinner is preceded by the *yontif seder* that is discussed on page 175, with lighting of candles, *kiddush*, and *motzi*. It is traditional to use a round *challah* on Rosh Hashanah, a symbol of the cycle of the year. *Sheheheyanu* is then recited, the blessing for all "firsts." And to begin the new year sweetly, it is customary to dip apple sections in a bowl of honey and to say:

יְהִי רָצוֹן שֶׁתְּחַדֵּשׁ עָלֵינוּ שָׁנָה טוֹבָה וּמְתוּקָה.
בָּרוּךְ אַתָּה, יְיָ אֱלֹהֵינוּ, מֶלֶךְ הָעוֹלָם, בּוֹרֵא פְּרִי הָעֵץ.

Y'hi ratzon, she'te'chadesh aleynu shana tova u'metukah.
Baruch ata Adonai Eloheynu Melech Ha-olam boray p'ree ha-eytz.

May it be Your will, to renew us for a good and sweet year.
You Abound in Blessings, Adonai Our Lord, You create the fruit of the tree.

SYNAGOGUE OBSERVANCE

The evening service of Rosh Hashanah is relatively short and much like other evening services, with a few exceptions. The distinctive melodies of the Days of Awe, which are reprised again and again during both Rosh Hashanah and Yom Kippur services, are introduced here. At the morning service for Rosh Hashanah, the themes of judgment and repentance are repeated. The recurrent image of God as a father-king is given voice in one of the most memorable prayers and melodies of all the Jewish holidays, *Avinu Malkenu*, "Our Father, our King."

One of the overarching metaphors of Rosh Hashanah and Yom Kippur is "the Book of Life." According to legend, on the first day of the year, the names of the righteous are written in this book, inscribed for another year of life. But those who are not entirely good or righteous, even the wicked, have the next ten days in which to turn away from their wrongs and repent before the book is closed and sealed on Yom Kippur.

After services, people generally have lunch with family and friends, go for walks, or search out a body of water for the informal ceremony called *tashlich*, from the Hebrew for "send off" or "cast away." *Tashlich* is a symbolic casting off of sins by emptying pockets into running water, built around the words of the prophet Micah: "And you will cast all their sins into the depths of the sea."[3] Some people fill their pockets with bread crumbs for this purpose and head for a duck pond; this is a favorite with children, especially on a day they may be asked to sit still so much. Some families take this time to apologize to one another for the wrongs of the past, and promise to try to be more patient and kinder in the coming year.

Taschlich is also a communal observance. Groups of friends, members of *havurot* and *minyanim*, and many congregations gather at a local stream or river, pond or lake for this purpose. Short, informal ceremonies have been created for *tashlich*, which includes songs about water and readings of all sorts. If the first day of Rosh Hashanah coincides with *Shabbat*, *tashlich* is not performed.

The second day of Rosh Hashanah is largely a repetition of the first day, unless the first day falls on a Sabbath, in which case *tashlich* is performed. In order to say the *sheheheyanu* a second night, many people serve some kind of fruit that is newly in-season.

THE TEN DAYS

Rosh Hashanah and Yom Kippur begin and end a ten-day period of reflection and repentance called, in Hebrew, *teshuvah*, which literally

---

Help us to break down the barriers which keep us from You:
falsehood and faithlessness
callousness and selfishness
injustice and hard-heartedness

from the Rosh Hashanah service

means "turning." The sabbath between the two holidays is called *Shab-bat Shuvah,* the "Sabbath of turning." In some synagogues, these ten days are observed with special services. In families and among friends, this is a time for saying, "I'm sorry" about thoughtless words, missed opportunities for kindness, and any offense given in the past year.

During this week of introspection and turning, some congregations offer an ethical will-writing workshop. An ethical will, a form of moral literature that dates back to Biblical times, is a personal statement of beliefs, hopes, and advice. A counterpart to a legal will that distributes material goods after a person's death, the ethical will is a way of communicating the values and insights of a lifetime to loved ones. But ethical wills are not legalistic or formulaic. Indeed they often take the form of a very personal letter to family and friends.

After reading and discussing examples of ethical wills, participants at these workshops sit with pen and paper and write their own. People who have done this say it is a powerfully clarifying exercise and a wonderful preparation for Yom Kippur. Ethical wills are usually stored with legal wills and other important personal documents, and some congregations keep copies in a special file.

Making Yom Kippur

AT HOME

Yom Kippur is called *Shabbat Shabbatot,* or the "Sabbath of Sabbaths." The meal prior to the start of the day-long fast is not begun with blessings, although a *motzi* may be said before any meal. However, as with Rosh Hashanah, the meal that precedes Yom Kippur can become a family tradition by virtue of special menus and rituals, such as standing and drinking a glass of water together to end the meal.

After dinner, people who have lost a close family member light a memorial, or *yahrzeit* candles. (See the chapter "Death" in Part Five.) Finally, Yom Kippur candles are lit with the following blessing:

בָּרוּךְ אַתָּה, יְיָ אֱלֹהֵינוּ, מֶלֶךְ הָעוֹלָם, אֲשֶׁר קִדְּשָׁנוּ בְּמִצְוֹתָיו, וְצִוָּנוּ לְהַדְלִיק נֵר שֶׁל יוֹם הַכִּפּוּרִים.

Baruch ata Adonai Eloheynu Melech Ha-olam asher kidshanu b'mitzvotav vitzivanu l'hadlik ner shel Yom HaKippurim.

You Abound in Blessings, Adonai Our Lord, You make us holy with commandments and call us to kindle the light of Yom Kippur.

After dinner, some people put a white tablecloth over the table that will remain empty until the following evening.

This is the last meal eaten before healthy adults undertake a complete fast from food and water, which ends the following sunset. Fasting is only the most obvious form of self-denial on the tenth day of the seventh month, which the Torah calls "a day for self-affliction"[4] None of life's pleasures are permitted in order to focus all attention on the task at hand, which is repentance.

Children under the age of 13 are not expected to fast during Yom Kippur, nor is anyone for whom a lack of food or water might cause physical harm. Pregnant and nursing women are forbidden to fast. People who cannot or do not fast, including children, often choose a modified fast, drinking water only or eating very little. Those who undertake a complete fast are often advised to cut back on caffeine consumption several days in advance because caffeine withdrawal is probably the most common cause of headaches, grouchiness, and other unpleasant symptoms.

SYNAGOGUE OBSERVANCE

Kol Nidre is the evening service for Yom Kippur, named for its opening prayer. The *Kol Nidre* prayer is set to a haunting melody that moves people deeply, year after year, though the content of the prayer is far less inspirational. *Kol Nidre* is an Aramaic legal document that declares all unfulfilled vows and promises null and void. It is pronounced ceremonially while a court of three, one of whom holds a Torah, stands as if in judgment. The full meaning of Kol Nidre has been the subject of debate for generations, though it clearly addresses the power of words and vows, a recurrent theme in the Yom Kippur litugry.

The evening service then continues with the stately, somber melodies of the Yom Kippur liturgy and the penitential and confessional language of the Day of Atonement. The communal confession, repeated several times during the holiday, called the *viddui*, is an alphabetical listing of communal sin that begins, "We abuse, we betray, we are cruel. We destroy, we embitter, we falsify."

Kol Nidre is the only evening service at which people wear *tallesim*, or prayershawls. There are other distinctive customs regarding clothing on this holiday as well. Some people dress in white, a sign of purity and some wear a bathrobe-like white garment called a *kittle*, which is sometimes worn at the Passover *seder* or by a groom to his wedding. Some refrain from wearing leather shoes, an ancient symbol of luxury. And others remove their shoes altogether during services and pray barefoot, a universal sign of humility.

The following morning, a full day's worth of services begin. Not all congregations hold all of the services listed here, nor is the order or content described here universal.

Shacharit, the morning service, traditionally includes a Torah reading from Leviticus, which describes the sacrificial rites for Yom Kippur in the Temple. Some congregations substitute another Torah reading, often Deuteronomy 29:9–30:20, which ends with the lines "I have put before you this day life and death, blessing and curse. Choose life . . ." The morning *haftarah* reading is Isaiah's angry sermon demanding justice of the Jewish people.

In some synagogues, *musaf*, the additional service, is part of Yom Kippur observance, and most of these services include the recitation of the martyrology, a list of the murders of Talmudic sages by the Romans. This section is often extended to include stories from the Holocaust.

The memorial or *yizkor* service is the time when a special memorial prayer for the dead is repeated. *Yizkor* is scheduled at different times of the day, depending on the synagogue custom; it is either at the end of the morning service, or immediately preceding or following afternoon prayers.

Mincha is the afternoon service, which traditionally includes a reading from the Torah that outlines the laws of incest,[5] though this too is often replaced with another Torah portion, Leviticus 19, called "the holiness code," which includes the injunction to "love your neighbor as yourself." The *haftarah* reading is the Book of Jonah.

Ne'ilah, from the Hebrew "to lock," is the concluding service. The name refers to the symbolic closing of heaven's gates and communicates the sense that time is running out. At *ne'ilah*, the liturgy changes in its reference to the Book of Life; "Write us in the Book of Life" becomes "Seal us in the Book of Life." Many people stand throughout this short service, which ends with a final *shofar* blast. In some congregations, *ne'ilah* is followed by a short evening or *ma'ariv* service. *Havdalah*, the ceremony that ends the Sabbath and holidays and which distinguishes between the holy and the profane, is the final service of Yom Kippur.

After services, the Yom Kippur fast is broken with little or no ceremony beyond the blessing over bread, *motzi*. Many people gather with family and friends for a break-the-fast meal. Some make it a point of inviting new friends to their homes for the break-fast, often a pot-luck meal of light, easy-to-digest foods.

A FEW WORDS ABOUT PRAYER

The words "prayer" and "sin" make many people uncomfortable. However, an understanding of their Jewish definitions can make them more accessible and even appealing. The Hebrew word for prayer, *tefila*, which can be translated as "self-judging," contains the notion that prayer is not about getting God to do something for you, but is a way of effecting change in yourself, a process of meditation, reflection, and stock-taking.

The Hebrew word for sin is *chayt*, a term based in archery that means "missing the mark." A sin is thus a missed opportunity for kindness or righteousness. During Rosh Hashanah and especially Yom Kippur, the liturgy's insistence on human sinfulness can become a reminder of times during the past year when a generous act was not undertaken, or when a kind word was not spoken. Indeed, the liturgy is replete with references to the ways that people hurt one another with words: through slander and insult, with words that embarrass, or with words spoken in anger. During the Days of Awe, prayer can be understood as the process of judging one's own language or conduct with others.

Perhaps the best example of the reflexive nature of prayer and sin is the Jewish approach toward atonement. Prayers to God do not wipe away sins committed against other people. The only way to do that is by asking the person you wronged for forgiveness. It is not necessary for the other person to accept the apology, only that the request for forgiveness to be offered sincerely. This is what is meant by "making *teshuva*," that is, "turning" away from your own sin by taking action.

Prayer is both a discipline and a spontaneous activity. It requires preparation and also a kind of passive receptivity. Sometimes it works, sometimes it does not. Prayer is not possible for every individual in every synagogue, which is why it is important to find a place where prayer is possible. But even in the most hospitable setting, it is difficult to sustain prayer for a long period of time. During the long services of Rosh Hashanah and Yom Kippur, there are times when individuals may feel the liturgy is downright hostile to prayer. Repeated references to a King-God, to judgment, and to sin can be off-putting. But then, a sentence or a phrase from the prayerbook may take your breath away. The challenge is to try to remain open to those flashes of insight that are available during the Days of Awe as they are at no other time during the year.

FURTHER READING

The Last Trial by Shalom Speigel (Behrman House, 1979). A book about the legends and interpretations attached to the story of the *akedah,* the binding of Isaac.

Ethical Wills; A Modern Jewish Treasure, edited by Jack Riemer and Nathaniel Stampfer (Shocken, 1983). A collection of ethical wills that spans nearly 200 years.

Days of Awe by S.Y. Agnon (Schocken, 1948). A treasury of legends, laws, and commentaries about Rosh Hashanah, Yom Kippur, and the days in between.

The Rosh Hashanah Anthology by Philip Goodman (Jewish Publication Society, 1973) and *The Yom Kippur Anthology* by Philip Goodman (Jewish Publication Society, 1971). Entries from the Bible, Talmud, and Midrash, the liturgies of the Days of Awe, histories, overviews of customs from around the world, stories for children, and poems and modern short stories that deal with the two holidays.

The Artscroll Machzorim (Mesorah Publishing Co, 1985). Four much-annotated volumes of the prayerbooks for the Days of Awe, two each for Rosh Hashanah and Yom Kippur, reflecting the difference between Ashkenazic and Sephardic practice.

CHILDREN'S BOOK

A Rosh Hashanah Walk by Carol Levin (Kar-Ben Copies, 1987). Children head out for *tashlich,* and consider the meaning of saying, "I'm sorry."

The Shofar that Lost its Voice by David E. Fass (UAHC, 1982). Ari is asked to blow the *shofar* for the children's service on Rosh Hashanah, but before the big day has an Alice-in-Wonderland type adventure inside his *shofar.*

Rosh Hashana; A Holiday Funtext by Judy Bin-Nun (UAHC, 1978). Great games and neat projects in a large-format paperback.

Minnie's Yom Kippur Birthday by Marilyn Singer (Harper & Row, 1989). Minnie turns 5 on the holiest day of the year, a tribulation with a happy ending.

Danny and the Silver Flute by Gerald C. Ruthen (United Synagogue Commission). A boy who doesn't know the words but prays with his flute.

Sukkot and Simchat Torah

Sukkot only makes sense in that it follows a narrow scrape with death and when it is experienced from inside a *sukkah,* the flimsy booth we make our literal home for a week. Sukkot is about the kind of happiness that can only come from looking through a leafy roof at the sunshine or the starry night and thinking, "I am glad I am alive."

At the very moment we are about to conclude the reading of the Torah, a project that we have worked on relentlessly and religiously for the past year, we grab another Torah scroll and lay it down and, without so much as a pause, start again. Simchat Torah means that learning never stops, and it contains one of the fundamental insights of the Jews: "How can I be sad, how can I despair, if there is something more to learn, something more to know?"[1]

Where Rosh Hashanah and Yom Kippur are intellectual and reflective, Sukkot (literally, "huts" or "booths") and Simchat Torah ("joy of the Torah") are sensual and expansive. Five days after the austere Days of Awe comes a festival cycle that celebrates pleasures and the senses: the joy of being human.

Sukkot is a seven (for some, eight)-day festival described three separate times in the Torah.[2] It is a celebration of the rewards of the growing season, of the harvest, of the fulfillment of labor, and of life itself. The primary symbol of Sukkot is the *sukkah:* a flimsy, temporary hut, reminiscent of the structures that the ancient Israelites constructed near their ripe crops during harvest time, a symbol of the fragility of life itself. In many ways, Sukkot is the autumnal mirror-image of Passover. Not only are both week-long festivals that begin at the full moon and involve a great deal of preparation, but the huts of Sukkot are also reminders of the shelters used during the years of wandering in the wilderness after the exodus from Egypt.

As Sukkot ends, another holiday begins, Shmini Atzeret, the Eighth Day of Assembly, is also ordained by the Torah and celebrated with a special synagogue service. However, in contemporary times, it is all but eclipsed by the holiday that falls on the very next day: Simchat Torah. When the Torah reading cycle was established during the 11th century, Simchat Torah became the ninth day of the autumn holiday cycle, as a celebration of both the completion and beginning of the year's Torah reading. Sh'mini Atzeret and Simchat Torah are combined and celebrated as one in Israel and by some liberal Jews. The official name for the combined holiday is Atzeret HaTorah, "the Assembly of the Torah," but is usually referred to as Simchat Torah.

Simchat Torah is celebrated with the kind of happiness and enthusiasm associated with Jewish weddings. The last of the autumn holidays —the end of three intense weeks—Simchat Torah closes the circle with a triumphant and joyful celebration.

PREPARATION

The biggest part of preparing for Sukkot is building a *sukkah*, the booth or hut in which Jews are supposed to live during the festival. According to tradition, the first nail is driven into the *sukkah* as soon as Yom Kippur ends, even before breaking the fast.

A *sukkah* is a temporary structure and can be made in any number of ways: as a kind of tent, as a lean-to built against the wall of a house, or as a free-standing hut. *Sukkot* (the plural of *sukkah*) have been constructed out of all kinds of materials, including bamboo, plexiglass, aluminum poles, and lumberyard 2 × 4's. Walls can be filled in with colorful fabric, old doors, canvas, pieces of plywood paneling, or just about any other material. There are kits and pre-fabricated models available, too.[3]

Inside the *sukkah*, it is customary to festoon every surface, especially the roof, with hanging fruits, dried gourds, leaves, and other harvest-type items. Virtually anything can be used for decoration: pictures, posters, paper chains, paper flowers, dolls, toys, and Rosh Hashanah cards.

The most important element of the *sukkah* is the roof, which may not be a permanent structure. The material needed is called *s'chach*, which is anything that once grew but has been cut. (Evergreen boughs, bamboo, palm branches and corn stalks make better *s'chach* than branches whose leaves quickly wither and fall.) The roof is supposed to be dense enough to provide some shade from the sun, but not solid enough to obscure starlight.

People who do not or cannot build a *sukkah* sometimes prepare for the holiday by helping their children assemble materials for a mini-*sukkah*, which can be made out of chairs or an empty appliance box. Making a table-top model of a *sukkah* (out of a shoe box, for example) is another good project that can be used as a centerpiece. Preparation can also take the form of buying and making special Sukkot decorations for the house and table. A *sukkah*-like canopy can even be raised over the dining room table for a week. Another way to get into the spirit of the harvest festival is to plan an outing to pick apples, pumpkins, and other fall fruits, and to buy gourds, corn stalks, and other decorations for home and *sukkah*.

The other symbols of Sukkot are the *etrog*, a citron, and the *lulav*, a green bouquet consisting of a palm frond and myrtle and willow branches; these are used in an ancient ritual performed at services and inside the *sukkah*, described below. Judaica shops stock *etrogim* and *lulavim* in advance of the holiday, and many synagogues order them for their congregations. Shopping for "the best" *lulav* and *etrog* is an ancient obsession, and one that suggests a family outing.

Simchat Torah is much more a synagogue-based holiday than Sukkot, so there tends to be far less home preparation. Some families make flags and banners for the festive processions held in the synagogue on Simchat Torah. Another unique project is to make a child-sized Torah, using two dowels and a long sheet of paper, decorated with original renderings of various Bible stories.

Another way to get ready for Simchat Torah is to go and look at a Torah; many people have never seen one up close. This is relatively easy to arrange by making an appointment with the rabbi, cantor, or religious school director of your synagogue, who will help you take the scroll out.

STUDY

In addition to the Torah readings prescribed for the holidays, the traditional text for study is the Book of Ecclesiastes, best known for its poetic listing of the seasons of life. "A time to plant and a time to uproot, a time for tearing down and time for building up." The reason why this particular book of the Bible is studied at this season is unclear, which makes a good starting point for discussion. Because the Torah is the focus of Simchat Torah, studying a commentary about the Torah seems most appropriate.

TZEDAKAH

Because Sukkot celebrates not only the harvest of this season, but also looks forward to a time when the harvest will feed everyone on earth, it is customary to send money to programs that feed the poor. The connections between Sukkot and current concerns about ecology, the environment, and agricultural policy also suggest donations to projects that help foster agriculture in poor countries.

In honor of Simchat Torah, donations to literacy programs and libraries seem especially appropriate. One worthy organization is the National Yiddish Book Center, which rescues and distributes Yiddish books that would have otherwise perished.

Making Sukkot

AT HOME

Building and decorating a *sukkah* can be a big, fun project, but using it is even more enjoyable. Although tradition encourages living inside the *sukkah,* in practice the major activity that takes place inside the little huts is eating. The *sukkah* becomes an *al fresco* dining room, and more.

Sukkot begins with the *yontif seder,* inside a *sukkah* if possible. In addition to the candles, wine, bread and the blessing for the new season, there is a special blessing regarding the *sukkah:*

בָּרוּךְ אַתָּה, יְיָ אֱלֹהֵינוּ, מֶלֶךְ הָעוֹלָם, אֲשֶׁר קִדְּשָׁנוּ בְּמִצְוֹתָיו, וְצִוָּנוּ לֵשֵׁב בַּסֻּכָּה.

Baruch ata Adonai Eloheynu Melech Ha-olam asher kid'shanu be-mitzvotav vitzivanu leyshev ba-sukkah.

You Abound in Blessings, Adonai Our Lord, You make us holy with commandments and call us to live in the *sukkah*.

There is no one dish or menu associated with the Sukkot meal in Ashkenazic tradition, though harvest foods seem most appropriate. It is a good holiday for beginning a family food tradition and, because it is a meal of thanksgiving, some people serve their first roast turkey of the autumn, and have their first taste of fresh apple cider.

A *sukkah* is an opportunity and an excuse for a continuous seven-day picnic. (You can put a tarp or other cover over the roof in case of rain.) A week of family breakfasts, solitary lunches, and informal dinners out of doors is a wonderful way to enjoy the waning light of the autumn; it's something to share with family and friends.

Sukkot is a holiday that has always been associated with hospitality. According to a mystical story, the spirits of different biblical ancestors visit each day: Abraham and Sarah, Isaac and Rebecca, Jacob and Rachel, Joseph and Leah, Moses and Miriam, Aaron and Abigail, and David and Esther. Sephardic Jews set aside a special chair for these guests. But the *sukkah* is a natural venue for gatherings of flesh-and-blood guests, too. There can be a party to help decorate the *sukkah*, to share the first night festivities, and to celebrate *Shabbat*. Some families try to have guests for dinner every night, or hold an annual "open *sukkah*" on a weekend afternoon.

A *sukkah* is not only a place for eating, though. It is also a place to sit quietly with a book and a cup of tea, to read aloud and study with

---

Recall, O Israel, our wanderings,
When life was harsh and insecure.
When cold winds blew,
The stars our only comfort.

May our lives be as upright as the palm,
The coming year as the sweet scent of the etrog.
            Vetaher Libenu, Prayerbook of Congregation Beth El, Sudbury, MA

friends, to sing every song that everyone can think of that contains a reference to food, flowers, or trees, to tell stories and stay up late talking, or to set up cots and sleeping bags and look up at the stars.

Not everyone can or wants to build a *sukkah* and there are other ways to enjoy its unique pleasures. One is to visit a friend's *sukkah*, the other is to make use of a synagogue's *sukkah*. Many congregations build a *sukkah*, which may well be available for members who wish to have a family or *havurah* meal there.

SYNAGOGUE OBSERVANCE

Holiday services are held on the first (and, in some congregations, the second) day of Sukkot. In addition to special liturgical additions to the prayer service, the rituals involving the *lulav* and *etrog* are most striking. The bouquet of tree leaves and the citron are ancient symbols of the harvest, and probably vestiges of a fertility rite of some sort. Over the centuries they have been given many religious interpretations: symbols of the parts of the human body, elements of the Jewish people, or the male and female parts of creation.[4] As a blessing is said, everyone who owns a *lulav* and *etrog* waves them in six directions: to the four points of the compass and upward and downward in a gesture demonstrating that God is everywhere. Then, celebrants—especially children—parade around the sanctuary, holding *lulavim* and *etrogim* aloft as they walk.

Making Simchat Torah

Simchat Torah begins at home with a *yontif seder:* candles, wine, *challah*, and a blessing for the season. In the synagogue, Simchat Torah obser-

---

Here where the end embraces the beginning,
Like the eternal bride and bridegroom joined as one,
Rejoice!

Vetaher Libenu, Congregation Beth El Prayerbook

vance begins with the evening service, when all the Torah scrolls are removed from the ark and paraded around the sanctuary in serpentine circles. It is considered an honor to carry the Torah, and in some congregations virtually everyone gets the opportunity.

The Hasidic model of celebration for Simchat Torah has inspired spontaneous and joyful observances in many American congregations. Live music, champagne, dancing, and singing may be part of these celebrations, which sometimes even spill into the street outside. One increasingly popular custom is to unfurl an entire Torah scroll in a huge circle around a room, enacting the full cycle of the year: from the final reading from Deuteronomy to the beginning of Genesis.

The mood of Simchat Torah resembles the joyful mood of weddings. Indeed, it is customary to call the person honored with reading the last portion of Deuteronomy "the bridegroom (or bride) of the Torah." The person who reads from Genesis is "the bride (or bridegroom) of the Beginning."

At morning services on Simchat Torah, some synagogues call the children up to the Torah, and a large prayershawl is draped over their heads for a special blessing. Simchat Torah has also become the occasion for welcoming children to religious school, sometimes with a gift of a mini-prayershawl, toy Torah, or prayerbook as a token of the beginning of their religious education.

FURTHER READING

The Sukkot/Simchat Torah Anthology by Philip Goodman (Jewish Publication Society, 1973). The anthology contains entries from the Bible, Talmud, and Midrash. The liturgy is included, as is a history, an overview of customs around the world, recipes, stories for children, and poems and modern short stories that deal with the holiday.

FOR CHILDREN

A Torah is Written by Paul and Rachel Cowan (Jewish Publication Society, 1986). Illustrated with black and white photographs, this book describes the work of writing and putting together a Torah scroll.

My Weekly Sidra by Melanie Berman and Joel Lurie Grishaver. (Torah Aura, 1986). A hands-on introduction to the Torah for children in grade 1 and up, this book provides a one-page plot synopsis for each Torah portion, along with projects to make and color. At the end of the Torah-reading year, the pages of the book can be cut out and taped together to create a kid-sized Torah scroll.

Hannukah

We watch the days grow shorter and shorter. We become frightened because it occurs to us that if this keeps up we will all freeze to death in the dark. We light candles in a transparently symbolic attempt to get somebody up there to notice and turn on the lights. We are literally whistling in the dark.[1]

Hannukah falls on the 25th day in the Hebrew month of Kislev, usually in December, at the darkest phase of the moon in the darkest season of the year. It is an intimate holiday, defined by the circle of light cast by little, colored candles arranged in rows. From the Hebrew word for "dedication," Hannukah recalls two rather different stories, one of which rests on a military victory, one which involves a miracle. However, at its emotional core, Hannukah—like the other holidays of the season—celebrates the return of the light in the heart of winter darkness.

Hannukah's story of religious nationalism, political intrigue, and military boldness is recounted in the Books of the Maccabees, part of the Apocrypha, a collection of ancient writings not included in the Hebrew Bible. During the second century B.C.E., Antiochus Epiphanes of Syria, ruler of the land of Israel, began a process of Hellenization that included persecutions of those who continued to practice Judaism. Antiochus ordered the desecration of the Temple in Jerusalem and the killing of those who opposed him. The Jewish guerrilla rebellion against this oppression was led by Mattathias and his five sons, the Maccabees, who defeated the Syrian forces and rededicated the Temple in 164 B.C.E. with an eight-day celebration.[2]

Although the rabbis who codified Jewish law and practice in the Talmud were disturbed by the prospect of a holiday that celebrated a military victory, it was clear that the Hebrew people were not about to give up their midwinter celebration of lights and merrymaking. Thus, the story of the miracle of the oil became the preferred justification for the lighting of candles, a custom that was probably borrowed from pagan solstice celebrations.

According to this story, the Maccabees found only a single jar of consecrated oil, which was used to keep the Eternal Flame alight in the Temple. There was only enough oil to last for one day, but lo and behold, the oil lasted for eight days. With the addition of this miracle, God was given a place in the Hannukah celebration.

PREPARING

Getting ready for Hannukah means getting ready for an eight-day party: decorating, shopping, wrapping gifts, and cooking. The eight-branched candelabra, called a Hannukah *menorah* or, more accurately, a *hannukiah*, is the primary symbol of the holiday. Judaica shops and synagogue gift shops usually stock a wide selection of these, which are made out of all sorts of materials in all shapes and sizes. Making *hannukiot* (the plural of *hannukiah*) is a favorite project for children.

Some families really go to town decorating for Hannukah, with banners, *draydls*, gold coins, *hannukiot*, and candles everywhere. And a shopping trip for a box of Hannukah candles and some new *draydls* (Hannukah tops) is a great way to begin the holiday.

STUDY

In addition to reading the Books of Maccabees, study for the holiday usually includes two stories which are found in the Apocrypha, both tales of heroic women: Judith, a widow who killed a general leading a siege against the land of Judah, and Hannah, the mother of seven sons who died with them rather than bow to a pagan idol.

Hannukah has inspired a great many Jewish children's books and songs. Buying new books or tapes and enjoying them in the week before the holiday begins is a good way to get everyone ready to celebrate.

TZEDAKAH

At Hannukah, which celebrates a Jewish victory over religious persecution, some people make contributions to organizations that work for
religious and political freedom for Jews and all oppressed people.

Making Hannukah

Hannukah is one of the most home-based and family-centered of the
Jewish holidays. Anytime after sunset, when family members and
guests are assembled, the *shamash* or helper candle is lit, and then used
to light the others. A *hannukiah* is filled from right to left, but lit left to
right, so the newest candle is always kindled first.

Every night, two blessings are recited:

בָּרוּךְ אַתָּה, יְיָ אֱלֹהֵינוּ, מֶלֶךְ הָעוֹלָם, אֲשֶׁר קִדְּשָׁנוּ בְּמִצְוֹתָיו, וְצִוָּנוּ לְהַדְלִיק נֵר
שֶׁל חֲנֻכָּה.

*Baruch ata Adonai Eloheynu Melech Ha-olam asher kid'shanu be-
mitzvotav vitzivanu l'hadlik ner shel Hannukah.*

You Abound in Blessings, Adonai Our Lord, You make us holy with
commandments and call us to light the Hannukah lights.

בָּרוּךְ אַתָּה, יְיָ אֱלֹהֵינוּ, מֶלֶךְ הָעוֹלָם, שֶׁעָשָׂה נִסִּים לַאֲבוֹתֵינוּ, בַּיָּמִים הָהֵם בַּזְּמַן
הַזֶּה.

*Baruch ata Adonai Eloheynu Melech Ha-olam
Sh'asa nissim lavoteynu bayamim hahem bazman hazeh.*

You Abound in Blessings, Adonai Our Lord, You performed miracles
for our ancestors in days of old, at this season.

On the first night only, a third blessing, the *sheheheyanu*, is added:

בָּרוּךְ אַתָּה, יְיָ אֱלֹהֵינוּ, מֶלֶךְ הָעוֹלָם, שֶׁהֶחֱיָנוּ וְקִיְּמָנוּ וְהִגִּיעָנוּ לַזְּמַן הַזֶּה.

*Baruch ata Adonai Eloheynu Melech Ha-olam, sheheheyanu vikiamanu
vihigianu lazman hazeh.*

You Abound in Blessings, Adonai Our Lord, You have kept us alive, You have sustained us, You have brought us to this moment.

Any number of *hannukiot* can be lit. In some households, everyone has his or her own *hannukiah*, and on nights when guests are invited they can be asked to bring *menorahs* and candles, too, so that dozens of flames are kindled. According to custom, the Hannukah lights are set in a prominent window, publicly announcing this is a house where Hannukah is celebrated, and making the night that much brighter.

On *Shabbat*, Hannukah candles are lit before the Sabbath lights. And every night after the holiday candles are lit, it is customary to sing *Maoz Tzur*, "Rock of Ages," and other Hannukah songs. (There are many records and tapes of Hannukah songs.)

The custom of giving Hannukah *gelt* (Yiddish for money)—gold coins or chocolate coins wrapped in gold foil—dates back to 17th century Poland. As Jews came into closer contact with Christians and Christmas, since the 19th century, Hannukah has also meant gift giving.

The extreme commercialization of Christmas and Hannukah drives many people of both faiths crazy. Because it is the business of America to raise every consumer's gift expectations to dizzying heights, many parents devise strategies to keep Hannukah from becoming an eight-day festival of greed. It is the custom in some households to create a sort of "designated gift-giver rule," which can be modified to suit any number of people and goes something like this: On night number one: Mom gives the gifts. On night number two, sister distributes presents. Night number three is for Dad. Four is for brother. Five is for gifts from maternal grandparents. Six for paternal grandparents. Seven is for going to a party, which is gift enough. And the last night is devoted to *tzedakah* when everyone in the household puts aside some money and decides on an appropriate organization, agency, or cause with which to share the season's bounty.

Traditional Hannukah foods tend to recall the story of the miracle of the oil with unswerving devotion to fried foods. For Ashkenazic Jews, Hannukah means potato pancakes, *latkes*, served with applesauce and sour cream. In Israel, jelly donuts, called *sufganiot*, are the official holiday treat.

Hannukah is commonly celebrated with parties, held on any and all of the eight nights. After candle lighting, there is singing, eating, and gambling: either with cards or with *draydls* (*sivivon* in Hebrew), four-sided tops. Actually, Jewish law is extremely hostile to gambling; the rabbis reasoned that a transfer of money in the absence of honest work was a form of theft. But at Hannukah, the rule is lifted and people are encouraged to enjoy themselves.

To play *draydl*, a game of dumb luck, each player antes up with nuts or chocolate coins, buttons or pennies. Each of the *draydl's* sides bears a Hebrew letter. If the *draydl* falls on נ (*Nun*), you get nothing; on ה (*Hay*), take half the pot; on ש (*Shin*), add something to the kitty; and on ג (*Gimel*), the winner takes all. The letters are an acrostic for the words, נס גדול היה שם —*Nes Gadol Haya Sham* "A great miracle happened there." (In Israel, the letters spell out נס גדול היה פא —*Nes Gadol Haya Po,* "A great miracle happened here.") The truth is, playing *draydl* is only slightly less tedious than frying potato pancakes. But little kids just love the tops. To play the "human *draydl*" game, children spin till they drop and the last one standing wins a prize.

Although Hannukah is by and large a home-centered holiday, it is also celebrated in synagogues with all sorts of family programs: dinners, song festivals, concerts, etc.

A WORD ABOUT CHRISTMAS

The proximity of Hannukah and Christmas raises a great many issues for Jewish and interfaith families. Christmas makes many Jews extremely defensive. For one thing, it is the time of year when they most acutely feel their differentness in an overwhelmingly Christian culture. It is also the season when children confront that sense of being different

---

I have a little *draydl*
I make it out of clay
And when it's dry and ready
Then *draydl* I shall play.

Hannukah song

for the first time, and at successive developmental stages every year. Christmas is when children ask their parents to explain why they are not allowed to take part in the dazzling festival everyone else gets to enjoy.

Interfaith families may find themselves fighting an annual symbolic battle over the Christmas tree. To the non-Jewish partner in an interfaith marriage, the tree may seem a secular symbol of the winter solstice. However, to the Jew, it is often *the* symbol of Christianity. Jewish agencies and synagogues often run workshops for interfaith couples at this season to help sort out just such dilemmas.

Families deal with the Christmas-Hannukah conundrum in very different ways. For many, Christmas is simply a holiday celebrated in other people's homes: a holiday to enjoy with non-Jewish friends or at the home of Christian grandparents, but not in "our" home, which is Jewish. At the other end of the spectrum, there are families that hang stockings and display other nonreligious decorations associated with Christmas.

Many people try to compensate for a lack of Christmas by trying to make Hannukah its equal, with a competing orgy of expectations and expensive gift-giving. Others resent that tactic and, citing the relative unimportance of Hannukah in the Jewish calendar of holidays, make as little fuss over it as possible. There is a middle ground. Hannukah can be celebrated with candles, stories, *tzedakah*, gatherings of family and friends, crafts, and gifts, without collapsing under the strain of Christmas expectations. The Jewish calendar has often accommodated itself to historical change and making Hannukah into a bigger party than it was in past centuries does not nullify its Jewishness.

However, for Hannukah to retain its own integrity, it cannot stand alone. If Hannukah is the only Jewish celebration of the year, then it does become that strange creature, the "Jewish Christmas:" a celebration of Christmas/solstice by Jews. But, no matter how many candles are lit, Hannukah will never be as big, flashy, and seductive to children as Christmas. Perhaps the best explanation of the differences between the two winter holidays comes from the mouth of a three-year old, who said, "Christine and Zack have Christmas. We have Hannukah and *Shabbat.*"

FURTHER READING

The Hannukah Anthology by Philip Goodman (Jewish Publication Society, 1976). The anthology contains entries from the Bible, Talmud, and Midrash. The liturgy is included, as is a history, an overview of customs around the world, recipes, stories for children, and poems and modern short stories.

The Power of Light by Isaac Bashevis Singer (Farrar, Straus, Giroux, 1990). A collection of eight short stories especially good for reading aloud—one for each night.

FOR CHILDREN

The Story of Hannukah by Amy Erlich (Dial, 1989). The vivid paintings by Israeli artist Ori Sherman almost leap off the pages.

Potato Pancakes All Around by Marilyn Hirsh (Jewish Publication Society, 1982). The story of Stone Soup, except that it's about making *latkes*.

Lights (Gesher Foundation, 1985). A book and video for the holiday, an animated allegory of the story of Hannukah.

Tu B'Shvat

Two men who were fighting over a piece of land brought their dispute to a rabbi. After listening to each man's case, the rabbi put his ear to the ground. After a moment he stood up and said, "The land says that it belongs to neither of you. You both belong to the land."

Talmud

Tu B'Shvat is a fascinating holiday. Once a very minor observance, Tu B'Shvat is in the process of becoming a far more important celebration in the Jewish calendar, complete with its own *seder*, the most positive celebration word in the Jewish lexicon.

Tu B'Shvat, which means the fifteenth of Shvat and usually occurs in February, is not even mentioned in the Torah. And whereas the Talmud describes it as "New Year of the Trees," it mandates no rituals, no blessings, and no synagogue observance. Tu B'Shvat may have been noted simply as a way of dating trees, so it would be possible to know when a fruit tree was old enough to be tithed, or when 10% of the fruit crop was due to the Temple priesthood.

Historically, Tu B'Shvat was always a way of maintaining a connection with the land of Israel, a hot, arid place where trees mean food, shade, and water, that is, life; where, in the month of Shvat, the winter rains end and the first signs of spring begin to appear. However, among Ashkenazic Jews the only observance of Tu B'Shvat was the eating of fruits, especially those grown in the land of Israel. Because it traveled well, carob (also known as *bosker* or St. John's bread) became the traditional food of the holiday. Although it was never a major holiday for Sephardic Jews either, they celebrate Tu B'Shvat with more festivity:

with readings from a book called *The Fruit of the Goodly Tree,* and with special fruit platters, meals, songs, and games for children.[1] After the founding of the state of Israel, Tu B'Shvat became a sort of international Jewish Arbor Day, a day for planting seeds in paper cups at religious school and for raising money for the Jewish National Fund, which supports the reforestation of Israel.

Beginning in the 1970s, American Jews rediscovered the Tu B'Shvat *seder,* which had been celebrated by a group of mystics living in the town of Safed during the 16th century. Modeled after the Passover talking-feast, the Tu B'Shvat *seder* featured four cups of wine and much eating of fruit, along with singing and praying. The mystics assigned various kinds of fruits to different categories, which corresponded to the "emanations" of God.[2]

The modern focus for Tu B'Shvat has broadened to include the relationship between people and the natural world, or in contemporary parlance, the ecology of the planet. In Jewish tradition, the primary symbol of this relationship is the tree. The Torah itself is called a tree of life, and the rollers around which the scroll is wrapped are also called trees of life: *atzay hayyim.* The planting of trees was seen as a holy activity. According to Jochanan ben Zakkai, "If you have a seedling in your hand, and someone says to you, 'Look, here comes the Messiah!' go and plant the seedling first, and then come out to meet the Messiah."[3] The Torah forbids the cutting down of an enemy's fruit trees in times of war, even if trees are needed for the siege of a city.[4] The confluence of the ancient Jewish concern for trees and the modern worry about the state of the earth's forests has contributed to interest in the midwinter holiday and its new/old *seder.*

PREPARING

Hosting or participating in a Tu B'Shvat *seder* means shopping for fruit and wine and decorating the table with greens and flowers. There are all sorts of arts and crafts projects for children, such as making a special *tzedakah* box in the shape of a watering can, or creating a forest of trees out of recycled cardboard boxes, or decorating cups for planting parsley seeds, which are then harvested for the coming Passover *seder.*

To get into the spirit, people peruse seed catalogs and select flowers for the coming spring. Other family activities might include visiting a botanical garden or even making a tour of your yard to see whether any of the trees need attention. Because Tu B'Shvat is called the New Year of the Trees, one rabbi even suggests blowing a *shofar* for your own trees.[5]

Study might include reading more about the holiday's history, and looking at existing *seders* or compiling a new Tu B'Shvat *seder*. The emerging ecological aspect of the holiday suggests study of environmental problems and solutions.

TZEDAKAH

The most common *tzedakah* custom for the holiday is to donate money to the Jewish National Fund for the planting of trees in Israel. There is also an old tradition of giving money for fruit, *ma'ot perot*, to the poor, so they can afford a taste of fruit from Israel on Tu B'Shvat. In that spirit, making a contribution to help feed needy people seems appropriate, too.

Some people make donations at this season to national and international organizations dedicated to protecting the environment. *Shomrei Adama*, "Guardians of the Earth," a group that combines a commitment to Jewish values with environmental concerns, publishes a Tu B'Shvat *seder* and other materials. For information about their programs and to make contributions, write: *Shomrei Adama/FRCH* (Federation of Reconstructionist Congregations and Havurot), Church Road and Greenwood Ave., Wyncote, PA 19095.

Making Tu B'Shvat

Tu B'Shvat is a holiday in the making. There are no home or synagogue rituals associated with the holiday except for the emerging Tu B'Shvat *seder*. Synagogues, *havurot*, and individuals are experimenting with this observance and there are many haggadot (plural of *haggadah*, which means "a telling") for the holiday, most of them photocopied collections of readings that are rewritten and updated annually, though a few have been published.

At some point in the future, a normative *seder* may emerge, but for now the Tu B'Shvat *seder* is in the hands of the people who are exploring its possibilities. There is no way of doing it "wrong," and many ways to proceed. Tu B'Shvat *seders* are sometimes part of a synagogue service, sometimes home observances. When they include a meal, it is usually vegetarian. In general, readings, poems, and songs are built around two ritual acts: the drinking of four cups of wine and the eating of many fruits.

The four cups of wine change in color from white to red. The first is white, intermediate cups are usually a mixture of the two, and the last is red. The same blessing is recited before each cup:

בָּרוּךְ. אַתָּה, יְיָ אֱלֹהֵינוּ, מֶלֶךְ הָעוֹלָם, בּוֹרֵא פְּרִי הַגָּפֶן.

Baruch ata Adonai Eloheynu Melech Ha-olam boray p'ree ha-gafen.

You Abound in Blessings, Adonai Our Lord, You create the fruit of the vine.

For the fruit, people set out festive platters with as many varieties as possible. One custom is to get fifteen kinds of fruit to correspond with the fifteenth of Shvat.

The fruit is usually divided into four categories, according to some system of metaphorical association with the elements, seasons, or human characteristics. One level consists of fruits with a hard outside and soft inside: nuts, pineapple, pomegranate, and coconut, which may be associated with winter, with the earth, and with the physical. A second level includes fruits with a soft outside and hard inner core: cherry, peach, and avocado, which may be associated with spring, with water, and with the emotions. A third category comprises fruits that are totally edible: strawberry, fig, grape, and raisin, which may be associated with summer, with the air, and with the cerebral. The fourth category is the most abstract and spiritual and is sometimes symbolized with inedible fruits, such as pine cones and acorns, or else it is given no physical representation at all.

The same blessing is recited before eating from each category of fruits:

בָּרוּךְ אַתָּה, יְיָ אֱלֹהֵינוּ, מֶלֶךְ הָעוֹלָם, בּוֹרֵא פְּרִי הָעֵץ.

Baruch ata Adonai Eloheynu Melech Ha-olam boray p'ree ha-ayts.

You Abound in Blessings, Adonai Our Lord, You create the fruit of the tree.

FURTHER READING

Seder Tu BiShevat; The Festival of the Trees by Adam Fisher (Central Conference of American Rabbis, 1989). This book actually contains two seders, one especially for use by children.

A Celebration of Nature edited by Ellen Bernstein (Shomrei Adama, c/o Reconstructionist Rabbinic College 1989). More of an activist seder, the readings include facts and figures about the state of the environment.

FOR CHILDREN

A Seder for Tu B'Shevat by Harlene Winnick Appelman and Jane Sherwin Shapiro (Kar-Ben Copies, 1984). An illustrated seder for families with children, containing activities, discussion questions, and songs.

Purim

Purim elevates laughter to a religious category. It is the one day when taking oneself seriously is a sin. At Purim, we make fun of everything, especially what we consider to be most sacred and reverent. Because religion without humor is blasphemy.[1]

The 14th of Adar, which falls near the vernal equinox, usually in March, is the Jewish equivalent of Mardi Gras, a giddy outburst of energy and excess. Purim, which celebrates a narrow escape from a disaster that probably never happened, takes its name from the Hebrew word *pur* or "lot," as in lottery; in the Purim story, the villain cast lots to determine a date for the slaughter of the Jews. The story, which appears in the biblical Book of Esther, is bawdy and improbable. But its ironic and dark undertone has struck a chord in generations of Jews who have suffered through and survived terrible persecution and loss.

According to the Purim tale, a large and prosperous Jewish community once lived in the land of Persia. The Jews were so well integrated into the society that one of them, named Mordechai, was a member of the court of King Ahasuerus. One day, the king banished his wife, Vashti, for refusing to obey his command to appear naked before his guests. To replace her, a beauty contest was held and won by Esther, a Jewish woman who happened to be Mordechai's relative.

As this Cinderella tale was unfolding, the courtier Haman was named Grand Vizier. Now Haman was a dreadful anti-Semite, indeed a descendant of the wicked Amalek—the archetypal enemy of the Jews described in the Torah[2]—so when Mordechai refused to bow down before him, Haman decided to massacre all the Jews in the kingdom.

Mordechai and Esther conspired to foil this plot by having Esther invite King Ahasuerus to her chambers, where she wined and dined him, and then revealed that Haman was plotting against him, that she was a Jew, and please wouldn't he spare her people. The king agreed to all her requests, and Haman was hanged on the scaffold that had been built for Mordechai, who then became Grand Vizier. As the sun set, Esther and the Jews of Persia lived happily ever after.

The name of God does not appear anywhere in this melodrama, which is probably based on a Persian legend given the fact that the names of its heroes, Esther and Mordechai, are alternate forms of well-known local deities, fertile Ishtar and war-like Marduk. Furthermore, Purim celebrations—typified by masks, revelry, and drunkenness—recall ancient Persian customs for the new year, which began in the spring.

Purim observance has changed over time, and customs vary from nation to city to synagogue. Still, it is the universal Jewish holiday of release, springtime, laughter, and excess. On Purim, it is a religious obligation to poke fun at Jewish tradition. On Purim, piety takes the form of jokes and outrageous behavior. According to the Talmud, the only holiday that will still be celebrated after the messiah comes, after the world is restored to peace and harmony, is Purim. Evidently, even in paradise it will still be necessary to make fun of ourselves.

PREPARING

Purim is mostly celebrated in synagogues and religious schools. Because many congregations encourage adults as well as children to dress up, getting ready for Purim can mean putting together a beautiful or silly costume. Mask-making is a time-honored arts and crafts project, as is the making of *graggers*, which are noise-makers used during the reading of the story of Esther.

The tradition of giving gifts to friends and to the poor is mandated in the Book of Esther. The custom of "sending portions," *mishloach manot* in Hebrew (*shalach mones* in Yiddish), is being revived today. So baking treats (or visiting a bakery) and decorating paper plates or bags can also be a way of preparing for Purim.

TZEDAKAH

Giving to the poor on Purim is based on the notion that merriment cannot be not complete unless everyone is able to celebrate. In some congregations, money is collected for *tzedakah* in the synagogue before the Purim story is read. Responding to the command in the Book of Esther that two portions be sent to the poor, some people make contributions to two charities.

Making Purim

AT HOME

The only home ritual associated with Purim is the Purim *seudah*, or Purim feast. Unlike all other holiday meals, which are eaten in the evening, this feast is generally a luncheon that features merrymaking, nonsense, and silliness of all sorts. Putting on a *Purimspiel* (Purim play) is often part of this celebration, the more foolish the better.

Among Jews of Eastern European descent, the traditional food for Purim is a three-cornered pastry called *hamentaschen*, "Haman's pockets," a delicacy that has been part of Purim celebration since at least the 12th century. Sephardic cooks make Purim ravioli and a deep fried confection called Haman's ears.

The other main Purim activity is delivering gifts of sweets to family and friends. Making surprise appearances at friends' houses with a bag of hamentaschen or a plate of fruit and candy is great fun for the givers as well as the recipients.

SYNAGOGUE OBSERVANCE

Jews do not refrain from work or play, or attend special services on Purim. The only religious obligation is that everyone—adults and children—listen to a reading of the Book of Esther, which is called the

Why is it pointless to put Jews in jail?
They eat lox on Sundays!

megilla, or "scroll." Although there are four other scrolls or *megillot* in the Bible (Song of Songs, Lamentations, Ruth, and Ecclesiastes), the book of Esther is known as "The" *megilla.*

After the evening service, the ten chapters of the *megilla* are chanted aloud, often in an abbreviated, hilarious performance. Sometimes the story is acted out by costumed players. Audience participation is required; whenever the villain's name is mentioned, boos, hisses, catcalls and the rude sound of the noise-makers, called *graggers* erupt as the audience does its duty and "stamps out" Haman's name.

There are other wild and crazy traditions associated with Purim. "Purim Torah" is the name given to making fun of all things sacred. Rabbis dress up like furry blue monsters and deliver absurd Purim sermons, synagogue newsletters are full of ridiculous articles and advertisements, and even the evening service that precedes the reading of the *megilla* is fair game, as traditional prayers are sung to the melody of "Home on the Range," or "I Want to Hold Your Hand."

Synagogues celebrate Purim with costume parties, parades, dances, theatrical offerings (Purimspiels), carnivals, beauty contests, and fairs. Gambling, forbidden every other day except Hannukah, is permitted on Purim. Drinking is not only permitted, but encouraged. Indeed, the Talmud says that Purim obliges every Jew to get so drunk that he or she cannot tell the difference between blessing Mordechai and cursing Haman.[3] And that is being truly drunk! In Israel, Purim is marked by a raucous parade called the *adloyada,* a word based on the Hebrew for "not being able to tell the difference."

FURTHER READING

The Big Book of Jewish Humor by William Novak and Moshe Waldoks (Harper & Row, 1981). A wonderful source of Purim laughter.

Along the same lines: Mad Magazine, stories by Woody Allen, videos of Marx brothers' movies, etc.

And the inevitable, *The Purim Anthology* by Philip Goodman (Jewish Publication Society, 1988). The anthology contains entries from the Bible, Talmud, and Midrash as well as an overview of customs from around the world, stories for children, and modern literature that deals with the holiday.

FOR CHILDREN

It Happened in ShuShan by Harriet K. Feder (Kar-Ben Copies, 1988). An appropriately silly telling of the Purim story, using pictographs. For pre-schoolers and early readers.

Passover

<hr>

The liturgy of the *seder* meal is a way of responding to the question, "Why?"
The answer to all of the questions asked at the Passover *seder* begin with the
words, *avadim hayinu,* because we were slaves. Through song, word, and
symbol we not only remember that we were slaves but also re-experience
ourselves as slaves. And we learn that our freedom, if it does not translate
into making others free, is a sham.[1]

No holiday in the Jewish calendar is more complex or evocative than
Passover. The spring holiday that celebrates the return of the sunlight
and the first spring fruits on the table also reflects on the profound
religious themes of the autumn festivals: awakening, life and death,
rebirth, and gratitude. Passover recalls the crucial event in the history
of the Jewish people in which a group of slaves became a nation pos-
sessed of the dream called Torah.

No other holiday inspires the same kind of loyalty as Passover. No
Jewish ritual word has more positive associations than *seder,* the Passover talking-feast. It is the most-practiced of all Jewish observances,
even more common than the lighting of Hannukah candles. Passover
memories—the holiday table, the crunch of *matzah,* songs, phrases, and
aromas—have inspired a kind of collective unconscious that recognizes
the *seder* as *the* Jewish celebration.

Passover can also be the most demanding of the Jewish holidays
because it requires a drastic change of diet during its week-long observance. The Bible forbids not only eating but even owning leavened
foods, as a reminder of the time when the Jews were a hunted people
who did not have even enough time to wait for dough to rise before

baking it. The Talmud elaborated the biblical injunction against leavened food into an entire system for breaking from the normal eating routines of the year. Homes and habits are turned upside down in order to help reenact the essential religious insights of Judaism: that once we were slaves and now we are free; that political liberation and personal change are both necessary for the redemption of the world, a world in which all forms of slavery will be forever abolished.[2]

Passover has several other names: the Festival of Spring, the Season of our Liberation, the Holiday of *Matzah*. But the most common of its names is embedded in the most dramatic story in Jewish history: It was the night before the last of the plagues that God unleashed on the Egyptians to force Pharoah to free the enslaved Israelites. The Jews were told to smear their doorposts with the blood of a lamb. According to the story, the angel of death stopped in all unmarked houses, taking the first-born of every family. But wherever Death saw the blood of the animal that the pagan Egyptians worshiped as a God, Death passed over—in Hebrew, *pasach*.

For this fragment to make sense, the rest of the story must be told too: the history of how the Jews came to Egypt, the story of Moses, the resistance of the midwives, and much more. This is both the method and message of Passover: to tell the story so vividly that it becomes part of the memory and consciousness of one generation to the next.[3]

PREPARING

No other holiday requires more preparation than Passover, or more choices. Thus, no two households prepare for Passover in the same fashion, and no two *seders* are quite the same. This chapter presents only a portion of the Passover menu, which is an endless and always-changing list of the ways that people make this *yontif*. Regardless of specifics, Passover preparations can be divided into two general areas: getting ready for the *seder*, and preparing for a week of doing without bread and other leavened foods.

Seder, which literally means "order," is the talking-feast held on the first and (for some people) second night of Passover. Patterned on the Greek and Roman symposium, where an evening was spent discussing a particular topic over dinner, the Passover *seder* was already being celebrated in the days of the Second Temple. The *seder* that is celebrated by Jews today was essentially set by the 11th century.

Planning for a *seder* begins sometime after Purim, when people draw up guest lists, look over cookbooks and choose a *haggadah*. *Haggadah*, literally, "a telling," is the name of the book that contains the order: the rituals and readings of the Passover *seder*. Because the *haggadah* is the script that determines the content and quality of the evening, selecting one that suits your needs is arguably the most important aspect of preparing for the Passover meal. A good place to start exploring the options is a synagogue library or other collection of Jewish books. Jewish bookstores usually offer a wide selection of *haggadot* (plural of *haggadah*), and rabbis, other Jewish professionals, and friends can make helpful suggestions.

Scores of *haggadot* are in use today. Some are nearly all-Hebrew, and others are mostly English with Hebrew blessings translated and transliterated. Some express contemporary political concerns, some are vividly illustrated, and many are annotated, with long footnotes explaining every aspect of the *seder*. Many *haggadot* published since the mid-70s refrain from referring to God as "He." The Reform and Conservative movements produce *haggadot*, as do other Jewish and secular publishers. There are art *haggadot* that feature museum-quality illustrations, and coloring-book *haggadot* for children. Some people use a number of different *haggadot* at the *seder*, comparing and contrasting the variations among them. But most try to purchase or borrow enough copies of the same edition so everyone can follow along together.

When shopping for a *haggadah*, it is also important to remember that virtually everyone customizes or edits the *seder*, itself a menu of sorts. Few people read every word in the book. For most, planning the celebration means deciding which readings will be deleted, what songs to sing, and how to encourage participation at the table.

Some people put together their own *seders*, cutting and pasting, collecting readings, poems, artwork, and songs from various sources to create their own *haggadah*. In some families, the *seder* changes from year to year, reflecting the growth of children. Each spring, a new *haggadah*, slightly longer and more sophisticated than last year's, is produced, filled with original drawings. Fifteen years' worth of these booklets describe family history in a unique way.

Passover is, first and foremost, a teaching holiday. Its central ritual, the *seder*, is an informal classroom where a special kind of information and a particular process of learning are being passed on. Indeed, according to tradition, if no one asks a question at the *seder* table, the meal cannot be concluded. Parents often gear at least part of the *seder* to their children's interest level and a great deal of planning and creativity can go into making Passover a wonderful experience for the young.

In addition to the *seder* text, many *haggadot* provide a lot of basic information about the holiday and how to celebrate it. Some include explanations and brief histories of various readings and ritual items, as well as descriptions and instructions for setting the Passover table and for preparing a *seder* plate and table.

The holiday table is never more elaborate than at Passover. Although the table is usually made festive with spring flowers, the real centerpiece is the *seder* plate, which contains six ritual items: a shank bone (usually a roasted chicken or turkey bone) and a roasted egg, both symbolizing the ritual sacrifices of the Temple; bitter herbs (horseradish or endive) and salt water representing the bitterness of slavery; a green vegetable (parsley, celery, or lettuce) suggesting the new season; and *haroset* (a sweet paste of fruit, wine, and nuts) symbolizing mortar, a reminder of the heavy labor the Israelites were forced to do. The Passover table itself is full of wonderful opportunities for children's participation.

Making *haroset* is something many children look forward to all year. Other *seder* plate projects might include harvesting parsley planted at Tu B'Shvat, roasting eggs, and grating fresh horseradish. And there are countless arts and crafts projects, too: making place cards, plate mats, napkin rings, or a *matzah* cover; designing a comic-book *haggadah;* or even creating a *seder* plate out of a decorated paper plate covered with clear Contact paper. If the *seder* includes a dramatization of part of the Exodus story, children can devise costumes, masks, or puppets.

One very exciting family project is baking *matzah.* According to Jewish law, in order to prevent fermentation, the *matzah* must be baked precisely 18 minutes after water is added to flour. Some synagogues run a *matzah*-baking family activity, which can become a great game of "beat the clock."[4]

In planning the *seder* meal, most cooks tend to stick to family favorites. Roast chicken, turkey, and brisket are among the more popular traditional main courses for Ashkenazic Jews; Sephardic meals often feature roast lamb. Spring foods, such as asparagus and strawberries, recall the seasonal aspect of the holiday. There are many Passover cookbooks on the market, and most Jewish cookbooks have Passover recipes and menus as well.

Preparing for the fast from leavened food is the second major task of getting ready for Passover. In practice, Jews prepare their homes in many different ways. The major task is removing *hametz,* a term that designates foods that are not "kosher for Passover." *Hametz* includes not only leavened foods, but also foods that can easily ferment, such as wheat, malt, and barley. Ashkenazic Jews also refrain from eating beans, peas, lentils, rice, corn, and legumes.

For some families, the days before Passover are taken up with a thorough house-cleaning, and the packing up of dishes and cookware and the unpacking of china and pots that are only used this one week every year. Children tend to find this process exciting, and it is the source of many powerful memories for adults who grew up with the tradition. However, in many other households, Passover simply means not buying or eating bread or other leavened foods. And although some people carefully shop for processed foods that are specifically designated as "Kosher for Passover" (which means they were prepared and packaged under rabbinical supervision), others simply read labels and avoid foods prepared with yeast and other leavening agents. (See also the chapter "What Jews Eat.")

Some people try to eat up all their leavened foods during the month before Passover. Others put leftovers (cereals, pasta, beer, liquors, and prepared foods such as ketchup, vinegars, and even confectionery sugar [it can contain corn starch]) in a box in the basement, or in a cupboard that is marked and taped or tied shut for the week. Because the Torah says that one should not have any *hametz* in one's possession during Passover there is an ancient custom, still practiced, of ritually "selling" *hametz* to a non-Jew for the duration of the holiday. The laws concern-

As it is said: You shall tell your child on that day.

Exodus 13:8

ing which foods are kosher for Passover and the rules for making a home kosher for the holiday are very complicated. There are many published guides about these matters, but first-hand advice from rabbis and other Jews who have done this for years is often the most helpful resource.

The ritual act of preparing a house for Passover is a search for *hametz* called *Bidikat Hametz*. Pieces of bread are hidden as the objects of a family hide-and-seek, which is traditionally conducted with a candle (it is more fun to do this in the dark) and a feather (for brushing the pieces onto a paper plate). The next morning, it is customary to burn what was found. The Hebrew blessings that precede and follow the search are printed in many *haggadot*.

It is customary to refrain from eating either bread or *matzah* between breakfast and the *seder*, as a way of increasing the pleasure of the first taste of *matzah*.

STUDY

The primary study text for Passover is the *haggadah*. But pehaps the best ways of putting the Passover story into context is to read the Book of Exodus, which tells the whole story of the departure from Egypt, the wandering in the desert, and the giving of the Torah. Many people also go back to the chapters in Genesis that tell the story of Joseph and explain how the Jews came to be in Egypt in the first place. It is also traditional to read Song of Songs, the biblical cycle of love poems that are filled with images of nature and sexuality, which addresses the springtime elements of the holiday.

Synagogues and other Jewish institutions sometimes offer seminars or workshops on making a *seder* in the weeks before Passover, which can be great sources of inspiration as well as basic information.

TZEDAKAH

Feeding the hungry is the theme of the *seder*, which includes the line, "Let all who are hungry come and eat." Traditionally, Jewish communities saw to to it that their poor could afford *matzah* and wine for the holiday. The American Jewish community continues to honor this tradition with special attention to the needs of the elderly and to recent immigrants. Individuals can participate directly in this *mitzvah* by making room at their *seders* for people who would otherwise have nowhere to celebrate the holiday: Jewish travelers, college students, and people in military service who are stationed locally. Furthermore, synagogues may be aware of members of their congregations who face a lonely holiday, for whom an invitation would be a great gift. It is also customary to give money to programs and agencies that feed the hungry at Passover. Many synagogues and other Jewish organizations collect canned goods and packaged foods that contain *hametz*, which are then donated to local food pantries before Passover.

Making Passover

AT HOME

Three core elements of making Passover are: retelling the story, remembering that "we were slaves in Egypt," and not eating *hametz*. The table rituals, the house-cleaning, the Passover cookbooks all enhance and celebrate these three basics.

Passover begins at the *seder* table. Although synagogues often hold community *seders* and some people attend them at resorts or on cruises (and thus avoid the lengthy preparations for the meal), the Passover *seder* is one of the most home-identified of all Jewish observances. Family traditions include everything from buying new toothbrushes, to filling the house with daffodils, to closely guarded recipes for Passover cakes, cookies, and candies. The descriptions that follow are meant to suggest possibilities: they are by no means definitive.

THE SEDER TABLE

The Passover table is an altar, a classroom, and a theater as well as a place for eating. The tradition of placing cushions or special pillows on the chairs comes from ancient days; tokens of leisure, they demonstrate that the people at this table are free men and women.

In addition to the *seder* plate described above, there are two other ritual objects placed on the table as well: a plate containing three *matzot* (plural of *matzah*) covered by a napkin or special *matzah* cover, and Elijah's cup, a goblet filled with wine, a symbol of hope that the prophet

Elijah, the harbinger of the Messiah, will come to announce the redemption of the world this very night.

THE ORDER

Variation is the rule regarding the *seder*. Some people change the order, and some delete rituals and readings while poems or original commentaries may be added. Some people prepare questions to spark discussion. The ceremony that precedes the meal can last for twenty minutes, forty minutes, or two hours. Some people spend a lot of time at the table after the meal, whereas others dispense with the post-dinner ritual altogether. Making a *seder* means making choices. The outline of the Passover *seder* that follows is not exhaustive; there are stories and songs not mentioned here that many people consider essential whereas others may delete several of the elements listed below. It is your table. Make the choices that suit you and your family.

The *yontif seder* described on page 175 is embedded in the Passover *seder*, but changed in several curious ways. Some scholars believe that parts of the Passover ritual exist for the sole purpose of getting children to ask "Why?"

PART I: INTRODUCTION

Lighting candles.

Kiddush is reciped over first cup of wine, and the wine is drunk.

Sheheheyanu: the prayer for having reached this moment.

Ceremonial hand-washing: without the traditional blessing.

Karpas: A blessing is recited over the green vegetable, which is then dipped into salt water and tasted by everyone.

Afikomen: The name of the middle of the three *matzot* on the covered plate, which is broken. The larger piece is usually hidden and then ransomed by the children after the meal, when it is eaten. *Afikomen* derives from the Greek word for dessert and the *seder* cannot end until everyone eats a piece of it.

PART II: TELLING THE STORY

The *Maggid:* the story. The telling of the Passover story begins with the line "This is the bread of slavery which our ancestors ate in Egypt when they were slaves. Let all who are hungry come and eat."

The Four Questions: Customarily asked by the youngest child capable of memorizing the words, the four questions are: Why do we eat *matzah?* Why do we eat herbs? Why do we dip our vegetables? Why do we recline? (In other words, what are we doing here?)

The Four Sons: A parable about the proper way to answer the Four Questions when asked by different kinds of children: wise, stubborn, simple, and those who do not know to ask.

The Ten Plagues: As each of the calamities that befell the Egyptians is recounted, a drop of wine is spilled from every glass. The most common explanation for this practice is that when any human life is lost or diminished, all people suffer, thus, our cups of joy are diminished as well.

Dayenu: A song that lists the miracles God performed to free the Jewish people from slavery.

The second cup of wine is drunk, and the blessing is recited.

PART III: PRELUDE TO THE MEAL

Ceremonial hand-washing, with the traditional blessing.

Motzi and the blessing over *matzah*.

Blessing over the bitter herbs.

Hillel sandwich. A mixture of bitter herbs and sweet *haroset* is prepared on *matzah* and everyone eats of the bitter-sweetness.

The meal is served.

PART IV: AFTER DINNER

The *afikomen* is "bought" back from children, and a piece is eaten by everyone.

Blessings after the meal, *birkat hamazon,* are sung.

The third cup of wine with the blessing.

The door is opened for the prophet Elijah.

Singing—traditionally, psalms of praise called *hallel.*

The fourth and final cup of wine with the blessing.

Conclusion: The traditional phrase that ends the *seder* is *L'shana haba-a b'Yerushalayim*—"Next year in Jerusalem," a statement expressing the hope that next year all will be free and none will be enslaved.

ELABORATIONS

The Passover *seder* has always inspired creativity and innovation. Laughter, enchantment, silliness, and argument are all appropriate to a celebration of the freedom to be fully human. The *haggadah* says, "To elaborate on the story is praiseworthy." The following examples—collected from the current practice of American Jews—demonstrate how people elaborate on the story, the *haggadah,* and the *seder:*

The entire *seder* can be a "pot-luck" affair. Not only can food courses be assigned to participants, so can parts of the *seder,* which turns the proceedings into a series of surprises with everyone on the edge of their seats to find out what happens next.

Before beginning or immediately after candle-lighting, have each person tell a personal Passover memory, talk about what the holiday means to them, or discuss the meaning of "freedom."

To keep people from getting too hungry to enjoy the *seder*, after the blessing for *karpas* (green vegetables) serve a first course of raw and/or cooked vegetables.

People do all sorts of things with the *afikomen*. Parents often hide the piece of *matzah*, which leads to a children's treasure hunt later. In order to get the *afikomen* back, parents pay the winner in coins, treats, or prizes. Alternately, older children can hide the *afikomen*, and make their parents search for it. In some households, pieces of *matzah* are hidden all over the house—one for each child who will be attending. When all the previously hidden bits of *afikomen* are found, all the children are given toys.

Giving gifts at Passover is becoming increasingly popular, either in association with the *afikomen*, or when the door is opened for Elijah. At that point, a bag of toys might be "discovered" on the doorsteps. In some families, an adult dresses up like the prophet and brings a sack of goodies in when the door is flung open.

Elijah's cup is on the table as a symbol of hope for redemption and a healed world. Some people put an empty cup in the center of the table and during the *seder* pass it around so that each person can pour a little wine from their own glass into it, symbolizing how each person needs to help bring the messiah, and how everyone must work to bring about a world of peace.

But Elijah's cup can also be the subject of fun; some people rig the glass to mysteriously drain during the course of the evening.

When the Jews arrived safely at the other side of the Sea of Reeds and the waters fell and drowned the Egyptian army, God stopped the angels from singing, saying, "How can you be happy when my creatures are dying?"

Talmud: Sanhedrin 39b

The *maggid,* the telling of the story, offers limitless possibilities for participation. The following suggestions are ways to encourage the sense of personally experiencing the redemption from Egypt:

People have devised skits, puppet shows, pantomimes, musicals, and even video productions that recount the story of the exodus from Egypt or some part of it. The story can be scripted, and parts can be drawn from a hat (Miriam, Moses, frogs, God, Pharoah, narrator, etc.). A costume box, masks, and hats heighten the drama.

Various kinds of "special effects" can be arranged at key moments; burning bushes have even been produced. Some people have adopted the Sephardic custom of getting up and walking around the table at the point in the story when the Israelites leave Egypt. Similarly, one can play music and dance around the table when they rejoice at having reached the other side of the Sea of Reeds.

Even the plagues have inspired a creativity. "Plague plates" are filled with things like origami frogs, plastic bugs, red food coloring (for blood), dolls (death of the firstborn), a burned out light bulb (darkness), and so on.

Some people sit in darkness, one of the plagues, for a few moments during which everyone names a modern plague: nuclear weapons, AIDS, homelessness, poverty, cancer, racism, anti-Semitism, and so on.

Many people try to achieve a balance between tradition and innovation. Although the *seder* may change drastically as children grow up, certain elements are always included: blessings, certain readings, even the same jokes told at the same juncture in the meal.

Parodies of songs and songsheets are ways to encourage participation. In addition to Hebrew songs, many people add familiar folk songs and spirituals such as "If I Had a Hammer," and "Go Down Moses." For a group that is unfamiliar with the Hebrew songs that traditionally follow the meal, playing tapes or records can add a nice touch.

If adults wish to have a longer, more traditional *seder* than their children can sit still for, children can be excused to play during discussions and more intellectual readings from the *haggadah.* However, at every important "event" of the *seder* (another cup of wine, the Four Questions, the Hillel sandwich), someone blows a whistle or bangs a drum to summon the kids back.

Where there are no young children or they have all gone to sleep, the *seder* can become an opportunity for intellectual and even esoteric discussion of the story and the other elements of the *seder*. These kinds of meals can go on until past midnight, or until everyone is satisfied that they finally understand what it all "really" means, at least for this year.

Of course, not everyone has such stamina, and by the end of the meal and after four (or more) cups of wine, some people end their *seders* on a lighter note. One family tradition consists of a contest (complete with a prize) for the person who can say all the verses to the traditional song "Who Knows One?" (*Echad Mi Yodeah,* included in most *haggadot*) the fastest.

Because many people attend two *seders,* on the first and second nights of Passover, it is common to differentiate the two: for example, a big group one night, a more intimate gathering the next; emphasis on teaching and entertaining children one night, followed by an adult *seder* —complete with a sitter for the children.

To keep the spirit alive and create some anticipation, some people even hold their second *seder* on the last night; after a week of eating "the bread of affliction," people can talk about the experience of living in the work-a-day world with one foot in the story of Exodus.

THE INTERMEDIATE DAYS

The only home observance after the *seder* and before the final day of Passover is the eating of *matzah* and the avoidance of *hametz.* As with the practice of *kashrut,* the range of the observance is very broad. Some people simply do not eat bread or other leavened foods, but otherwise make no change in their kitchens and simply tailor their orders at restaurants. Some people, who do not otherwise follow the rules of *kashrut,* will totally clean their homes of *hametz* for the week.

The challenge of cooking without leavening can get tedious as the week goes on, so some people try to plan pot-luck dinners with family and friends to ease the strain (and potential monotony) of Passover cooking.

Although it is traditional to say the *havdalah* prayer over wine at the end of Passover, the holiday tends to just peter out, at least for Ashkenazic Jews. However, a Sephardic custom called *Maimuna* is fast gaining popularity among all parts of the American Jewish community. Named to honor Maimon ben Joseph, father of the great 12th century rabbi

Maimonides, *Maimuna* is still celebrated with festive, elaborate traditions in communities of Moroccan Jews and in the state of Israel. People wear their finest clothes and eat at tables decorated with flowers and wheat stalks. Traditional *Maimuna* feasts are meatless, dairy meals, featuring buttermilk, sweets, and special pancakes called *muflita*. Many individuals and synagogues have adopted the custom as a way to provide a sense of closure to Passover.

SYNAGOGUE OBSERVANCE

Home observance tends to overshadow all other aspects of Passover. However, the first (and for some second) days are commanded to be days of rest in the Torah, as is the last day (or two), and special holiday services are held. On the last day of Passover, a memorial service is held and the *yizkor* prayer is recited in memory of loved ones who have died. Some congregations hold a community *seder* on the first or second night. Community *seders* are often planned on evenings during the middle of Passover, and these may be interfaith, interracial teaching-and-sharing ceremonies of great beauty and meaning.

LAG B'OMER

Shavuot marks the giving of the Torah to the Israelites 49 days after they were freed from slavery. The holidays of Passover (liberation) and Shavuot (revelation) are connected by the counting of the Omer.

An *omer* was the measure of grain set apart for offerings at the Temple. On the second day of Passover, the first of 49 measures of barley were given, one per day, as an offering or gift to God. Over the years, these 49 days came to be associated with terrible persecutions of the Jews and certain mourning practices came to be observed. Some people do not cut their hair, and some rabbis will not officiate at weddings during the counting of the Omer, except on the 33rd day of the Omer, in Hebrew, Lag B'Omer.

Lag B'Omer is considered a semi-holiday, and has long been associated with weddings and picnics. However, it was never widely celebrated and its origins and proper observance have long been the subject of rabbinic debate. Today, Lag B'Omer is mostly known as an occasion for outdoor congregational and community events: family field days, picnics, softball games, and races.

FURTHER READING

SOME *HAGGADOT* TO CONSIDER

Passover Haggadah; The Feast of Freedom (Rabbinical Assembly, 1982). A Conservative movement publication.

A Passover Haggadah (Central Conference of American Rabbis, 1974). A Reform movement publication.

Gates of Freedom, A Passover Haggadah by Chaim Stern (New Star Press, 1981). Reform.

The Shalom Seders: Three Haggadahs, compiled by New Jewish Agenda, (Menorah/Public Resource Center, 1984). Three alternative versions.

Haggadah for the Liberated Lamb by Roberta Kalechofsky, (Micah Press, 1984). The vegetarian's Passover handbook.

A Sephardic Passover Haggadah prepared by Rabbi Marc D. Angel (Ktav, 1988).

OTHER BOOKS

Exodus and Revolution by Michael Walzer (Basic Books, 1985). A political-philosophical reading of Exodus.

Exploring Exodus by Nahum Sarna (Schocken, 1986). A theme-by-theme reading of the book of Exodus by a biblical scholar.

The Passover Anthology by Philip Goodman (Jewish Publication Society, 1961). Entries from the Bible, Talmud, Midrash and modern fiction, among others.

The Passover Gourmet by Nira Rousso (Adama Books, 1987). One of many excellent resources for Passover cooking.

FOR CHILDREN

The Four Questions by Lynn Sharon Schwartz (Dial Books, 1989). The text tells the story of Exodus and explains the *seder*. The illustrator, Ori Sherman has created a vivid menagerie that reenacts the tale and then eats the Passover meal.

The Animated Haggadah. A videotape and accompanying book (Scopus Films, 1985, 1987). Using the technique of "claymation," the book and tape are funny, sophisticated, and vivid teaching tools that introduce a lot of Hebrew in addition to knowledge of the Passover story and *seder.* Some parents report that the "scary parts" are a little overwhelming for some young children. An activities book for ages 5–10 is also available.

Everything's Changing—It's Pesach by Julie Jaslow Auerback (Kar-Ben Copies, 1986). A rhyming view of how a home—especially a kosher kitchen—gets turned upside down in preparation for Passover.

Only Nine Chairs by Deborah Uchill Miller (Kar-Ben Copies, 1982). This "tall tale" gets sillier and sillier as it imagines what would happen if there weren't enough chairs for the *seder.* Pre-school and up.

The Carp in the Bathtub by Barbara Cohen (Lathrop, 1972). Leah and Harry make friends with the fish that Mamma is going to cook for Passover.

Holocaust Remembrance Day and Israel Independence Day

Nothing is so whole as a broken heart.

Rabbi Nachman of Bratslav

In one of its earliest sessions, the Israel Knesset (parliament) declared that Israel Independence Day (Yom HaAtzma'ut), would be celebrated on the fifth of Iyar—the Hebrew date corresponding to May 15, 1948, when Israel became a sovereign nation. Three years later, the Knesset proclaimed Holocaust Remembrance Day (Yom HaShoah), on the 27th of Nisan, 14 days after the start of Passover and eight days before the celebration of Israel's birth.

The addition of these holidays to the Hebrew calendar reflect the profound impact of these two historical events on the Jewish psyche. The world could never be the same after the *Shoah*, the Holocaust that killed one-third of the pre-war world Jewish population. Nor could the future be the same after the realization of the dream of returning to the land promised in the Torah to the children of Abraham. The relationship between the two holidays is undeniable, but not easy to explain. It is not that the establishment of Israel compensates for the Holocaust, or is a product of the slaughter of European Jewry. But Israel is, undeniably, a response to the horror, an affirmation of life and Jewish continuity against that overwhelming death and destruction.[1]

Outside of Israel, Yom HaShoah and Yom HaAtzma'ut are still in formative stages, holidays-in-the-making. It is not easy to shape traditions, rituals, and universal metaphors out of raw emotion, and the historical ramifications of the Holocaust and Israel are still unfolding.

The death camps continue to haunt the dreams of survivors and their children. And although Israel is a source of pride and hope, it is also a source of tension and struggle.

HOLOCAUST REMEMBRANCE DAY

It is terrible to remember. It is worse to forget. These are the twin realities of Yom HaShoah. In the tension between them, observances are taking shape. To many people, it seems almost blasphemous to try to speak about the Holocaust, to attempt to make sense out of the senseless slaughter of six million Jewish men, women, and children, and three million other souls. The photographs, film footage, diaries, and memoirs of survivors are excruciating. And yet, the responsibility to remember is absolute and, in some sense, sacred.

In Israel, on what is called "Holocaust and Resistance Remembrance Day," all public entertainments are closed. A three-minute siren blast is heard throughout the country, and everyone stands at attention. In America, commemorations of the Holocaust include a wide range of events including civic ceremonies attended by public officials and clergy of all faiths. There are classroom presentations about the Nazi horror tailored to the age and ability of students to understand what is incomprehensible. Some synagogues and Jewish community centers mark Yom HaShoah with displays of art, photographs, or books, and with seminars, lectures, and film series.

It is difficult to generalize about synagogue observance of Holocaust Remembrance Day. Although some liturgies have been published and used, many congregations create original services for Yom HaShoah. Readings from Lamentations and Psalms are often used, but the most common source for commemorations held in hushed and darkened sanctuaries is literature from the Holocaust: the testimony of victims, survivors, and witnesses.

Common elements of many Yom HaShoah services are silence, darkness, and candles. Silence has been suggested as the most appropriate response to the unspeakable horror. Darkness recalls the darkest period of Jewish and human history. Candles both recall the dead and affirm light and life, even in the heart of the blackest night.

Fasting has been suggested as an appropriate way to mark Yom HaShoah. Some people abstain from eating sweet foods, or eat very little all day. But so far, the ritual that seems to have become the central act of Yom HaShoah is the lighting of six memorial candles, one for each of the six million Jews who were killed. This is done both in synagogues and at home, and some light a seventh candle in memory of non-Jews who were killed in the Holocaust, or to honor the righteous non-Jews who risked their lives to help Jews.

Yom HaShoah is not associated with any home observance. The Holocaust is still too close and too awful to bring to the table. However, because it is a time when children may be introduced to or reminded of the events of the Holocaust at school, families sometimes use the opportunity to discuss the thoughts and feelings these lessons provoke. Good books about the Holocaust have been written for readers of all ages; reading one as a family may be one way to help children begin to absorb the story as is watching a film version of *The Diary of Ann Frank.* For adults there is a huge literature of fiction, poetry, philosophy, and history, as well as a large selection of documentary and feature films available for home viewing.

Donations to virtually any Jewish organization seems appropriate *tzedakah* at Yom HaShoah because the vitality of the Jewish community repudiates the attempted annihilation of the Jewish people. Some earmark money at this time for projects devoted to keeping the memory of the Holocaust alive, such as the Simon Weisenthal Center.

ISRAEL INDEPENDENCE DAY

After nearly 2,000 years in exile, the formation of a Jewish state in the land of Israel transformed the self-image of Jews everywhere. Even Jews who do not live there feel somehow connected to, committed to, and responsible for Israel's existence. Although Israel Independence Day is, by and large, a secular event, it is impossible to forget its context in Jewish tradition. From the Torah, where God promises Abraham, "I give all the land that you see to you and your offspring forever,"[2] to the annual Passover wish, "Next year in Jerusalem," the land of Israel has been a focal point of the Jewish hope for redemption. Thus, there is a sense that the modern state of Israel has something to do with God and God's purpose. The power of the dream that is Israel lies in its attempt to fuse a religious, messianic vision with the normalization of Jewish existence in the world.[3]

In Israel, Yom HaAtzma'ut is celebrated with flags, bands, fireworks, picnics, parties, and dancing in the streets. Many American Jews try to schedule trips to Israel to coincide with this gala celebration. In the United States, Israel Independence Day is the occasion for public gatherings of all sorts, the Israel Day Parade in New York City being the largest. Local community centers and synagogues hold dances, concerts, film series, seminars, and lectures that feature Israeli culture and concerns. Religious schools and day schools usually schedule programs and parties in conjunction with the celebration.

Again, although this holiday is not home-centered, family activities might include Israeli singing or music, foods that are popular in Israel, reading about Israel, watching Israeli movies, and so forth.

Tzedakah for Israel Independence Day has come to mean supporting the state of Israel by purchasing Israel bonds, by making a contribution to any Israeli charity, and by buying Israeli goods and products.

There are two other modern-historical holidays celebrated almost exclusively in Israel. Yom HaZikaron (Remembrance Day) is observed the day before Yom HaAtzma'ut in Israel, and honors the memory of those who died fighting for Israel's independence and continuing existence. Yom Yerushalayim (Jerusalem Day) is celebrated three weeks after Israel Independence Day, and commemorates the capture of Jerusalem during the Six-Day War of 1967.

FURTHER READING

For more about the history of Yom HaShoah and Yom HaAtzma'ut, see the appropriate chapters in *The Jewish Way* by Rabbi Irving Greenberg.

Both the Holocaust and the land of Israel have inspired excellent works of history, fiction, and every imaginable form of commentary. For specific recommendations, see also "People of the Library." Ask rabbis, Jewish educators, librarians, and friends for suggestions.

FOR CHILDREN

Promise of a New Spring: The Holocaust and Renewal by Gerda Weissman Klein (Rossel, 1981). An introduction to the Holocaust for the very young, kindergarten and up.

The Number on my Grandfather's Arm by David A. Adler (UAHC, 1987). A little girls asks a very hard question. Grade 1 and up.

The Yanov Torah by Erwin and Agnes Herman (Kar-Ben Copies, 1985). The story of how one Torah survived the Holocaust and was eventually brought to America. Grade 3–4.

Escape from the Holocaust by Kenneth Roseman (UAHC, 1985). An interactive book that poses several answers to various "What would you do?" situations set during the Holocaust. Junior high.

Anne Frank: The Diary of a Young Girl (Doubleday, 1967).

What's in Israel? by Chaya Burstein (Kar-Ben Copies, 1983). Activities, puzzles, projects and things to color. Perfect for the airplane trip to Israel, or just to learn about the country. For pre-school to grade 2.

And Shira Imagined by Giora Carmi (Jewish Publications Society, 1988). On a tour with her family, Giora's imagination vividly illustrates the land of Israel. A picture book for pre-school to grade 2.

A Kid's Catalog of Israel by Chaya Burstein (Jewish Publications Society, 1988). Photographs, crafts, history, biography, holidays in Israel: a catalog for the school-aged child to junior high.

Kids Love Israel, Israel Loves Kids by Barbara Sofer (Kar-Ben, 1988). A travel guide for families, complete with maps and suggestions for activities.

Shavuot

Shavuot celebrates the moment when the Jewish people stood before God at Mount Sinai and received a scroll containing all the secrets of the universe as a memento of their encounter. The scroll was the Torah. She is called a tree of life.[1]

Seven weeks after Passover—seven weeks after leaving Egypt—comes Shavuot, Hebrew for "weeks." The early summer holiday recalls the giving of the Torah at Mount Sinai, the encounter of a whole people with the Holy. The Torah is sometimes called a *ketubah,* the marriage contract that describes the covenantal relationship between the people of Israel and God. Shavuot can be thought of as the celebration of this wedding anniversary.

Shavuot is celebrated with greens and flowers, with milk and sweets and a reading of the Book of Ruth, who came to be part of the Jewish people not by birth, but by her own choice. In the same way Passover encourages every member of every generation to feel as though he or she had experienced slavery and liberation, Shavuot insists that revelation—receiving the Torah—is experienced by every Jew, by every descendent of the marriage that occurred at Sinai.

The Bible, however, makes absolutely no connection between Shavuot and the Torah. The references to Shavuot in Exodus, Leviticus, and Deuteronomy describe an agricultural pilgrimage holiday, a day when people came from all over the land of Israel to the Temple, bearing gifts from the first fruits of the wheat and fruit harvest as an offering to God.[2] The agricultural and seasonal aspects of Shavuot are still reflected in its many names: The Day of the First Fruits, the Day of the

Harvest, the Feast of the Flowers (in Persia), and the Feast of the Roses (in Italy).

But after the destruction of the second Temple in 70 C.E., the holiday was reconstructed around the new center of Judaism: the Torah. The agricultural roots of the holiday are echoed in seasonal decorations and especially in Israeli celebrations that include public processions featuring singing and dancing. But for the most part, Shavuot may be the most mystical of all the Jewish holidays, a day that celebrates revelation.

PREPARING

There are few symbols and rituals associated with Shavuot. In recognition of the late spring-early summer season, it is customary to decorate both home and synagogue with green plants and flowers. An old European craft associated with Shavuot is the papercut. Called *shavuoslech, raizelech,* or *shoshanta* (the latter two words refer to roses), these were hung on windows, and light would filter through a floral design.[3] Baking bread for the *yontif seder* is another Shavuot custom. And some people go to the *mikvah* for the ritual of purification to get ready to receive the Torah.

STUDY

Study is the primary way of preparing for this holiday. It is traditional to read *Pirke Avot,* "The Chapters of the Father," a very accessible section of the Talmud, during the weeks between Passover and Shavuot. In line with the custom of the *tikkun,* or study session, some people try to read a little bit of each book of the Bible, with special attention to Exodus 19-20 (the Ten Commandments), the Book of Ruth, and Ezekiel 3:12, the strange vision of "the wheel."

TZEDAKAH

The themes of learning and agriculture suggest donations to organizations devoted to education, feeding the poor, and restoring the earth.

Making Shavuot

AT HOME

Shavuot begins with a festival meal, including all the blessings of the *yontif seder:* candles, a festival *kiddush, sheheheyanu,* and *motzi.* Because the Torah mentions the offering of two loaves of bread made from newly harvested wheat, it is customary to have two loaves on the table. Some people bake two loaves of challah side-by-side and connected, so that they look something like the popular image of the double tablets of the Ten Commandments.

Shavuot meals feature dairy foods, especially cheese. For Ashkenazic Jews, blintzes (sweet cheese wrapped in a thin pancake) are traditional. Sephardic cuisines include dishes flavored with rosewater. Eating outside is a nice way to welcome the summer season.

The custom of late-night Shavuot synagogue study sessions can be translated to the home, where children can participate. Shavuot can become a special night for staying up very late and reading stories from or about the Bible. Some families rent all the Bible movies they can find and stay up late watching them from sleeping bags on the living room floor.

SYNAGOGUE OBSERVANCE

Synagogue observance of Shavuot begins in the evening with a holiday service that often starts later than usual. Afterwards, many congregations have instituted some form of a *tikkun.* This custom dates back to the 16th century mystics of Safed who stayed up all night long to read and study from the Bible, from various rabbinic writers, and from the *Zohar,* a mystical book. Modern Shavuot study sessions take many forms: a series of seminars led by members of a congregation, discussion of modern as well as ancient Jewish texts, writing modern *midrashim* or imaginative commentaries on a biblical passage. Some synagogues run study sessions until late into the night or all night long, stopping only at sunrise, when the morning service is held and breakfast is served.

The Torah portion of the morning service includes the reading of the Ten Commandments. The *haftarah* portion comes from Ezekiel, and includes the hallucinatory vision of the *merkavah,* God's chariot or throne, which is attended by marvelous strange creatures: angels, divine beings. The prophet's description of wheels within wheels has been given many interpretations, and remains a stunning work of imagination. The Book of Ruth is also read on Shavuot. Ruth, the archetypal Jew-by-choice, demonstrates that it is not birth or family identity but acceptance of the Torah that distinguishes Jews from other peoples.

Many congregations hold confirmations or graduation ceremonies on Shavuot, which has long been associated with Jewish study.

FURTHER READING

"Ruth," by Cynthia Ozick in *Congregation: Contemporary Writers Read the Jewish Bible*, edited by David Rosenberg (Harcourt, Brace Jovanovich, Inc., 1987). A beautiful, personal and learned essay.

The Shavuot Anthology by Philip Goodman (Jewish Publication Society, 1974). The anthology contains entries from the Bible, Talmud, and Midrash. The liturgy is included, as is a history, an overview of customs around the world, recipes, stories for children, and poems and modern short stories that deal with the holiday.

Tisha B'Av

Tisha B'Av, the ninth day in the month of Av, is a day of mourning for, the destruction of the Temples in Jerusalem, first in the year 586 B.C.E. by Nebuchadnezzar, King of Babylonia, and again seven centuries later in 70 C.E. by General Titus of the Roman empire.

The destruction of the Temple was, quite literally, the end of a world to the Jews of those times. The end of the Temple meant the end of a way of life; of a religion of sacrifices and priesthoods, and of national identity for the Jewish people, who were dispersed and exiled in the aftermath of the military defeats. The destruction of the Temple was also interpreted as a sign that God had withdrawn from the world and from God's people. Over time, other sad events were associated with and commemorated on the Tisha B'Av, among them: The end of Bar Kochba's revolt (125 C.E.), the expulsion of Jews from England (1290 C.E.), from Spain (1492), and from Vienna (1670).

Tisha B'Av is a day of fasting observed with mourning customs, such as not shaving and sitting low to the ground. It also culminates a three-week period of semi-mourning when weddings and other celebrations are avoided. Those who observe Tisha B'Av light memorial candles and attend services, where there is no singing or chanting. The Torah may be draped with dark or black covers. The text for Tisha B'Av is the Book of Lamentations, a long poem that keens over the destruction of Jerusalem and the first Temple.

Tisha B'Av is the least-known of the traditional holidays and is largely ignored by American Jews. In some part this is due to the fact that it falls during the middle of the summer, when many congregations are on summer schedule and many people are on vacation. Also, for many modern Jews, the destruction of the Temple does not evoke the emotions of grief and mourning called for by Tisha B'Av. In some sense, Holocaust Remembrance Day has taken its place as a communal day of grief and mourning. And because Tisha B'Av is a holiday mourning the exile of the Jews, some have argued that the founding of the state of Israel suggests that the tone of the day deserves to be changed from one of mourning to one of hope. Indeed, there is a legend that the messiah will be born on Tisha B'Av.

Because it is the only event on the Jewish calendar during the summer months, the Jewish camping movement has made Tisha B'Av a focus for teaching and creative programming. Campers participate in poetry-writing workshops, discussion groups, dramatic readings and services in candle-lit recreation halls.

THE LIFE CYCLE

Birth

The first *mitzvah*—the first "commandment"—in the Bible is "Be fruit-ful and multiply." For Jews, having children is both a religious obliga-tion and the crown of human life, the source of greatest happiness. The birth of Jewish babies is thus greeted with rituals that are both solemn and joyful.

All parents know that *their* baby is the center of the universe, a "fact" that is acknowledged by the Jewish view of time. Every Jewish baby is a link in the chain that extends back to the birth of Isaac, the first Jewish baby, and extends forward to the day when the world will be peaceful and whole. After all, any baby might grow up to be the messiah, the person who will lead the world to redemption. The Jewish traditions and rituals described in this chapter give voice to the powerful feelings that surround the birth of every baby: gratitude, awe, fear, humility, continuity, and hope.

Names

The choice of a name is the first Jewish decision parents are called on to make. And for Jews, a name is a complicated gift. It bestows not only personal identity but also familial and religious connection; a baby named Daniel or Rebecca is often a living testament to a grandparent who has died, and a link to every Jewish Daniel and Rebecca back to the Bible.

Jewish tradition is very attentive to names and naming. *HaShem,*

The Name, is one of the most common ways of referring to God. The Torah contains several dramatic and important name changes. Once Abram and Sarai accepted the covenant with God, they became different people with different names: Abraham and Sarah, the parents of the Jewish people. Even more striking is the transformation of Jacob, "supplanter," into Israel, "wrestler with God." There is a story that the Jews enslaved in Egypt were saved from complete assimilation by keeping two identifying signs that set them apart: the custom of circumcision and their Hebrew names.

There are 2,800 personal names in the Bible, fewer than 5% of which are used today. Throughout history, Jews have given their children names from many sources, reflecting the fashion and culture of their time as well as their own unique tradition. For example, Esther, a quintessentially Jewish name, is Persian in origin and shares its root with Astarte and Ishtar, the great fertility goddess of the ancient Middle East. The Eastern European custom of naming children after deceased relatives dates back to the Egyptian Jews of the sixth century B.C.E., who probably borrowed the idea from their non-Jewish neighbors.

The practice of giving a secular name for everyday use and a religious name for prayer and on Jewish legal documents developed during the Middle Ages in Eastern Europe.[1] This custom is still very much alive in America, where the connection between the secular and Hebrew name is sometimes as tenuous as an initial sound; thus a baby girl named for her grandmother Shayna becomes Susan, and Max is named in memory of Uncle Moshe.

Since the founding of the state of Israel, the lexicon of Jewish names has expanded with the introduction of biblical names that had not been heard for generations, such as Amnon, Yoram, Avital, and Tamar. Israelis also translate names from Yiddish to Hebrew so, for example, Gittel (good one) becomes Tovah. Inspired by the land of Israel, chil-

With each child, the world begins anew.

Midrash

dren are named Kinereth, (a sea), Arnon, (a wadi), Barak (lightning) and Ora (light).

Today, Jewish-American parents have made biblical names popular again, and the pre-schools are full of Samuels and Rachels, Benjamins and Sarahs. Modern Israeli names are also growing in popularity: Ariella, Levi, Noam, and Shoshana. Increasingly, parents are choosing identifiably Jewish names (from Abigail to Zachariah) because they work well in three settings where American Jews are likely to find themselves: in secular life, in synagogues, and in Israel.

Covenant: Brit

A covenant is a contract, an agreement that acknowledges the participation and assent of various parties. Covenant is the name of the relationship between the people of Israel and God. With the birth of every Jewish child, that covenant is renewed again, with ritual and celebration.

The ancient ceremony for bringing sons into the covenant of Israel is *brit milah*, a religious ritual that includes circumcision as a physical sign of the bond between the Jewish people and God. For daughters, American Jews are creating a new ceremony, *brit habat* or "covenant for a daughter," to invoke the joys and responsibilities of entering the covenant of the people of Israel.

In many ways, the covenant of circumcision and the covenant for a daughter are as different as two ceremonies can be. *Brit milah* is the oldest continuous Jewish rite, celebrated with remarkable consistency throughout the world. *Brit habat,* which is called by many names, is a recent invention, a rite of passage in the making, no two quite the same. What these two celebrations have in common, however, is the element of covenant, expressed with joy, gratitude, and wonder. *Brit* ceremonies give parents a way to express the complex feelings occasioned by the birth of a baby, and a way to express new feelings of connection to Jewish tradition.

The Covenant of Circumcision: Brit Milah

In the covenant of circumcision, the removal of the foreskin takes place within a religious ceremony as a physical token signifying the unique relationship between a Jewish boy and God. In America, the Ashkenazic Hebrew or Yiddish term, *bris*, is probably the most familiar name for ritual circumcision. *Brit milah* is also called the "covenant of Abraham" because he was the first to practice circumcision as a Jewish ritual. According to the biblical story, Abraham responded to God's command and circumcised himself (at the age of 99) and all the men of his household, including his 13-year-old son Ishmael. Isaac, the first born of a circumcised Jew, underwent *brit milah* on the eighth day, which set the precedent for the ritual's timing ever since.

The importance of circumcision as a mark of peoplehood is a recurring theme in the Bible, and in every generation this covenant has been renewed. During periods of persecution when it singled Jewish men out for execution, circumcision became an act of defiance and courage. In the 20th century, stories from the Holocaust and from the Soviet Union testify to the steadfastness of Jewish practice of *brit milah*—no matter what the consequences.

The liturgy of *brit milah* was established before the first century C.E., and the laws that regulate and explain it are contained in the Talmud. *Brit milah* takes place on the eight day of life,* even on *Shabbat* or a holiday, including Yom Kippur. However, if the baby is ill or weak, Jewish law requires that the rite be postponed until it is completely safe for the baby. A *bris* may occur anytime before sundown, but it is customary to schedule it early in the day, because the tradition says that one should be eager to perform a *mitzvah*. A *bris* may be held anywhere, though today most take place at home.

A father is responsible for his son's *brit milah*, and technically he performs the circumcision; the *mohel*,** or ritual circumciser, acts as his representative. The only people who absolutely must be present at a *bris* are the baby, the *mohel*, and one honored assistant called the *sandek*, often a grandfather, who holds the baby. However, because a *bris* is

---

* According to the Jewish calendar, a day begins with the preceding nightfall, so if a boy is born on Monday night, his bris would be on the following Tuesday.
** The Yiddish pronunciation is "moyl;" the Hebrew is "mo-hel."

considered a joyful event, it is customary to invite friends and family members.

CHOOSING BRIT MILAH

Nearly all Jews, even those with little or no connection to community or congregation, or with little or no understanding of the ritual or its meaning, choose to fulfill what is arguably the most difficult of all the commandments. Even so, for many American Jews, *brit milah* is no longer an automatic response but a decision made after considering a series of questions: Is it safe? Will my baby suffer? What is the best way to have it done? Why should we continue this tradition at all?

Until recently, virtually all Americans, regardless of religion, circumcised their sons for reasons of health and hygiene. As recently as the 1960s, approximately 98% of all boys born in the United States were circumcised. But after an official announcement by pediatricians that routine circumcision was not medically warranted, that figure dropped to 59% in 1985.[2] The medical debate shifted somewhat back in favor of universal circumcision again in the late 1980s. However, Jews have never performed *brit milah* as a health measure. It is a religious obligation.

As far as safety is concerned, complications following circumcision are extremely rare. It also seems obvious that Jewish tradition, which is so concerned with the sanctity of life and health, would not require an act that might jeopardize either. And clearly, Jewish sons have survived the procedure for 3,500 years.[3]

Although some physicians and *mohelim* (plural of *mohel*) numb the area, *brit milah* is generally performed without anesthesia. And al-

Such shall be the covenant between Me and you and your offspring to follow which you shall keep: every male among you shall be circumcised. You shall circumcise the flesh of your foreskin, and that shall be the sign of the covenant between Me and you.

Genesis 17:10-11

though there can be no definitive answer about pain, anyone who has attended more than one *bris* knows that babies are easily comforted after the procedure.

Some Jewish parents, feeling more confidence in professional medicine than ritual practice, decide to have their sons circumcised by a physician in the hospital before they take the baby home. Apart from the fact that a medical circumcision is not the same as a *brit milah*, which is a religious ritual performed on the eighth day with the deliberate intent of bringing a son into the covenant, there are other salient differences between a hospital "circ" and a *bris* performed by a *mohel*.

In many hospitals, residents of varying experience perform the procedure. In order to immobilize the baby, his limbs are strapped to a board where he may be held for as long as ten or fifteen minutes. After the procedure is over, there may be no one to immediately comfort the baby. At a *brit milah*, the baby is held by loving hands throughout the procedure, which is performed by an expert at the operation. The baby is given some wine, which is thought to lessen the pain and may help him fall asleep afterwards. When the ceremony is over, he is returned to his mother, who can nurse and comfort him.

As to the "why" of *brit milah*, the most compelling reasons are not always the most rational. For many parents the answer to that question is: If we stop doing *brit milah*, we stop being Jews. *Brit milah* is a physical connection to the ancient Jewish past and to all subsequent generations to the present day. It is also one of the few ritual practices on which virtually all Jews still agree. Choosing not to circumcise a son may, in effect, cut him off from full membership in the Jewish community, or present him with the choice of undergoing a painful operation as a adult.

THE MOHEL

Traditional *mohelim* learn their skills by apprenticeship to and supervision by an accomplished, established *mohel*. The Reform and Conservative movements now certify as *mohelim* physicians who take a course on the theology, Jewish law, folklore, and liturgy of *brit milah*. As it happens, more and more *mohelim* of all denominations are board-certified physicians.

On the day of a *brit milah*, the *mohel* examines the baby first. If there is the slightest question about the child's health, Jewish law obliges that the circumcision be postponed. The *mohel* then usually acts as the "master of ceremonies" for the *bris,* leading prayers and explaining the ritual as well as performing the circumcision. Sometimes, a rabbi, cantor, the parents, or others will share the liturgical honors. After the ceremony, the *mohel* again examines the baby, gives instructions for caring for the circumcised penis, and then remains "on call" for questions about healing.

Word of mouth recommendation is the best way to find a *mohel,* and because rabbis and cantors go to many circumcisions, they are probably the best people to consult. Local movement offices may also be able to provide a list of names, and some *mohelim* place advertisements in Jewish newspapers.

THE CEREMONY

The liturgy of *brit milah* is ancient and, as with most Jewish life-cycle rituals, the ceremony is very brief, no more than five or ten minutes long. A *bris* consists of three parts. The first is as normative and universal as any part of Jewish religious life: a blessing is recited, the circumcision is performed, and another blessing follows. The second part begins with *kiddush,* the blessing over wine, and includes a longer prayer that gives the baby his name. The third section, required by Jewish law, is the *seudat mitzvah,* the ritual meal of celebration.

There are variations and many customs attached to this simple outline. The father may hand the circumcision knife to the *mohel,* demonstrating that he bears responsibility for the act. Sephardic Jews follow the blessing over wine with the scent of fragrant spices—Moroccan Jews use dried rose petals—and recite the blessing over spices, familiar from the Sabbath *havdalah* service.

Recently, there has been interest in adding parental participation to the ceremony in the form of readings, prayers, or a short *d'rash,* or teaching. Because the comfort of the baby is paramount, additions to the liturgy tend to be simple and brief. Sometimes, the baby is passed from one generation to the next, from great-grandparents to grandparents to parents. If an older sibling is mature enough to participate, he or she might carry the baby into the room, or light a candle, or say a few words.

Many parents talk about the baby's name after the circumcision. This is a time for remembering Uncle Jake, for whom little Jacob has been named, and to hope this child will grow up to be as learned, as quick to laugh, as devoted a friend and father, as his namesake. Another new tradition, added after the naming or at the meal of celebration, is to have guests offer personal blessings for the new baby: "May he be blessed with long life. May he grow up in a world free of want and fear. May he inherit his mother's good looks and his father's appetite." Wishes like these can be recorded in a guest book, or on a tape or video recorder.

There is also renewed interest in the old custom of distributing *kibbudim* or "honors," to family members and friends during the ceremony. The most important of these is the role of the *sandek*, from the Greek, *syndikos*, or "patron." The *sandek* assists the mohel by holding the baby during the circumcision. The other traditional ceremonial roles are that of *kvatterin* (godmother), who carries the baby from the mother to the room where the *bris* takes place, and *kvatter** (godfather), who in turn brings the baby to the chair of Elijah. According to the ancient legend, the prophet Elijah, who is associated with the coming of the messiah, attends every *bris*. The special chair set aside for the prophet is a symbol of hope that this baby will bring peace and redemption to the world.

Covenant for a Daughter: Brit Habat

In the early 1970s, feeling a lack of ritual forms for expressing their joy, parents began to create ceremonies to welcome baby girls into the covenant of the Jewish people. What began as a tentative, experimental practice is now so much a part of Jewish life that most rabbi's manuals include some sort of welcoming or naming ceremony for daughters.**

---

* *Kvatter* and *kvatterin* are entirely ceremonial roles. There is no Jewish role analogous to that assumed by Christian godparents who become responsible for the child in case of his parents' death. The Jewish community as a whole is responsible for the education and support of orphaned children.

** Many rabbis officiate at "baby namings." These are not so much ceremonies as they are a kind of introduction of the baby to the community. In general, the rabbi says a few blessings while the parents and baby stand on the *bimah*, the platform in front of the Torah, during a worship service.

Covenant ceremonies go by many names; *simchat bat* (joy of the daughter), *brit hayyim* (covenant of life), *brit bat Zion* (covenant for the daughters of Zion), *brit ohel* (covenant of the tent), *brit hanerot* (covenant of candles), *brit Sarah* (covenant of Sarah), *brit rehitzah* (covenant of washing) *brit mikvah* (covenant of immersion), *hachnasat habat* (welcoming a daughter) and *brit habat* (covenant for a daughter).

In fact, ceremonies for baby girls are not new. Sephardic tradition is rich in rituals and customs to celebrate a daughter's birth, including a ceremony called *Seder zeved habat*, "celebration for the gift of a daughter." The Jews of Spain held a special party at home after the mother's recovery called *las fadas*, a celebration probably adapted from non-Jewish folk beliefs that welcomed good fairies.[4]

Of the many new ceremonies being written and celebrated in America today, it may be that a single, standard liturgy for daughters will eventually become as normative as the words associated with *brit milah*. However, it is just as likely that the ceremony will continue to be given many interpretations like the Passover *seder*, which retains its identity even as it is interpreted anew every year.

WHERE AND WHEN

There are no rules for *brit habat*, but current practice offers a variety of choices. *Brit habat* can take place at home or in the synagogue. Although a sanctuary or social hall encourages more of a community celebration, some people feel that home is the best place for this occasion. When *brit habat* takes place at home, the baby's parents usually lead the ceremony, often with a rabbi's assistance. When it is held in a synagogue, the rabbi tends to officiate, sometimes with parental participation. In general, grandparents are usually given the most important *kibbudim* or honors at *brit habat* ceremonies, often with the honorary roles and titles from *brit milah*. For example, the *sandek* (or, if a woman, *sandeket*) holds the baby during part of the ceremony, and the *kvatterin* and *kvatter* may carry her to and from the room.

Generally, parents schedule *brit habat* for a time when the mother is recovered enough to enjoy the event, and when it will be possible for out-of-town family members to attend. Various intervals are used and justified on traditional grounds. For example, holding the ceremony on the eighth day mirrors the ancient customs of *brit milah*. However, because mothers often do not feel ready for a party so soon after giving birth, this is a relatively infrequent choice. Thirty days after birth is a popular choice because it allows the family enough time to recover. This interval also has a basis in tradition because the rabbis of the Talmud believed a child was only viable after 30 days.

Brit habat often takes place sometime during the Sabbath. In many congregations, both parents take the baby up to the *bimah* during Friday night or *Shabbat* morning services where the rabbi pronounces some blessings and makes a few comments, and the parents address their new baby and the congregation. Another option is to hold a separate ceremony immediately following the morning service so the *seudat mitzvah* can coincide with the *Shabbat* midday meal, either in the synagogue or at home. Finally, some parents schedule *brit habat* for the end of Shabbat at *havdalah*. The ceremony that separates the Sabbath from the other days of week can also signify the separation of the baby from her mother's body.

ELEMENTS OF THE CEREMONY

There are literally hundreds of *brit habat* ceremonies in circulation. Some are short and simple, others are long and elaborate. Some use a lot of Hebrew, and others use very little. It is difficult to generalize about these ceremonies, but, despite the variety, there are a few nearly universal elements:

1. The introductory section begins with the greeting, "Blessed is she who enters," *B'rucha haba'a.* Songs may be sung, and candles are sometimes lit. There are usually prayers or readings by the parents, rabbi, and/or cantor. *Kiddush,* the blessing for wine that is part of all signficant Jewish rituals, is recited here as well.

2. The second part of the ceremony is about covenant. Using blessings and symbolic actions, a baby daughter is entered into the people of Israel. Although daughters are most commonly entered into the covenant simply by saying a blessing, many parents feel that *brit habat* requires symbolic action as well as words. Washing the baby, or bathing her feet or hands, is an earthy yet gentle physical act that seems to have struck a responsive chord, especially because the Torah is rich with water imagery, much of it associated with women: Rebecca and Rachel make their first appearances at wells, and Miriam the prophetess is associated with a well of living water that sustained the Israelites in the wilderness.

Generally, the covenant-making is followed by some version of the threefold wish recited at *brit milah*; "As she has entered the covenant, so may she enter a life devoted to Torah, *huppah*, and the accomplishment of good deeds."

3. In the third section, the baby's name is announced and her namesake(s) recalled. Anything said about how a name was chosen can be very moving, especially because most American Jews name children to honor the memory of a family member who has died. The Hebrew or biblical meaning of a name can also suggest ways for parents to talk about their hopes and dreams for a daughter.

Other kinds of readings, prayers, poems, and songs are added here and family and friends may be invited to offer spontaneous prayers and wishes for the new baby: "May she live to be 120. May her life be filled with laughter and people who love her. May she sleep through the night soon." If the group is small and the baby placid enough, she might even be passed from person to person as they speak. (With the tape or video recorder on!)

4. The end of the ceremony is signaled by one, some, or all of the following three prayers: *Sheheheyanu*, the prayer of thanks for any new blessing, which may be the most common element of all *brit habat* ceremonies; the traditional blessing for a daughter, which is recited on Friday night as part of the *Shabbat seder*, and the priestly benediction, which concludes various Jewish rituals and services, and which some parents include in the *Shabbat* blessing of their children.*

5. *Brit habat* concludes with the *seudat mitzvah* or celebratory meal. The Jewish term for this kind of party is *simcha*, a word that means both joy and celebration.

Celebrating

According to Jewish law, all major life-cycle events are marked, concluded, and celebrated with a *seudat mitzvah*, "the meal of the *mitzvah*."

---

* See the index for references to these and other blessings.

The celebrations to honor the birth of a new baby range from catered sit-down dinners to pot-luck buffet brunches. However fancy or plain, large or small, these meals traditionally begin with the blessing over *challah (motzi)* and end with the *birkat hamazon,* blessings after meals.

The meal can also be an informal continuation of the *brit* ceremony, a time for guests to offer their blessings and wishes for the baby and family. Telegrams or messages from people who could not be present might be read aloud, or older siblings can be given a chance to shine during a day in which they are eclipsed.

TZEDAKAH

Traditionally, Jews mark happy occasions like births with contributions of *tzedakah,* righteous giving or charity. Giving *tzedakah* is a way of both sharing the joy of the occasion and of acknowledging that personal happiness is incomplete in a world so badly in need of repair. A donation to honor the birth of a child is a kind of investment in a more just world for all children.

In ancient Israel, it was customary to plant a cedar sapling at the birth of a boy and a cypress for a girl. The cedar symbolized strength and stature, the cypress symbolized gentleness and sweetness. Eventually, branches were cut down from each tree to hold up a wedding canopy. Some parents have revived this custom, planting a sapling in the yard when a baby is born. And many people have a tree planted in Israel's Children's Forest in honor of a birth.

God commands us to perform countless acts of love.
How can we begin to obey such a difficult commandment? It is not such a mystery really.
Every lullaby, every diaper change, every smile, every sleepless night, every wordless prayer of thanks for this perfect baby—in these and the unending ways we care for and teach and protect our children, we perform countless acts of love.
And the world is made holier. And so are we.

adapted from Midrash

FURTHER READING

The Jewish Baby Book by Anita Diamant (Summit Books, 1988). A complete guide to all the Jewish decisions that new parents are called on to make: from the selection of a name to distinctive birth announcements, to a year's worth of celebrations.

What to Name Your Jewish Baby by Anita Diamant (Summit Books, 1989). A listing of some 500 Jewish names including biblical and Israeli names.

The New Name Dictionary: Modern English and Hebrew Names by Alfred Kolatch (Jonathan David Publishers, 1989). The most comprehensive source of names.

The Jewish Women's Resource Center, a project of the National Council of Jewish Women, New York Section, maintains a library of birth ceremonies and other rituals pertinent to women's lives. Their pamphlet "Birth Ceremonies" contains many examples of *brit habat*. To find out about ordering this and other publications:

> The Jewish Women's Resource Center
> National Council of Jewish Women, New York Section
> 9 East 69th Street
> New York, NY 10021

Bar and Bat Mitzvah

Parents' Blessing

May you live to see your world fulfilled,
May your destiny be for worlds still to come,
And may you trust in generations past and yet to be.

May your heart be filled with intuition
and your words be filled with insight.
May songs of praise ever be upon your tongue
and your vision be on a straight path before you.
May your eyes shine with the light of holy words
and your face reflect the brightness of the heavens.
May your lips ever speak wisdom
and your fulfillment be in righteousness
even as you ever yearn to hear the words
of the Holy Ancient One of Old.[1]

According to the rules of Hebrew grammar, no one is ever *bar mitzvahed*. One *becomes* a *bar mitzvah*, "son of the commandment," or *bat mitzvah*, "daughter of the commandment." There is more to this distinction than grammar. The ceremonies called *bar* and *bat mitzvah*—the preparation and study, the public recognition, and the celebration—do not confer the status of *bar* or *bat mitzvah*. At the age of 13, Jews automatically become *bar* or *bat mitzvah*, full-fledged members of the community.

Still, the ceremony associated with this change of status has become one of Judaism's most potent rites of passage. *Bar* and *bat mitzvah* mark and celebrate a fundamental and irrevocable life change: the end of childhood. Although no one treats a 13-year-old as an adult, the beginning of adolescence is a momentous transition, one that many human cultures have marked with ritual and ceremony.

Traditionally, *bar/bat mitzvah* is understood as a ceremony that welcomes a young Jew into the formal, adult prayer life of the community. In a religious culture that stresses communal rather than individual prayer, it is a unique moment, the only ceremony that features one Jew acting solely on his or her own behalf. In celebrating the transition from childhood to puberty, *bar/bat mitzvah* ceremonies are also family rituals; moments that mark the beginning of major changes in family dynamics.

History

Bar mitzvah does not appear in the Bible, which gives the age of 20 as the time when adult obligations begin.[2] However, by the first century C.E., adulthood was universally held to begin at 13 for boys and 12 for girls, a view codified in the Talmud, which states, "At age 13, one becomes subject to the commandments."[3] The earliest reference to any ceremony to mark this change dates from the Second Temple period, when a special blessing was recited for 13-year-old boys who had completed their first Yom Kippur fast.[4] But, until the Middle Ages, the religious distinction between a 10-year-old and a 13-year-old was strictly theoretical. Children were regularly counted for the purposes of creating a *minyan*, the quorum of ten needed for certain prayers, so that reaching the age of 13 was not associated with any particular rituals or celebrations.[5]

That approach to ritual maturity changed drastically sometime between the 14th and 16th century in Germany and Poland, where minors were no longer permitted to read from the Torah or to be counted in a *minyan*. From that point in history, *bar mitzvah* became an important life-cycle event throughout the Jewish world. Boys were called to the Torah to symbolize the attainment of adult status in the prayer life of the community.

The central act of this rite was receiving the honor of an *aliyah*, of being called to bless and/or read from the Torah. However, other elements were soon added to the ceremony. As early as the 16th century, *bar mitzvah* boys were delivering *d'rashot*, discourses on the Torah portion they had read. In the 17th and 18th century, some synagogues permitted accomplished students to lead part of the service as well. As with every joyful occasion, or *simcha, bar mitzvah* carried with it the obligation of a *seudat mitzvah:* a commanded meal of celebration.

BAT MITZVAH

Because girls' coming of age was not connected with the performance of public religious rites, the notion of a parallel synagogue ceremony for girls was unthinkable before the modern era. In some German communities, families would hold a *seudah,* or party, on the occasion of a daughter's 12th birthday, and although a girl might deliver a speech and her father recite a blessing, this was not a religious celebration.

Bat mitzvah is a 20th century innovation. Although the Reform movement officially instituted equality between the sexes in the late 19th century, the first recorded *bat mitzvah* did not occur until 1922. It was celebrated by Judith Kaplan (Eisenstein), the eldest daughter of Mordecai Kaplan, the founder of the Reconstructionist movement. The practice did not become commonplace until the 1950s, first in Reform congregations and then in Conservative synagogues.

For many years, *bar* and *bat mitzvah* were distinctly different. Boys were usually expected to read or chant a Torah or *haftarah* portion on Saturday morning whereas girls were limited to a Friday night reading from the *haftarah.* The differences between *bar* and *bat mitzvah* have been steadily diminishing to the point that today, in many congregations, they are virtually indistinguishable. *Bar* and *bat mitzvah* are, therefore, treated interchangeably in this chapter.

Current Practice

Bar and *bat mitzvah* have a strong hold on the American Jewish community's loyalty and sense of identity. For many parents, the prospect of a child's turning 13 years old is the impetus for the first contact with the organized Jewish community since their wedding. Indeed, *bar* and *bat mitzvah* are the main reasons many American Jews send their children to religious school, or even affiliate with a synagogue.

Many synagogue religious schools have a curriculum that prepares students for *bar/bat mitzvah.* In addition to basic Hebrew reading, there may be smaller tutorial sessions with teachers and the rabbi or cantor, focusing on the text the student will be reading: a portion of Torah, the first five books of the Bible, and/or a reading from the *haftarah,* selections from the prophets associated with each week's Torah portion. Some parents also hire private tutors to work with their children on these readings.

To offset the tendency to stress a one-time performance over the process of Jewish learning, some congregations have instituted special programs for children studying for *bar/bat mitzvah.* The content of Torah portions might be explored in depth, and guest teachers may be invited to the classroom to talk about more "grown-up issues;" everything from sexual ethics to Israeli politics. Rabbis may schedule a private meeting with each child. There are often *mitzvah* requirements, such as doing volunteer work of some kind or collecting money for charity, and some synagogues schedule an annual weekend retreat for their *bar/bat mitzvah* class.

In theory, *bar/bat mitzvah* can take place at any service where the Torah is taken out and read. In practice, however, virtually all of them take place on *Shabbat.* Children are commonly assigned a date more than a year in advance. Some people try to schedule the occasion for the first *Shabbat* after the 13th birthday, though in large congregations with many dates to assign, the results can be rather random and there may even be two *bar/bat mitzvahs* scheduled for the same day.

Bar/bat mitzvah ceremonies vary enormously from one congregation to the next. In some synagogues, the *bar/bat mitzvah* leads part of the service, reading prayers in Hebrew and English, and leading songs and responsive readings. In other congregations, participation is limited to reading a Torah portion and making a speech of some kind. In some congregations, the liturgical participation for *bar/bat mitzvah* is always the same, whereas in others more accomplished students are given more to do.

At some synagogues, *bar/bat mitzvah* ceremonies are not held at the morning service but late in the afternoon, coinciding with the closing service of *Shabbat* and *havdalah.* But many people object to this practice, feeling that *bar/bat mitzvah* belongs within the context of communal worship, and that proximity to Saturday night overly "socializes" the event.

Synagogues tend to have a more or less standard format for *bar/bat mitzvah* ceremonies. Some rabbis and congregations are flexible and open to creative changes in the service, whereas others insist on closer adherence to congregational style. These are subjects to discuss early in the *bar/bat mitzvah* process. Children with special needs who wish to become *bar/bat mitzvah* are almost always accommodated with sensitivity and respect.

Despite the great variety in how *bar/bat mitzvah* are conducted, three elements are virtually universal: the *aliyah*, the speech, and the celebration.

THE ALIYAH

Receiving an *aliyah* means being called up to the *bimah* to recite the blessings for the Torah reading and/or to read from the scroll. A *bar mitzvah* may read or chant as little as three verses or as much as the entire weekly Torah portion. In some congregations, he will only read from the *haftarah*, and in others from both the *haftarah* and Torah.

On the day of a *bar mitzvah*, it is also customary to honor the young man's relatives with *aliyot* (the plural of *aliyah*). Parents, grandparents, siblings, uncles, aunts, and cousins may be called up to recite the Torah blessings, open the ark where the Torah is stored, and lift or "dress" the Torah.

THE SPEECH OR D'RASH

At some point in the service, the *bat mitzvah* usually delivers a speech of some kind. Although these are very personal and tend to include a fairly formal "thank you" to parents, siblings and teachers, the notorious, canned "Today I am a fountain pen" recitations of the 1950s are somewhat less common today.

More often, the *d'rash*, sometimes written as part of a religious school class or in consultation with the rabbi or parents, recalls its original purpose; of showing how the *bat mitzvah* has mastered some aspect of Jewish learning. Her remarks may focus on the content of the portion for the week, or just start from there. Many teachers see the *d'rash* as an opportunity for a young person to make an important statement about who she is and what she believes in. There is also almost always a second speech delivered by the rabbi. Often called the rabbi's "charge," this tends to be a kind of personal sermon addressed to the *bat mitzvah*.

ALTERNATIVES

Although an overwhelming majority of families choose to hold *bar/bat mitzvah* in a synagogue, they have also been celebrated in living rooms, function halls, and back yards. Do-it-yourself *bar/bat mitzvahs* tend to be small, intimate, and modest. This choice is sometimes made by people who are active in a *havurah* or *minyan*, small, self-directed groups of Jews who meet for study, community, and worship.[6] As Jewish religious services do not require the presence of a rabbi, the proceedings may be led by a learned family member or friend, or by the *bar mitzvah* himself. Some people consult with a teacher or rabbi for advice and assistance, or hire someone to run the service.

Obviously, this kind of *bar/bat mitzvah* places many more responsibilities on the planners because they must determine the nature and content of the service, and design and implement a curriculum for the *bar/bat mitzvah*. On the other hand, doing it at home or anywhere outside a synagogue means that the entire service can be tailored to reflect the beliefs and values of the family.

The most common alternative to the synagogue *bar/bat mitzvah*, however, is the *bar/bat mitzvah* in Israel. Families sometimes decide to travel to Israel and hold the ceremony at the Western Wall in Jerusalem (for boys only*) or at the historical ruins of Masada (for both boys and girls.)

This kind of trip—perhaps the first one to Israel for the whole family—can have a very powerful impact, and many people who have made this choice consider it a turning point in their Jewish commitment. Tour companies that specialize in *bar/bat mitzvah* trips to Israel make all necessary arrangements; they even provide the Torah. Some families celebrate a *bar/bat mitzvah* twice: within the context of their synagogue or *havurah*, and again in Israel.

---

* Orthodox rulings restrict public and communal observances and services for women at the Wall.

Celebrating

Although tradition dictates that there be a festive meal (*seudat mitzvah*) to mark the occasion of a *bar/bat mitzvah*, there are no Jewish laws or regulations regarding the celebration, also called a *simcha*. The most potent messages about how to celebrate *bar/bat mitzvah* emanate from congregational custom and children's peer groups.

Many American Jews put enormous amounts of energy and money into the celebration of *bar/bat mitzvah*, partially in response to social pressure. If everyone in the congregation puts on lavish, elegant parties, it may seem cheap not to do the same. Likewise, hiring clowns, offering a children's menu, and buying expensive party favors may seem mandatory if your child has been so entertained. Then again, some parents use the *bar/bat mitzvah* reception as a way to repay business obligations.

Many people have ridiculed and bemoaned the commercialization of *bar/bat mitzvah*. And there are legendary accounts of bad taste: huge ice sculptures in the shape of the *bar mitzvah* boy, monkeys wearing *yarmulkes*, even a caped super-hero character called "Captain *Bar Mitzvah*." One therapist compares this kind of conspicuous consumption to potlatch, a ceremonial feast among certain Indian tribes where the hosts actually destroyed property to demonstrate their wealth.[7]

This is not a new dilemma. During the Middle Ages, rabbis in many communities promulgated laws limiting the number of guests who could be invited to *bar mitzvah* celebrations, and even regulated what kinds of finery could be worn. In part, these laws were an attempt to stave off anti-Semitic sentiments about Jewish riches and ostentation; however, the rabbis were also concerned about unseemly excess that could overwhelm the religious significance of the day.

In reaction to modern excesses, and to help keep the focus on the ritual rather than social aspects of the day, some families plan more intimate parties, and less formal receptions. Although there is still great pressure to conform, there is a growing desire to personalize these celebrations. From this perspective, "personalize" means more than engraved matchbook covers or *yarmulkes* with the *bat/bar mitzvah*'s name inside. Making a celebration that genuinely reflects a family's beliefs and tastes can start with designing an invitation that features the *bat/bar mitzvah*'s own artwork or poetry, or contains a request that guests bring a can of food for distribution at a local shelter.

Increasingly, *tzedakah* (righteous giving, or charity) is becoming a focus for *bar/bat mitzvah* celebrations. In the small, close-knit Jewish communities of the past, beggars were invited to wedding and *bar mitzvah* feasts. Today, many families symbolically invite the poor to their celebratory meals by setting aside a voluntary tax of 3%; of the money spent for food to MAZON, A Jewish Response to Hunger, which funds soup kitchens, food pantries, and other feeding programs in the United States and around the world. (See the chapter "Good Deeds.")

It is, however, important to remember that children have social pressures of their own to contend with. Young adolescents want their party to be just like their friends' parties, and ignoring or dismissing the strong emotions of children at this age can be counterproductive. It makes sense to listen to their concerns and even compromise on details that seem crucial to a 13-year-old. Still, at this age, parents are making most decisions that affect their children's lives, and setting limits is as much part of planning a *bar/bat mitzvah* party as deciding on the menu. Besides, virtually every decision parents make about the *bar/bat mitzvah* celebration becomes a lesson. If parents pay more attention to the color scheme than to the Torah portion, the child learns that the religious ceremony is secondary to putting on a pretty show.

New Traditions

Traditionally, *bar/bat mitzvah* marks the beginning of commitment, the commencement of Jewish adulthood. In a community where synagogue attendance is the norm, a *bar/bat mitzvah* demonstrates this new status by wearing a *tallit* (prayershawl), or being asked to recite the blessings for Torah reading.

In practice, however, *bar/bat mitzvah* is often the end of Jewish commitment, marking graduation from Jewish study, permission to stop attending services, even withdrawal from synagogue membership. For the recent *bar/bat mitzvah* who attends services only during holidays or to attend a friend's *bar/bat mitzvah*, there is a real question about the lasting Jewish impact of this much anticipated ceremony.

To address this issue, Jewish families and institutions are exploring new ways of enacting the status of *bar/bat mitzvah:* at home, in religious school curricula and in synagogue custom. What follows are some of the ways people are attaching new meaning and privileges to the status of *bar/bat mitzvah*.

BEFORE THE BAR OR BAT MITZVAH

Some families inaugurate the *bar/bat mitzvah* year or "season" with special time for the child and parents. A weekend trip out of town, without siblings, is perhaps the most dramatic way to start. During the course of walking on the beach, visiting the museum of natural history, or eating at a grown-up restaurant, conversations about and plans for the coming year can begin. This is a good time to get input from the child, to set the tone for the celebration, and to begin the process of working together to create a meaningful day for the whole family.

Take the *bar/bat mitzvah* shopping for a *tallit.* Or help your child design and make a *tallit* bag.

Augment the religious school curriculum by selecting a few Jewish books and reading them together. Let the child select the titles. Make formal dates for your discussions at an ice cream parlor.

Work together on a family history and create a family tree.

In the week or two before the *bar/bat mitzvah,* go away for another weekend, or just take a long walk together to talk about the past year, about the ceremony, and also about what is going to happen in the coming year.

Some innovative religious schools run a weekend retreat for *bar/bat mitzvah* candidates, alone or with parents. Some schools offer a curriculum where parents and children take a course together.

DURING THE SERVICE AND CELEBRATION

Some, though not all, congregations welcome changes to the *bar/bat mitzvah* script. The addition of special readings, poems, prayers, and even music can add personal meaning to the ritual.

Most liberal congregations have dispensed with the traditional *bar/bat mitzvah* blessing that says, "Blessed is the One who has freed me from responsibility for this child's conduct." However, some synagogues have instituted ways for parents to participate in the *bar/bat mitzvah*. Fathers and mothers may be given the opportunity to address their child publicly, talking about their thoughts, feelings, and wishes on this occasion. And in some congregations, the Torah scroll is passed from grandparents to parents to the *bar/bat mitzvah,* in a gesture that symbolizes the passing of the tradition from one generation to the next.

There are countless ways of personalizing *bar/bat mitzvah* celebrations. In some communities, it is customary to have a candle-lighting cake ceremony at the reception. (Although as far as anyone can tell, this practice originated with Long Island caterers who were interested in selling large cakes.) Rather than have a paid master of ceremonies read a script about the "meaning" of each of the 13 candles on the cake, the *bar/bat mitzvah* can take the microphone and invite 13 guests to light one candle each, while explaining what each person means to her or him.

If there are floral centerpieces at the *simcha,* the *bar/bat mitzvah* and his or her family can deliver them to a local nursing home after the party. Alternately, money that might have been spent on flowers may be donated to some worthy cause, with a note on each table explaining that decision. Likewise, leftover food may be donated to local shelters for the homeless.

There are many ways to make *tzedakah* an important part of *bar/bat mitzvah.* In some families, a percentage of all money spent on the event is donated to charity, or a portion of all cash gifts is earmarked for *tzedakah.* If parents know that a particular relative plans to give money as a gift, they may request that donations be made to a charitable endowment instead; the *bar/bat mitzvah* then becomes trustee for this fund and decides which charities should receive interest payments.

THE YEAR AFTER

Many religious schools offer post-*bar/bat mitzvah* education in the form of confirmation or high school classes. Families can mark this new educational status with, for example, a special dinner on the first night of "Hebrew High."

Parents may give their child a *tzedakah* goal. The *bar/bat mitzvah* might be given a sum of money to distribute to charities of his or her choosing over the course of the year. Or some percentage of a weekly allowance or babysitting earnings might be earmarked for *tzedakah.*

Working in a food drive, or raising money for a local cause can all be encouraged in Jewish terms: as acts of *tzedakah*.

In addition to obligations, privileges might also be associated with becoming *bar/bat mitzvah:* anything from a night out with the other grown-ups to see a Jewish play, to a later bedtime.

At home, the *bar/bat mitzvah* can lead *Shabbat* blessings, or take charge of other aspects of family celebrations.

Synagogues can be enlisted to make the year after *bar/bat mitzvah* special. The new members of the community might be given special honors such as dressing or carrying the Torah, or reciting the blessings before and after the Torah is read. On the anniversary of a *bar/bat mitzvah,* the rabbi might acknowledge the occasion. The family can treat a *bar/bat mitzvah* as a kind of birthday, with a special meal or a gift.

Finally, it is important to remember that *bar/bat mitzvah* is a rite of passage not only for children, but also for parents and families. Looking in the mirror, parents suddenly see people who are old enough to have a child of *bar/bat mitzvah* age, a child who is maturing sexually, a child who is beginning to have strong opinions about everything under the sun. Watching a son or daughter stand, Torah in arms in front of the whole congregation, can be a revelation for parents who see both baby fat and new self-confidence, and realize their family unit no longer includes yesterday's beloved little one. And as the child begins a new stage of·development, the family must also change if it is to remain healthy. Parents need to recognize their child's new maturity, and to respond to it appropriately.

Marriage

To the Jewish imagination, the wedding is a prototypical act of creation. The *Zohar*, the great book of Jewish mysticism, states, "God creates new worlds constantly. In what way? By causing marriages to take place."[1] The wedding is the premiere life-cycle event. Although the core of the ritual is simplicity itself, the customs, symbols and rituals associated with Jewish weddings spill over into more than a year's worth of celebration and joy.

Until recently, it seemed that conspicuous consumption and the urge to assimilate would overwhelm the Jewish wedding. However, modern practice has begun to move the focus of the wedding away from the guests, the menu, the gifts, and the spectacle, and onto the "new world" created by the love of the bride and groom.

Reb Nachman of Bratslav, a 17th century Hasidic master, is credited with a wonderful story on this subject:

A group of people who have been to a wedding are walking home when one says, "That was a beautiful wedding. The food was out of this world." One of her companions says, "It was a great wedding. The band was terrific." A third friend chimes in, "I never had more fun at a wedding. I got to talk to people I hadn't seen in years."

But Reb Nachman, who overhears this conversation, says, "Those people weren't really at a wedding."

Then a fourth person joins the group and says, "Isn't it wonderful that those two people found each other!" At that Reb Nachman says, "Now *that* person was at a wedding!"

At their best, Jewish weddings are simultaneously reverent and hilarious; delicious and *schmaltzy;* intimate and communal; mysterious, romantic and revealing. And everyone who has been there feels like they witnessed some sort of miracle.

Symbols, Laws, and Customs

The Jewish wedding is the focus for a whole season of preparation and celebration. There are parties and rituals, customs and symbols, and documents and gifts to fill the months from the first announcement of an engagement to the wedding day and after. The following discussion of symbols, laws, and customs are only selections from the much longer wedding menu.

THE HUPPAH

Jewish marriage ceremonies take place beneath a *huppah,* which is basically a canopy supported by four poles. Although there are customs and conventions about the most appropriate location for a wedding, a *huppah* can be raised anywhere, reflecting the Jewish notion that almost any place can be made a holy place by human action and intention.

The *huppah* is a multifaceted symbol of home, garment, bedcovering, and a reminder of the tents of the ancient Hebrews. During the 16th century, the vogue was for a portable canopy held aloft by four friends, a custom that remains popular to this day.

Some couples have embraced the old custom of using a prayershawl, or *tallit,* as a canopy, a symbol that affirms a commitment to creating a Jewish home. People also commission or make beautiful canopies using batik, silk-screen, weaving, quilting, and embroidery. These become instant heirlooms and are often displayed in the married couple's home, on a wall or even suspended as a canopy over the bed. Some couples raise their *huppah* again later in life over a son's *brit milah* or a daughter's *brit habat* ceremony. (See the chapter called "Birth.")

TIMING

Although a *huppah* can be raised almost anywhere, Jewish law is far more prescriptive about the timing of weddings. Marriages do not take place on the Sabbath, nor on the major holidays and festivals, including

Rosh Hashanah, Yom Kippur, Passover, Shavuot, and Sukkot. Weddings are forbidden on *Shabbat* not only because the work and travel involved could violate the Sabbath spirit of rest, but also because of the injunction against mixing one *simcha* (or joy) with another. The combining of two kinds of happiness risks that one or both of them will not be given their full due, which is why double weddings are discouraged.

THE KETUBAH

The Jewish marriage contract is one of the oldest elements of the Jewish wedding. It is also one of the least romantic. In its traditional form, the *ketubah*—a word derived from the Hebrew for "to write"—does not mention love, trust, the establishment of a Jewish home, or God. The *ketubah* is a legal contract, plain and simple: it is written in Aramaic, the technical language of Talmudic law, not the poetic biblical Hebrew of Song of Songs.[2]

When it came into use during the first century C.E., the *ketubah* was considered a great advance for its time, in part because it provided women with legal status and rights in marriage. Over the centuries, it has changed very little. Indeed, a contemporary traditional *ketubah* is very much like a marriage contract from over 1,000 years ago, complete with phrases such as:

> And I here present you with the marriage gift of virgins, two hundred silver zuzim, which belongs to you, according to the law of Moses and Israel; and I will also give you your food, clothing and necessities, and live with you as husband and wife according to the universal custom. And this maiden consented and became his wife. The trousseau that she brought to him from her father's house in

---

From every human being there rises a light that reaches straight to heaven. And when two souls that are destined to be together find each other, their streams of light flow together, and a single brighter light goes forth from their united being.

the Baal Shem Tov
founder of Hasidism

---

silver, gold, valuables, clothing, furniture and bedclothes, all this the bridegroom accepted in the sum of 100 silver pieces.

Obviously, these terms have nothing to do with relationships between women and men today. Thus, since the early 1970s, rabbis, calligraphers, brides and grooms have been writing new *ketubot,* the plural of *ketubah.* These documents not only express mutual and egalitarian obligations and commitments, they can also be a way for couples to give voice to their feelings for each other and hopes for their marriage. Some new *ketubot* make additions to the original text, but many are wholly original. Beautifully calligraphed, illustrated, and illuminated *ketubot* may be commissioned or purchased in Judaic shops or through catalogs.

Whatever the exact content, the text of modern *ketubot* tends to be simple and brief, in keeping with other Jewish ritual documents. Generally, modern *ketubot* are written both in English and Hebrew, and signed by the bride, groom, witnesses, and rabbi, cantor, or other officiant. One example of a modern *ketubah* reads:

> On the first day toward *Shabbat,* the _____ day of _____, in the year five thousand _____ since the creation of the world according to our accustomed reckoning in _____, _____ (bride's name) and _____ (groom's name), in the presence of beloved family and friends entered into this covenant with each other.

> We promise to consecrate ourselves, one to the other as husband and wife, according to the tradition of Moses and Israel; to love, honor and cherish each other; to work together to create a home faithful to the teachings of Torah, reverent of the Divine, and committed to deeds of lovingkindness. We promise to try always to bring out in ourselves and in each other qualities of forgiveness, compassion, and integrity. All this we take upon ourselves to uphold to the best of our abilities.

> Groom _____
> Bride _____
> We affirm the mutual agreement of the bride and groom. All this is confirmed and abiding.

> Witness _____
> Witness _____

> Rabbi _____

RABBIS AND WITNESSES

In a Jewish wedding, the bridal couple actually marry each other with their own words and actions. However, it is customary to have an officiant, a person called a *mesader kiddushin*, literally, one who "orders (or leads) the sanctification." Although any knowledgeable Jew can recite the necessary blessings at a wedding, cantors and rabbis almost always perform this honor. Most rabbis and cantors also meet with the couple in advance of the wedding. These meetings often involve discussions about marriage and the establishment of a Jewish home, as well as plans for the ceremony.

Two impartial witnesses are required to make a Jewish wedding "kosher" or binding. Neither of the witnesses may be related to either the bride or groom, so they can have no emotional, social, or economic stake in the marriage. Because they are such important participants, it has been suggested that witnesses assume a special kind of responsibility for the marriage, to offer aid and support especially in times of trouble.

The Wedding

The essence of the Jewish wedding ceremony can be summed up in a few words: the bride accepts an object worth more than a dime from the groom, and the groom recites a ritual formula of consecration. If these two actions are witnessed by at least two other people, a wedding has taken place.

Over the centuries, some of the customs and traditions that surround this simple ceremony have taken on almost equal authority and importance; some of these are described on the following pages, in brief.

The Baal Shem Tov said that if a couple was fighting, they should read the ketubah aloud to one another to help them remember the day of their marriage, when they affirmed their love for each other.

THE PROCESSIONAL

In a standard Hollywood wedding, the father escorts his daughter down the aisle and gives her away. The Jewish custom is very different. Both parents lead their children—sons as well as daughters—to the *huppah* and to marriage. No one is "given away." Indeed, the Jewish processional demonstrates how a marriage is a union of families, not just individuals.

In some communities, it is customary for members of the processional to light the way with candles; a hand-held *huppah* can also be part of the processional. But the most common way of welcoming the bride and groom to the *huppah* is with music. In ancient times, the sounds of flutes greeted the bride and groom, and Yemenite brides are sometimes preceded by a group of singing women. In America, string quartets, organs, choirs, soloists, or the guests themselves perform this customary honor.

UNDER THE HUPPAH

Before the 11th century, the Jewish wedding was comprised of two distinct rituals separated by as much as a year. The first of these was betrothal or *kiddushin*, from the same root as the word *kadosh*, or holy. After betrothal, the bride and groom were considered legally wed, and a formal bill of divorce was necessary to dissolve the marriage. Even so, the marriage was not consummated until after the next ceremony, the nuptials or *nissuin*. Nissuin derives from the verb *nasa*, which means to carry or lift, and may refer to the days when a bride was carried through the streets to her new home. The nuptials are not accomplished by words, but in a symbolic act of intimacy called *yichud*. Betrothal designates the bride and groom *for* each other only; nuptials give them *to* one another.

It has been ten centuries since these two ceremonies were made into one, but Jewish weddings still show the seam where they were joined. The presence of two cups of wine, one for each ceremony, is a reminder of the time when two separate ceremonies were begun with *kiddush*, the prayer of sanctification recited over wine.

CIRCLING

Just before the ceremony begins, it is customary for the bride to circle the groom, either three times or seven times. Circling is a magical means of protection, so the bride builds a wall against evil spirits by walking around the groom. The bride's circle has also been interpreted as a gesture that binds the groom to her.

Many Jews abandoned this custom, both because of its magical connotations and because of the apparent subservience in the bride's action. Recently, however, some couples have reclaimed the gesture, interpreting it as a bride's way of defining the space the couple will share. The action itself has also been made more egalitarian by having bride and groom circle each other in turn or walk around each other simultaneously, holding each other's hands.

BETROTHAL (KIDDUSHIN)

Most Jewish weddings begin with two introductions. The first one is addressed to the people gathered, especially the bride and groom. The second, a prayer asking for God's presence at and blessing of the marriage, is called the ''*Mi Adir.*''

> Splendor is upon everything
> Blessing is upon everything
> May the One Who is full of this abundance
> Bless this groom and bride.[3]

Next comes the recitation of *kiddush,* which begins virtually all Jewish observances and celebrations. There has been a recent revival of an old European custom of using a special wedding cup or a matched pair of goblets made by Jewish artists.

The next blessing, the betrothal blessing, was once recited a full year before the nuptials. Thus, it includes a very specific warning that betrothed couples are not sexually permitted to one another until after the next ritual takes place.

> Praised are You Adonai, Ruler of the universe, who has made us holy through Your commandments and has commanded us concerning sexual propriety, forbidding to us those who are merely betrothed, but permitting to us those who are married to us through *huppah* and *kiddushin.* Blessed are You, Adonai, who makes Your people Israel holy through *huppah* and *kiddushin.*

This blessing tends to be translated very loosely. For example:

> Praised are you Adonai, Ruler of the universe, who has made us holy through Your commandments and has commanded us concerning marriages that are forbidden and those that are permitted when carried out under the canopy and with the sacred wedding ceremonies.

The wine is drunk after this blessing is recited. In some communities the first cup of wine is shared with members of the immediate family.

Next comes the core of the ceremony; the groom's giving and the bride's acceptance of a ring. As he gives her the ring, the groom recites the words that literally marry them. It is called the *Haray aht*, and because it is essential that both bride and groom understand the meaning of these words, the phrase is recited both in Hebrew and English, or whatever language the couple knows best.

Haray aht m'kudeshet li b'taba'at zu k'dat Moshe v'Yisrael.

By this ring you are consecrated to me in accordance with the traditions of Moses and Israel.

The bride is not legally required to say or do anything when she receives the ring. However, in many ceremonies today, the bride replies either with a line from Songs of Songs ("I am my beloved's and my beloved is mine"), or with the same words the groom addressed to her (adapted for gender), which, in effect, equalizes the wedding ritual.

Haray ata m'kudash li b'taba'at zu k'dat Moshe v'Yisrael.

By this ring you are consecrated to me in accordance with the traditions of Moses and Israel.

The Jewish wedding liturgy contains no wedding vows or "I do's." However, because an expression of intention is such a powerful image in American culture, and because couples often feel a need to say "yes" during the ceremony, many rabbis and couples add vows either just prior to or immediately following the ring ceremony. Most rabbis and cantors avoid the "To have and to hold, to honor and obey" formulas common to secular and Christian wedding ceremonies. Instead, vows or promises can be personal and specific. Sometimes they are taken from the *ketubah,* or are written by the bride and groom themselves.

The ring ceremony completes betrothal/*kiddushin.* At this juncture it has been customary, almost since the beginning of the combined betrothal-and-nuptials wedding in the 12th century, to make a clear separation. Traditionally, this is done by reading the *ketubah* or part of it, and generally, this is when the rabbi makes a short speech. Sometimes, there are personal additions to the ceremony as well: songs, poems, or personal prayers by family members and friends.

NUPTIALS (NISSUIN)

This ceremony consists of two elements: the seven wedding blessings, *sheva b'rachot,* and the seclusion of the bridal couple, called *yichud.*

Although a wedding *requires* only two witnesses to be valid, a *minyan*—ten adult Jews—must be present for the seven blessings to be recited. Generally, the rabbi or cantor chants the wedding blessings, but there is also a long tradition of honoring special guests by asking them to read or chant one or more of them. In one Sephardic tradition, parents cover the bride and groom with a prayershawl before the seven wedding blessings are recited.

Although the seven blessings comprise the longest part of the wedding liturgy, only the last two have anything to say about weddings or brides and grooms. Read as a whole, however, they situate the bride and groom within the entire span of Jewish time. The seven blessings mention the beginning of time in Eden when life was perfect, and the end of days when that perfection, or wholeness, will be restored. A nexus between the first and the last, every wedding becomes the embodiment of union and unity. And because Judaism has no concept of individual redemption, the *huppah* provides the whole community with a glimpse into the unbroken, healed reality that once was and will be again.

The seven blessings are as follows:

1. You abound in Blessings, Adonai our God, who creates the fruit of the vine.*

2. You abound in Blessings, Adonai our God, you created all things for Your glory.

3. You abound in Blessings, Adonai our God, you created humanity.

4. You abound in Blessings, Adonai our God, You made humankind in Your image, after Your likeness, and You prepared from us a perpetual relationship. You abound in Blessings, Adonai our God, you created humanity.

5. May she who was barren rejoice when her children are united in her midst in joy. You abound in Blessings, Adonai our God, who makes Zion rejoice with her children.

6. You make these beloved companions greatly rejoice even as You rejoiced in Your creation in the Garden of Eden as of old. You abound in Blessings, Adonai our God, Who makes the bridegroom and bride to rejoice.

7. You abound in Blessings, Adonai our God, who created joy and gladness, bridegroom and bride, mirth and exultation, pleasure and delight, love, fellowship, peace and friendship. Soon may there be heard in the cities of Judah and in the streets of Jerusalem, the voice of joy and gladness, the voice of the bridegroom and the voice of the bride, the jubilant voice of bridegrooms from their canopies and of youths from their feasts of songs. You abound in Blessings, Adonai our God, You make the bridegroom rejoice with the bride.

The seven blessings conclude the marriage service. Some rabbis give the wedding sermon at this point, and others end with the official secular pronouncement ". . . by the power vested in me by the state of . . ." Some cantors and rabbis conclude with a benediction.

THE BROKEN GLASS

The shattering of a glass to mark the end of the wedding is a practice that dates back to the writing of the Talmud and has become one of the

---

* The words, "Baruch ata Adonai Eloheynu Melech ha-olam" introduces most Jewish blessings. The most familiar English translation for the Hebrew is "Blessed art Thou, Lord our God, King of the Universe." This is one of several English versions of this formula that do not address God as a male monarch.

most kaleidoscopic of all Jewish wedding symbols. The broken glass is a joyous conclusion that encourages merriment at the meal of rejoicing to follow. In modern times weddings have become rather solemn, and the shattering gives permission for levity to break out. There is an irony in this because, according to one traditional explanation, the glass-breaking may have originated at one particularly raucous wedding party, as a way of calming things down.[4]

By the 14th century, the broken glass was generally interpreted as a reminder of the destruction of the Temple of Jerusalem, and of the fact that even at moments of personal joy, Jews remember that terrible loss. This remains the dominant interpretation, although it is generally broadened to include all of the losses suffered by the Jewish people, and also the need for the repair and redemption of the whole world. The breaking is not only a reminder of sorrow, but also an expression of hope for a future free from all violence.

There are other interpretations as well: A broken glass cannot be mended; likewise, marriage is a transforming experience that leaves individuals forever changed. The fragility of glass also suggests the frailty of human relationships; even the strongest love is subject to disintegration. In this context, the glass is broken to "protect" the marriage with the implicit wish that, "As this glass shatters, so may our marriage never break."

Loud noises are also an ageless method for frightening and appeasing demons whom, it was widely believed, were attracted to the beautiful and the fortunate: people like brides and grooms. And the breaking of a glass has the sexual connotation of a symbolic enactment of breaking the hymen. In a more general way, the breaking glass hints at the intensity and release of sexual union, which is not only allowed to married couples but required of them.

The sound of breaking glass signals the end of the ceremony. The silence that surrounded the *huppah* ends with an explosion. People exhale, shout *"mazal tov!"* clap their hands, embrace, talk, and sing the traditional wedding song, *"Siman tov u'mazal tov"* as the couple departs.

YICHUD

After they leave the *huppah*, bride and groom traditionally spend ten or fifteen minutes alone together. *Yichud*, or seclusion, is a custom that dates from ancient days when a groom would carry the bride off to his tent to consummate the marriage. Although consummation has not immediately followed the wedding ceremony for many centuries, these moments of private time have remained as a demonstration of the couple's new level of intimacy.

Yichud has been described as a period of bonding, an island of privacy and peace before the public celebration begins. It is a time for bride and groom to hold one another, to face one another, to let it all sink in.

Celebrating

"Reception" is too formal a word for the celebration of a wedding. *Simcha* is more accurate. *Simcha* mans joy as well as the celebration of a joyous event, and the purpose of Jewish wedding parties is to increase the joy of the bride and groom. The Talmud says that anyone who enjoys a wedding feast but does nothing to rejoice the hearts of the bride and groom has transgressed against the "five voices:" the voice of joy, the voice of gladness, the voice of the bridegroom, the voice of the bride, and the voice that praises God.

The meal that follows a Jewish wedding is a *seudat mitzvah,* a meal that fulfills a religious commandment to rejoice. At a wedding, everything that increases happiness—words of Torah, blessings, songs, dances, toasts, riddles, jokes, and parodies; indeed anything that make the bride and groom laugh—is considered a religious act, a way of praising God.

In order to ensure the *mitzvah* of entertaining the bride and groom, some couples have revived the role and title of *badchan,* which means "joker." The *badchan's* job is to act as master of ceremonies for the celebration by making toasts, telling jokes, and organizing and eliciting performances from other guests. Sentiment as well as foolishness plays a part in this assignment, thus a *badchan* may start by reading a love poem, then lead the guests in a song or *"mazel tov"* cheer, crown the "royal" couples with paper crowns, and tell the band when to play a slow song for romantic dancing.

Perhaps the best-known of all Jewish wedding dance customs is the moment at which the bride and groom are raised up on chairs and whirled around each other holding either end of a handkerchief. The custom may have originated as a way for the bride and groom to catch a glimpse of one another over the physical barrier that separated the rejoicing of the women from the men. But it may also be an echo of the privileges of royalty, who have been carried in chairs and on litters from earliest times.

THE FIRST YEAR

Since Biblical times, a couple is referred to as "bride and groom" for their entire first year together. That year begins with a week of parties. According to one tradition, a *minyan* of friends gather with the couple each night for a week for a meal, blessings, and songs; this practice is also called *sheva brachot* for the seven blessings recited nightly in their honor.

The year-long public recognition of the special status of bride and groom is a way for the couple and the community to savor the joy and gladness of the wedding. The designations "husband" and "wife" only apply after the first anniversary.

Intermarriage

When a Jew announces his or her decision to marry a non-Jew, red lights tend to start flashing. For the most part, the Jewish community perceives intermarriage as a threat to the continuation of the Jewish people. Relatively few rabbis officiate at interfaith marriages, and couples who feel personally rejected by this position rarely understand its basis in Jewish law.

A Jewish wedding has legal standing when two witnesses see the bride accept a ring from the groom and hear him say, "With this ring you are consecrated to me according to the laws of Moses and Israel." A rabbi does not marry a bride and groom, they marry each other with these words and gestures. Thus, if one of the parties is not bound "by the laws of Moses and Israel," the marriage has no standing.

Another reason for rabbis' reluctance to participate in intermarriage ceremonies is that the major function of Jewish weddings is to establish Jewish homes and families. According to traditional Jewish Law, children born to non-Jewish mothers are not considered Jews. Recent demographic evidence has shown that very few children of mixed-faith marriages identify with the Jewish world.

Strong feelings about intermarriage tend to overwhelm and ignore the dilemmas facing many intermarrying couples. However, there are individuals in most cities and towns—among them counselors at Jewish agencies, rabbis, and cantors—who are willing to listen and discuss the ways intermarrying couples can affirm their connection to Judaism through the wedding. Many rabbis suggest that couples seek out a judge or justice of the peace to perform a ceremony that includes Jewish references and symbols.

Some rabbis and cantors do officiate at weddings between Jews and non-Jews, not as a matter of course but on a case-by-case basis. Such rabbis agree to officiate when the non-Jew has no religious affiliation and both people express a willingness to create a Jewish home. These interfaith weddings, which may not include all the liturgical elements of a traditional Jewish wedding, are seen as ways of encouraging couples to become members of the Jewish community, and to raise Jewish children.

But the only option that satisfies the entire Jewish community is the conversion of the non-Jewish partner to Judaism. Once a non-Jew has become a Jew, intermarriage is no longer an issue. See the chapter "New Traditions" for more regarding conversion. However, it must be noted that Orthodox Jews and the state of Israel recognize only those conversions supervised by Orthodox rabbis.

FURTHER READING

The New Jewish Wedding by Anita Diamant (Summit Books, 1985). A guide to the traditions—contemporary as well as traditional—of the Jewish wedding. This book of customs is geared to helping brides and grooms create Jewishly meaningful wedding ceremonies for themselves.

The Jewish Marriage Anthology by Philip and Hanna Goodman (Jewish Publication Society, 1965). This book contains excerpts from the Bible, Talmud, and Midrash, as well as historical essays, short stories, poems, songs, and customs that relate to Jewish weddings.

The Jewish Way in Love and Marriage by Rabbi Maurice Lamm (Harper & Row, 1980). A comprehensive compendium of Jewish wedding law and custom from an Orthodox point of view.

New Traditions

The Jewish community is changing. More people are choosing to become Jews. Many Jews are creating families through adoption. Feminism has transformed the ways Jewish women and men conceive of themselves in relation to each other and in relation to the Holy. Divorce, once rare, is commonplace. For a tradition that sanctifies the passage of time in so many ways, the need for ritual responses to these important changes is clear. The need is being met with a broad range of celebrations and rites of passage.

Of course, little of this is entirely "new" to Judaism; conversion and adoption are featured in the biblical stories of Ruth and Moses, and the Talmud is very specific regarding divorce. However, the traditional Jewish canon does not always address the emotional and spiritual needs of people who are choosing Judaism, adopting children, divorcing spouses, or exploring the limits of gender today. Which is why the apparently contradictory term "new traditions" makes sense. Jews are reimagining and restructuring ancient ceremonies and creating new ritual forms, new pieces of the frame.

Conversion

The Jewish attitude toward conversion has changed dramatically. Although tradition required that rabbis try to rebuff people interested in converting, today the door is wide open. Where conversion for the purpose of marriage was once treated as suspect, today rabbis and Jewish organizations welcome and even solicit interest from non-Jews planning to marry or already married to Jewish spouses.

In large part, this change is a response to the fact that as many as half of all American Jews marry non-Jews, and thus the fear that there will be no "next generation" of American Jews. There is also a renewed and self-confident sense that Judaism is an intrinsically fulfilling way of life that appeals to people for many different reasons. For whatever reason it is pursued, however, choosing Judaism is a major and momentous decision. One who makes this decision seriously and sincerely is called a "righteous proselyte" or *ger tzedek,* from the same root as *tzadik,* or "righteous/holy person."

The Reform and Conservative movements in many cities offer "Introduction to Judaism" courses, which can be a good way to begin exploring the possibility of conversion. These courses vary both in content and form, but they generally cover a broad range of subjects: history, theology, Sabbath and holiday observance, Israel, the Holocaust, an introduction to the Hebrew alphabet, and some basic prayers. Students are also encouraged to make Jewish choices by attending worship services and trying out home observances.

Although many people begin by taking a class, the primary experience of becoming Jewish is private study with one rabbi. Serious candidates for conversion find a rabbi with whom they meet privately for some period of time. The content and duration of these meetings depend on the rabbi's requirements and the student's level of interest and diligence. When a rabbi determines that a student is ready, he or she will explain and schedule the ritual elements of conversion.

Jewish law requires *mikvah* (ritual immersion) for men and women, and circumcision or ritual circumcision (drawing one drop of blood from an already circumcised foreskin) for men. Converts also meet with a *bet din,* which means literally "house of law," and is a Jewish court that usually consists of three rabbis who examine the candidate about his or her knowledge of Judaism. Not all liberal rabbis require their students to participate in all these rituals, although the tendency is to do them all in some form.

Mikvah, immersion in a ritual bath accompanied by two short prayers, is required of all converts to Judaism, regardless of sex or age. Like virtually all religious traditions, Judaism treats water as the symbol of rebirth and renewal. The *mikvah* also represents the source of human life, the waters of the womb. According to one legend, the "living water" of *mikvah* flows from the mystical source of all water and all life, the river whose source is in Eden.[1]

Circumcision and ritual circumcision pose the biggest dilemmas for male converts, and this is a subject best discussed with a rabbi. The importance of *brit milah*, the covenant of circumcision, is discussed in the chapter on "Birth."

Although people often get anxious about meeting with a *bet din*, the fact is that this gathering is not really a "test." People are virtually never "failed" because rabbis do not bring unqualified candidates to a panel of their peers. As a rule, liberal *bet dins* tend to be far less concerned with dates and facts and Hebrew fluency than they are with a candidate's motivation for conversion and his or her understanding of basic Jewish concepts and practices.

Historically, conversion to Judaism has been a private occasion. Indeed, focusing attention on conversion was seen as an abrogation of respect because it is considered inappropriate to refer to a Jew by choice as a "convert." A Jew by choice is a Jew. Period. This is a position shared by some converts to this day who prefer to keep this life-change entirely private.

However, some Jews by choice wish to publicly acknowledge their life-passage, to make it a *simcha*, the celebration of a joyful event, not only for an individual, but also for their family, and indeed the entire Jewish community. There are many ways of celebrating conversion; some are intimate, some very public.

People may bring a few close friends or family members to the *mikvah* or even to the meeting with the *bet din*; after the formal conversion is over, everyone shares a festive meal. Sometimes, a recent convert to Judaism is acknowledged at a worship service. The rabbi may call the person up to the Torah for a blessing and to introduce the congregation's "newest Jew" by his or her new Hebrew name. Some Jews-by-choice address a speech or *d'rash* to the congregation and then sponsor a festive meal afterwards: a *seudat mitzvah*.

Finally, conversion raises many complex issues within the Jewish world about "who is a Jew." The Orthodox community and the state of Israel recognize conversions performed only under Orthodox auspices, a position that may have ramifications for the children of Jews converted by Reform, Reconstructionist, and Conservative rabbis. This is a subject to discuss in depth with a rabbi.

Adoption

If you turned to this section first, you may already know that as many as one in six American couples has difficulty conceiving. This explains why more and more American Jews are turning to adoption as a way of completing their families.

For many people, adoption is a difficult choice that usually means acknowledging the loss of a cherished dream. Experts agree that the need to grieve for the loss of that dream—the expectation of a biological child—is crucial before starting the adoption process. Although adopting a child is rarely easy, there are well-established networks to guide and comfort people through the process.

Adoption is no longer a rarity in the Jewish world, nor is it a stigma. The emerging Jewish view of adoption has been eloquently expressed by Rabbi Daniel Shevitz, the father of two adopted sons, who writes, "As long as there are children in need of homes, and loving homes in need of children, adoption should be encouraged as an act of piety and love." [2]

Jewish law on adoption is sketchy, though the rabbis of the Talmud looked kindly on the actions of Pharaoh's daughter, the most famous of all adoptive mothers. And there is a tradition saying that one who raises a child is called its parent, not the ones who conceived it.

Today, Jewish adoptive parents have some special resources available to them. Many Jewish family agencies provide support services for adoptive families, ranging from help with special-needs children to family counseling, to Hannukah parties. Stars of David is a nonprofit, national support network for Jewish adoptive families. Founded in 1984, Stars of David has active chapters in cities from coast to coast. Members include Jews of all affiliations, interfaith couples, single parents, prospective parents, interracial couples with biological children, and grandparents. It publishes a national newsletter for its members and local programs include holiday parties, lectures and panel discussions, and general information-sharing. (For more information, see "Further Reading" at the end of this chapter.)

According to Jewish law, the adoption of a baby who was born to a non-Jewish mother requires a formal conversion, which entails ritual immersion, *mikvah*, for both girls and boys, and circumcision, *brit milah*, for boys. *Mikvah* is the only ritual requirement for the conversion of girls. Baby girls are named either immediately following immersion or sometime later in a synagogue or at home, in a *brit habat* or adoption ceremony. An uncircumcised adopted male newborn is given a *brit milah* on the eighth day after birth, or as soon as possible. For a baby adopted at four months or older, circumcisions are generally done under anesthesia in a hospital, with both a physician and a *mohel* (ritual circumciser) in attendance. If a boy was circumcised without religious ceremony, a ritual is performed in which a *mohel* draws a drop of blood from the site of the circumcision and recites the appropriate blessings. (See the chapter on "Birth" for more on circumcision.)

Again, liberal rabbis interpret Jewish law in different ways. The Reform and Reconstructionist movements recognize the Jewishness of children not born of a Jewish mother who are given a Jewish upbringing both in religious school and at home, who celebrate Jewish holidays, and who publicly identify with the Jewish people. Parents who are in the process of adopting a non-Jewish child are well-advised to discuss these issues with a rabbi.

Because the rituals provided by tradition may not acknowledge the special feelings of joy, gratitude, and awe that adoptive parents feel, new Jewish adoption ceremonies, such as the one that follows, are being created and usually performed in addition to *mikvah* and *brit milah*. As there is no precedent for these rituals, their timing, location, and content are entirely determined by the parents, often with assistance from a rabbi.

Brit Imuts
Covenant of Adoption[3]

The baby is carried into the room by one grandparent and handed to others if they are present. The parents explain the nature of the ceremony and tell the story of the baby's name, commonly selected to honor the memory of a relative who has died.

The baby is placed on the knees of his adoptive parents, who then take the following oath.

"We solemnly swear, by the One who is called loving and merciful, that we will raise this child as our own. We will nurture him, sustain him, and guide him in the paths of Torah, in accordance with the duties incumbent upon Jewish parents. May God ever be with him. We pray for the wisdom and strength to help our child _____, become a man of integrity and kindness."

May the One who saved me from all evil, bless this boy, and let him be called by our name and the names of our ancestors and may he multiply throughout the land.*

The priestly benediction** is recited, followed by the *sheheheyanu*.

The child is showered with wishes and blessings from family and friends.

Kiddush is recited, and a meal to celebrate the occasion, a *seudat mitzvah*, is served.

Women's Lives

Until the modern era, Jewish public life was an all-male arena. In the synagogue, women sat in the balcony, in the back or behind a curtain. With the exception of weddings and funerals, Jewish women were ritually invisible: except at home. At home, women were responsible for the lighting of *Shabbat* candles, and the preparation of *challah*. They were also charged with obeying the laws of ritual purity; going to the ritual bath, *mikvah*, after menstruation. Clearly, they were also responsible for a great deal more. The fact that Jewishness is a traditionally matrilineal status alludes to the importance of the woman who shapes the hearts of her children.

In the past, most of Jewish women's spiritual life resided in informal and unrecorded events, in prayers, songs, conversations, and wisdom heard around the kitchen table. It is tempting to imagine a counter-history, a counter-practice of Judaism known only to the women. Clues

---

* This prayer is based on the words of the patriarch Jacob, spoken when he adopted his two grandsons, Menashe and Ephraim.
For a girl, the following quotation from the book of Ruth may be substituted: "Be blessed of the Lord, daughter and have no fear. I will do on your behalf whatever you ask. For you will be a fine woman."
** See index.

of such a tradition remain: Sephardic brides bring their friends to the *mikvah* where they have a party with music and abundant sweets. *Brisitzah*—a feminine version of the Yiddish word *bris* or covenant—is all that remains of an Ashkenazic custom, a ritual perhaps, at the birth of a daughter.[4]

The remnants are tantalizing, but the questions are even more compelling: In the Torah, a woman who delivered a boy child was kept apart from the community for 33 days.[5] If she bore a daughter, she vanished for twice that time. What happened in that extra month? Who attended mother and infant daughter? What special songs and jokes and secrets were whispered to the next generation of mothers? Which amulets did the midwives carry to the woman who had miscarried?

Today, these sorts of questions are the subjects of national conferences, poetry, and informal study groups. Laywomen, rabbis, scholars, and students research, write, and teach about Jewish women's history. Poets no longer refer to God as "Father" or "King," but as "Shelter" or "Breath." And today, women are exploring ways to observe the unmarked events and passages of their lives such as puberty, weaning, infertility, abortion, miscarriage, a last child's departure for college, and menopause.

One of the most popular forums for this process of recovery and discovery is the Rosh Hodesh group, a gathering that has roots both in ancient Jewish lore and modern feminism. Rosh Hodesh, literally "the head of the month," is the semiholiday that celebrates every new moon. In the past, Rosh Hodesh was a special holiday for women, a day on which women were forbidden to do their usual work.

The reason given for this special dispensation comes from a legend about the golden calf, the idol that the restive Hebrews fashioned when Moses was gone to talk to God on Mount Sinai. According to the story, when the men asked them to add their rings and golden jewelry to help create the calf, the women refused. Thus, God gave the new moon as a holiday to women so that they would be rejuvenated like the moon in the sky.

Today, groups of Jewish women gather on or around the time of the new moon, in the spirit of feminist consciousness-raising groups, to talk about what it means to be a Jewish woman. In synagogue classrooms and one another's living rooms, they discuss their names and for whom they were named. They study the Torah with special attention to the matriarchs and other female characters. Groups often focus on the women associated with each Hebrew month (Esther and Vashti in Adar, the month of Purim; Ruth and Naomi in Sivan, when Shavuot falls).

Some Rosh Hodesh groups create and enact rituals to mark and sanctify their members' varied life-passages: everything from getting pregnant to menopause, and from graduating from college to celebrating a 50th birthday. The rituals, some of which are published, include singing, hand-washing, wish-giving, dancing, and meditating.

In addition to the creation of new forms of religious expression, women are also rethinking ancient ones. *Mikvah*, for example, which many liberal Jews had dismissed as demeaning to women, is being re-examined and reclaimed as a ritual of spiritual renewal for women and men at special times of life: before *bar/bat mitzvah*, before weddings, before the high holidays, and in the ninth month of pregnancy.

Many of the new traditions of Jewish women are private. A mother whispers the *sheheheyanu*, the prayer for all new beginnings to her 13-year-old daughter who has begun to menstruate. A woman at menopause goes to the *mikvah* accompanied by two close friends, bearing flowers and chocolate. Both privately and publicly, a new body of Jewish custom and ritual is coming into being.

Divorce

Divorce has always been a fact of Jewish life, which means that there has always been a body of law attached to this unhappy transition. Although Jewish law, *halachah*, permits a few instances where a wife can dissolve a marriage, it is by and large a male perogative. According to traditional practice, a husband commissions a religious divorce decree called a *get*, which is formally delivered to his wife. If she accepts it, the divorce is then certified by a court of three rabbis, a *bet din*.

In fact, no more than 10% of all divorced American Jews ever seek a Jewish divorce, which are readily available from Conservative and Orthodox rabbinical courts. Since between one-third and one-half of all Jewish marriages end in divorce, it seems clear that most people consider civil divorce sufficient, valid, and final.

However, as the divorce rate among Jews has increased, and as rabbis have been called on to do more family and marriage counseling, many people have expressed the need for a formal Jewish conclusion to a relationship that began with Jewish blessings. Thus, some liberal rabbis have begun to offer a Jewish divorce ritual to help give the parties a sense of resolution and closure.

This form of divorce differs substantially from a traditional Jewish divorce and is not recognized as legitimate by Orthodox and many Conservative Jews. Because divorce is one of the most divisive issues in the community, affecting remarriage and the status of children as Jews, this is an issue to discuss with a rabbi.

Liberal *gittin* (the plural of *get*) and accompanying divorce rituals are egalitarian, reciprocal agreements that can be initiated by either partner. The *get* may be written either in English or Hebrew, or in both languages. It may include specific clauses relevant to the couple who are divorcing, but the core of the document is a formal statement of dissolution. For example:

> I, _____, son/daughter of _____ and _____, of my own free will grant you this bill of divorce. I release you from the contract which established our marriage. From this day onward you are not my husband/wife and I am not your wife/husband. You belong to yourself and are free to marry another.[6]

Such a document can be executed in a rabbi's study or any place agreeable to the parties involved. It is then signed by at least two witnesses. In order to physically enact the dissolution of the marriage covenant, a corner of the document can be cut or ripped. This kind of ritual divorce can be done with little or no ceremony. However, some people add other readings at this time, especially the familiar lines from Ecclesiastes:

When a marriage ends, the altar sheds tears.

Talmud

For everything there is a season

and a time for every purpose under heaven

a time to be born and a time to die

a time to plant and a time to uproot . . .

a time for tearing down and a time for building up

a time for weeping a time for laughing

a time for embracing and a time to refrain from embracing.[7]

FURTHER READING

CONVERSION

Choosing Judaism by Lydia Kukoff (UAHC, 1981) Personal accounts of the process of becoming a Jew.

ADOPTION

And Hannah Wept, Infertility, Adoption, and the Jewish Couple by Michael Gold (Jewish Publication Society, 1988). Solid information and advice, along with a thorough discussion of Jewish law on various aspects of infertility and adoption.

The Jewish Baby Book by Anita Diamant (Summit Books, 1988). See especially the section on adoption. But the chapters regarding *brit milah, brit habat,* and birth announcements, all have application to ceremonies for welcoming an adopted child into a Jewish family and community.

Chag Sameach! by Patricia Schaffer (Tabor Sarah Books, 1985). A children's book that features Jewish children of many races celebrating the holidays. For information, write to: Tabor Sarah Books, 2419 Jefferson Ave., Berkeley, CA 94703.

Stars of David publishes a newsletter which is sent to all members. For more information, write to: Stars of David, Temple Shalom Emeth, 16 Lexington Street, Burlington, MA 01803.

WOMEN'S LIVES

Miriam's Well; Rituals for Jewish Women Around the Year by Penina V. Adelman, (Biblio Press, 1986). The most comprehensive treatment of Rosh Hodesh rituals, Adelman's book contains a year's worth of Rosh Hodesh rituals that focus on various women's life stages, from menarche to birth to menopause. Liturgical sources range from traditional to new age.

Midlife and its Rite of Passage Ceremony by Irene Fine (Women's Institute for Continuing Jewish Education, 1988). An interesting discussion of midlife rituals, especially *Simchat Hochma,* celebration for a "wise woman."

For information about this and other books about Jewish women's prayers, stories, and rituals:

Women's Institute for Continuing Jewish Education
4079 54th St
San Diego, CA 92105

The Jewish Women's Resource Center of the National Council of Jewish Women, New York Section, maintains a library of new liturgies and a regularly updated bibliography. Upon request, they will send a listing of materials available for purchase:

Jewish Women's Resource Center, NCJW
9 East 69 Street
New York, NY 10021

Also see: "This Month is for You: Observing Rosh Hodesh as a Woman's Holiday," by Arlene Agus in *The Jewish Woman,* edited by Elizabeth Koltun (Schocken Books, 1976). This essay mentions the many traditional sources for Rosh Hodesh observance, and also includes an outline for a women's celebration of the holiday. A pre-birth Rosh Hodesh ceremony appears on pp. 33–34 of *The Jewish Baby Book,* and *The New Jewish Wedding* includes a discussion of *mikvah* for brides and grooms.

DIVORCE

The Jewish Women's Resource Center (above) has materials on divorce and *The Jewish Wedding Book* contains a somewhat longer discussion of traditional views on divorce.

Death

The primary principle underlying every Jewish law, ritual, and custom having to do with death and mourning is *kavod*, a word that means "honor" and "respect." The Jewish approach to bereavement is also based on respect for the powerful emotions of loss.

Unlike the widespread American practice of encouraging mourners to hide or repress their grief and get back to work within a matter of days, Jewish law and custom create time for grief and provide a methodology for grieving. The specific laws regarding the mechanics of burial —even to selecting a coffin—give mourners guidance during a time when making necessary decisions is so difficult. And after the funeral, mourners are given a structure to encourage feeling their loss, and thus heal.

Although this chapter provides an introduction to Jewish burial and mourning practices, when a death occurs, it is important to seek out assistance and support from members of the Jewish community: rabbis, Jewish funeral home personnel, members of your synagogue, or the deceased's congregation. It is relatively easy to find such help, even for people who are unfamiliar with Jewish burial and mourning practices or for those coping with a loss in a strange city. Hospital chaplains of all denominations are always aware of local Jewish resources.

Death and Burial

From the moment of death until a body is buried, Jewish law and custom are entirely focused on honoring the deceased. Gestures of respect include closing the eyes and mouth, lighting a candle, which is a symbol of the soul, and opening a window for the soul's release. Psalms and personal prayers are recited.

The traditional prayer said on witnessing or hearing of a death is a statement of total acceptance:

בָּרוּךְ אַתָּה, יְיָ אֱלֹהֵינוּ, מֶלֶךְ הָעוֹלָם, דַּיַּן הָאֱמֶת.

Baruch Ata Adonai Eloheynu Melech Ha-olam Dayan Ha-emet.

Holy One of Blessing Your Presence fills creation You are the True Judge.

Jewish tradition stresses that the body should not be left alone from the time of death until burial, which takes place as quickly as possible. The custom is to have someone read Psalms beside the body, a duty that can be performed by family members, friends, or by synagogue members. On request, Jewish funeral homes will provide a ritual guardian, or *shomer*, for this purpose.

If a death occurs in a hospital, family members inform the staff of their wishes regarding respectful treatment for the body. Autopsies are generally not permitted by Jewish law, mostly because they are seen as a desecration of the body and thus an abrogation of respect. However, because the rabbinic principle that saving a life takes precedence over most other laws, by extension, autopsies, organ donation, and donation of the body for medical research may be authorized. These issues are usually discussed on a case-by-case basis with a rabbi.

Although some people make their own burial and funeral arrangements in advance of their own deaths, family members are often left to make the decisions surrounding burial. Jewish tradition is quite specific in this regard: embalming, viewing the body, and holding a wake are considered disrespectful to the body and to the memory of the deceased.

Mahogany caskets with silver hardware may be purchased from a Jewish funeral home for the price of a luxury car. However, according to Jewish tradition, respect for the dead is expressed not by "burying money," but by contributing to *tzedakah*, especially to charities and causes that were important to the deceased. A plain wooden coffin is seen not as a sign of cheapness or disrespect; instead it is a way to promote the natural processes of death and decomposition, a way of returning to the earth, to the source of life. A desire for simplicity can be expressed to representatives of a Jewish funeral home with a request for "the least expensive kosher casket available." In this context, "kosher" means "in conformance with Jewish law," in other words, a casket made of plain wood by Jews for the purpose of burying a Jew.

According to Jewish tradition, the body is prepared for the grave with the utmost simplicity. No attempt is made to preserve or prettify the body, which is washed and cleaned according to specific regulations. Everyone, male and female, rich and poor, are buried alike, wearing nothing but plain, white shrouds, without pockets. Jews are sometimes buried wearing a *tallit;* however, the fringes on the prayer-shawl will be cut because they are reminders of *mitzvot* or obligations that are binding only in this world.

These practices are known to Jewish funeral home personnel; however, it may be necessary to ask for them to be performed.

CREMATION

In Jewish law, the prohibition against cremation is absolute. Someone who chooses to have his or her body burned after death is treated like someone who has cut him or herself off from the Jewish community. In traditional circles, official forms of mourning are not permitted for one who has been cremated; survivors may not be permitted to say *Kaddish* or sit *shiva.* Although the response is rarely so drastic in liberal circles, many rabbis will not officiate at a memorial service for someone who has been cremated.

The Jewish distaste for cremation is also based on respect for the natural process of the decomposition of the flesh, which is abetted by

---

A baby enters the world with closed hands. A person leaves the world with open hands. The first says, "The world is mine." The second says, "I can take nothing with me."

Midrash: Ecclesiastes Rabbah

Jewish burial methods. Jewish burial is seen as a way of returning the body to its source, of reuniting one part of creation with the rest of it. Cremation is not only seen as a repudiation of the natural pace of "dust to dust," but as the desecration of that which was created in God's own image. In modern times, the Holocaust has cast cremation into an especially problematic light. The very word conjures up images of ovens, chimneys, and the charred remains of thousands of Jewish bodies that were never "laid to rest."

Despite the legal, historical, and emotional arguments against it, some Jews express wishes and even make arrangements for their own cremation after death, often with the intention of sparing their families the trauma and expense of a funeral. A loved one's wish to be cremated often creates an emotional dilemma for family members who would prefer to follow a more traditional Jewish path. The son or daughter of a parent who wishes to be cremated is asked to choose between not obeying Mom or Dad's last wishes, and doing something that violates a personal belief or need. For many people, visiting a grave is an important part of healing after a loss.

Although it is difficult to speak about these matters with a healthy parent, sibling, or spouse, this is a conversation worth having. The counsel of a sympathetic rabbi can also be extremely helpful.

The Funeral

Jewish funerals take place as soon as possible following death, although they may be postponed until relatives and friends can arrive, as a way to honor the dead. Burials are not permitted, however, on *Shabbat* and most holidays.

Funeral services usually take place at a funeral chapel or in a synagogue, though they may also be conducted at a home or at the cemetery. Although anyone knowledgable about Jewish burial customs may conduct a funeral, it is a function performed almost exclusively by rabbis. The decision about whether or how much family members want to participate in the funeral service, with special readings or prayers, for example, is entirely personal and is made in consultation with the officiating rabbi. Many families leave the service entirely up to him or her.

Compared with the specific rules and requirements for treatment of the body and burial, there are almost no liturgical requirements for a funeral service. Psalm 23, "The Lord is My Shepherd," is nearly universal and certain prayers are traditional, especially the *"El Maley Rachamin,"* God Filled with Compassion:

God who is full of compassion, dwelling on high
Grant perfect peace to the soul of _____.
May s/he rest under the wings of Your Presence
Holy and Pure, Who shines bright as the sky.
And may his/her place of rest be as Eden
We pledge *tzedakah* for the sake of her/his memory.
We pray that You comfort her/his soul in eternal life, under the protection of your wings.
Adonai, You are our heritage.
May s/he rest in peace.
Amen.

The single most important element of the funeral is the eulogy, or *hesped,* which honors the dead and expresses the loss felt by his or her passing. Typically, eulogies are delivered by rabbis, who meet with mourners in advance of the funeral to talk about the one who has died and to solicit suggestions for his or her remarks. Sometimes members of the family write the eulogy or part of it for the rabbi. In some cases, a relative or close friend will deliver it.

The tearing of a mourner's garments, called *k'riah,* is an ancient, physical enactment of the feeling that the world has been torn apart. *K'riah* is often done just prior to the funeral service, although it can take place at the grave, or when someone first hears of the death. For men, the tear is usually made on the lapel of a sport coat or jacket. Women will tear a sweater, dress or blouse. It is also common to substitute a torn black ribbon, which is then worn on the lapel for the next seven days.

At the Cemetery

It is considered both an honor and duty to help bury the dead.[1] Carrying someone to his or her grave is seen as a way of paying loving tribute.

And it is common for everyone present to participate in the burial by using the shovel, a process usually initiated by close family members. By inviting participation in the physical act of burial, Jewish custom makes it extremely difficult to deny the reality of death, which makes it possible for grief and healing to begin. Those in attendance generally do not leave the grave until the body is placed into the earth and the coffin is covered with earth.

There is usually a brief service at the graveside as well, consisting of Psalms and the recitation of the *Kaddish*. *Kaddish*, from the word *kadosh* or holy, is a familiar and much-recited prayer which has several forms, all of which praise God. Written in Aramaic, the *Kaddish* does not mention death at all, but praises God for the gift of life. Sometime during the Middle Ages, however, it became associated with mourning and today its recitation evokes the pain of loss and the consolation of remembrance for Jews everywhere. There is a legend that angels brought *Kaddish* to earth. The 20th century writer S. Y. Agnon imagined that the prayer was first recited by a human mourner to comfort God, Who also grieves over the deaths of men and women.[2]

The recitation of the *Kaddish* at the graveside begins the mourner's obligation to repeat this prayer during the formal period of mourning, and again at appropriate occasions, such as during a synagogue service.

MOURNER'S *KADDISH*

Exalted and hallowed be God's greatness
In this world of Your creation.
May Your will be fulfilled
And Your sovereignty revealed
In the days of our lifetime
And the life of the whole house of Israel
Speedily and soon.
And say, Amen.

May You be blessed forever,
Even to all eternity.
May You, most Holy One, be blessed,
Praised and honored, extolled and glorified,
Adored and exalted above all else.

Blessed are You.
Beyond all blessings and hymns, praises and consolations
That may be uttered in this world,
And say, Amen.

May peace abundant descend from heaven
With life for us and for all Israel,
And say Amen.

May God, Who makes peace on high,
Bring peace to all and to all Israel,
And say, Amen.[3]

Mourning

The Talmud says, "Do not comfort the bereaved with their dead still before them."[4] In other words, it is considered inappropriate to offer words of condolence to mourners until after the funeral. But after the burial, indeed even as the mourners walk from the grave, the focus shifts from honoring the deceased to comforting the bereaved.

Jewish tradition designates official mourners very narrowly to include people who have one of seven relationships with the deceased: father, mother, son, daughter, sister, brother, or spouse. The laws and customs regarding mourning apply only to this small and intimate circle. This does not mean that cousins, grandchildren, and friends are not bereaved or should not express their grief. However, the tradition was concerned that people might spend too much time in the official ritual forms of mourning, which call for some withdrawal from the world and from joyful activities.

Jewish mourning practices are arranged in a series of concentric circles that reflect and respond to the diminishing intensity of grief and concurrently reintroduce mourners to the world of the living:

Aninut, the period between death and burial, is a time filled with shock and even denial. Mourners essentially do nothing but prepare for the burial, funeral, and the mourning period to follow. They make necessary phone calls, meet with the rabbi, and spend time with only their closest friends. This is generally not a time when visitors call. *Aninut* ends with the sound of earth being thrown onto the coffin.

Shiva, from the Hebrew word for seven, refers to the seven days that include and follow the funeral.* This is the most intense period of formal mourning. People often refer to this period as "sitting *shiva*" because of the custom of sitting on or near the floor, an ancient gesture of being struck low by grief. Funeral homes sometimes provide *shiva* benches or low stools. Some people remove cushions from couches and chairs and simply sit lower to the ground. Only mourners, not guests, sit on or near the ground.

Shiva begins as soon as the mourners return from the cemetery. Hands may be washed at the door, a symbolic acknowledgement of the sad duty just completed at the grave. A seven-day candle, usually provided by the funeral home, is lit. Then, a meal is served. This *seudat havra'ah,* or "meal of consolation," is a graphic reminder of the fact that life must go on, even for those with the taste of death in their mouths. It is considered a great act of kindness, a *mitzvah,* for friends to provide and serve this meal to mourners. Eggs and other round foods, such as lentils, are often served as a symbol of the continuing cycle of life, but this is not a festive meal. It is eaten quietly.

During *shiva,* mourners refrain from doing business or experiencing pleasure. They do not go to work, watch television, or even leave the house. Mirrors are covered to discourage vanity. Mourners often do not shave, wear new clothing, or have sex. Some Jews do not wear leather shoes, because, in the ancient world, they were a sign of luxury and worldliness.

The purpose of *shiva* is not to make mourners feel better or to cheer them up, but to encourage them to grieve and to share their grief. *Shiva* means taking time to remember and cry, to feel anger, loss, sorrow, panic—whatever feelings are present—fully and without distraction. For seven days, the mourners speak of the life that is over; they tell and retell stories, and laugh at fond and happy memories. Some families read and discuss books about Jewish mourning customs and books about death and dying during *shiva.* This is also a time for mending family fences.

If mourners are observing the custom of not going out during *shiva,*

---

* Because Shabbat and certain holidays affect the counting of these seven days, rabbis can help determine when *shiva* begins and ends. Some people choose to observe shiva for fewer than seven days, though the minimum is usually three days.

a daily *minyan* is held in the home so that the bereaved can say *Kaddish.* The task of organizing a *minyan* is often done by a synagogue committee set up for that purpose.

PAYING A SHIVA CALL

Visiting a house of mourning is considered a *mitzvah,* a good and holy thing to do. Many rules of etiquette are suspended where people are sitting *shiva.* One enters without ringing the bell or knocking; mourners are not hosts, nor are guests emissaries of good cheer. There is very little that can be said at times like this, but words are not as important as the presence of friends. It is enough that people come just, in the words of the prophet Ezekiel, to "Sigh in silence." [5]

Because bouquets and wreaths serve to soften or even beautify a scene of mourning, it is considered inappropriate to send or bring flowers to a Jewish house of mourning. A donation to charity in the name of the deceased is considered a far more meaningful tribute. Gifts of food are, however, traditional. But rather than bringing the sixth plate of brownies, it may be more helpful to call whomever is taking responsibility for food in the house to find out what is most needed: a dinner casserole, a trip to the grocery store, a few hours of babysitting for small children, or someone to take out-of-town relatives to the airport. These arrangements, among others, may be performed by a synagogue committee, sometimes called a *chevra kadisha,* which means literally "holy fellowship." [6]

Shiva ends on the morning of the seventh day. The memorial candle is blown out in silence, and sometimes mourners go for a walk around the block, as a way of taking a first step back into the real world.

Sheloshim refers to the 30 days following burial and includes the seven days of *shiva.* During *sheloshim,* many of the prohibitions against work and pleasure are lifted. Mourners return to their jobs, sit on real chairs again, go out of their homes, wear perfume, have sex. However, some restrictions still apply, and some people will not attend parties or other social functions, go to movies, or listen to music. Some Jews go to services every day to say *Kaddish,* others attend services every *Shabbat* with the same intention. On the 30th day, all outward signs of mourning are suspended, except for those who have lost a parent, who continue to abstain from attending joyful events and continue to say *Kaddish* regularly.

Avelut, which literally means "mourning," is the 12-month period observed only by people who have lost a parent. It is counted from the day of death and ends after 12 Hebrew months. Jewish law requires that mourners recite *Kaddish* daily for eleven months, which means attending a prayer service where a minyan will be present. However, many observe *avelut* by saying *Kaddish* at *Shabbat* services every week for a year.

The year of mourning also mandates refraining from "joyous" activities, so some people do not go to movies or parties. The practice is a way of reminding oneself, "I am not finished mourning. I am not entirely ready to be soothed."

Another way to observe the year of remembering a parent, or other loved one who has died, is with gifts to charities that were especially important to the deceased. Similarly, some people volunteer and work for a social service agency or religious organization in memory of a parent.

UNVEILING

The dedication of a gravestone takes place anytime between the end of *sheloshim* and the anniversary of the death. A cloth or veil is removed from the grave marker in the presence of the immediate family and perhaps a few close friends. As unveiling is *not* a second funeral, and although rabbis sometimes officiate, it is common for family members to gather on their own to read Psalms or prayers, or just reminisce. There is no set ceremony for an unveiling.

Simplicity tends to be the rule regarding Jewish gravestones. As the

---

People used to bring food to a house of mourning. The wealthy brought it in baskets of silver and gold, the poor in baskets of willow twigs, and the poor felt ashamed. Therefore our sages taught that everyone should use baskets of willow twigs out of deference to the poor and in hopes of fostering unity.

Talmud, Mo'ed Katan 27a-b

Talmud puts it, "We need not make monuments for the righteous—their words serve as their memorial."[7] Generally, the marker includes the full Hebrew and secular names of the deceased, the Hebrew date of death, and the secular calendar dates of birth and death. There are usually a few Hebrew letters on the stone that stand for, "Here is buried," or "May his/her soul be bound up in the bonds of life." Jewish symbols, such as the six-pointed star of David, are commonly inscribed, as are quotes from scripture or personal notes.

The custom of leaving pebbles on a gravestone may date back to biblical days when people were buried under piles of stones. Today, pebbles are usually left as tokens that people have been there to visit and remember.

YARZEIT AND YIZKOR

Yarzeit, from the Yiddish for "a year's time," is the anniversary of a death. A special 24-hour memorial candle is lit on the eve of the day of the death, and also on the eve of Yom Kippur. It is also traditional to light these candles at the end of the festivals of Sukkot, Passover, and Shavuot. No special prayer is associated with this act of remembrance. Sometimes, silence is the most eloquent tribute.

Yizkor, which means "remember," is the name of a prayer and also the name of the short Memorial Service that takes place four times every year: on Yom Kippur and at the end of Sukkot, Passover, and Shavuot. The prayer consists of a series of paragraphs that all begin with the words, "May God remember," or *Yizkor Elohim*. It is recited by anyone who has ever lost a parent, a child, a sibling, or a spouse. The Memorial Service also includes paragraphs for those mourning other relatives and friends.

Liberal Practice

The traditions surrounding death present mourners with choices. During the past several generations, Jews tended to choose less and less from the traditional menu, shortening the duration of mourning, including *shiva*, and ignoring the obligations and prohibitions for the month and year following a death.

That trend is beginning to reverse itself. Rabbis and other Jewish educators report growing interest in seminars and classes about the traditions and customs of death and mourning. It is no longer a matter of rejecting or ignoring the tradition, but of studying it to discover how it applies and how to apply it. The most common alteration in mourning practices among liberal Jews is the choice to attend a weekly rather than a daily *minyan* during the month of *sheloshim* and the year of *avelut*.

There are other ways to bend the rules respectfully. For example, although the tradition is not to leave the house during *shiva* or listen to music, some people make long, meditative walks a regular part of those seven days, or spend time listening to music that was especially beloved by the deceased.

Traditional Jewish burial and mourning customs respond to two fundamental needs: practical and psychological. During the emotional crisis that follows a death, it is comforting to have a set of clear directions to follow. Equally compelling is the way that Jewish burial and mourning customs reflect modern insights into the healing processes of grief. The image of Jewish tradition as a mirror, a tool of reflection, seems particularly apt for mourners. During the week of *shiva*, the mirrors in a mourner's house are draped to encourage people to look within and also to seek answers from those gathered around them in sympathy. Recovering from the death of a loved one is never easy or speedy, and there is much evidence that people who do not fully explore the depth of their feelings immediately following a death tend to suffer more depression and disorientation years later. The "schedule" of Jewish mourning customs insists both that people take time to fully grieve, and that they re-enter the world of the living step by step.

The memory of the righteous is a blessing.

Proverbs 10:7

FURTHER READING

Jewish funeral homes often provide their clients with pamphlets containing basic information about customs and rituals that mourners find accessible and useful.

OTHER GOOD RESOURCES INCLUDE:
Open Hands: a Jewish Guide on Dying, Death and Bereavement
  and
Willow Baskets, Colored Glasses: A Friend's Guide to Comforting Mourners

These two pamphlets, written by Rabbi Rami M. Shapiro, provide a liberal overview of Jewish traditions. Shapiro discusses the variety of choices that can be made at the time of a death, and helpful guides for visiting a house of mourning. For information:

Temple Beth Or
11715 SE 87th Ave
Miami, FL 33176

Talking About Death: A Dialogue Between Parent and Child by Earl A. Grollman (Beacon Press, 1991). A book of answers to parent's questions.

The Jewish Way In Death and Mourning by Rabbi Maurice Lamm (Jonathan David Publishers, 1969). The classic and authoritative guide to Jewish tradition and all the laws on death, burial, and mourning from an Orthodox perspective.

"A Plain Pine Box." This television documentary, produced by ABC, tells the story of a Minneapolis congregation that decided to make coffins for its own members, sold for the price of the lumber. For rental information:

Alden Films
P.O. Box 449
Clarksburg, NY 08510

FOR CHILDREN
How it Feels When a Parent Dies by Jill Kremetz (Alfred Knopf, 1983). From Kremetz's much-praised series of books, illustrated with photographs.

Bubby, Me and Memories by Barbara Pomerantz (UAHC, 1983). When a grandparent dies.

CHAPTER NOTES

PART ONE: INTRODUCTION

Making Jewish Choices

1. The phrase came from the 1866 poem "Awake my people," by Judah Leib-Gordon, A Russian-Hebrew poet of the *Haskalah*, the Jewish enlightenment. The exact line is, "Be a man abroad and a Jew in your tent."

2. William Novak and Moshe Waldoks, *The Big Book of Jewish Humor* (New York: Harper & Row, 1981) p. 288.

3. "The Divine Authority of the Mitzvah," Herman E. Schaalman, *Gates of Mitzvah*, edited by Simeon J. Maslin (New York: Central Conference of American Rabbis) p. 103.

4. Schaalman, p. 103.

5. Hasidism was a mystical revival of the 18th century. This idea is attributed to Rabbi Yehudah Aryeh-Leib of Ger, in *S'fas Emes*, a five-volume classic of Hasidic spiritual insights, and was suggested to the authors by Rabbi Nehemia Polen.

6. Exodus 24:7

7. Reprinted from *The Complete Poems of Charles Reznikoff* with the permission of Black Sparrow Press.

PART TWO: HOME

A Little Sanctuary

1. Deuteronomy 6:4–9, 11:13–21. Translation from *Vetaher Libeynu, Purify Our Hearts*, the prayerbook *(siddur)* of Congregation Beth El of the Sudbury River Valley, Sudbury, Massachusetts. p. 35.

2. This translation/adaptation, taken from the verse written on the *mezuzah* parchment is by Rabbi Rami Shapiro.

3. *Baruch ata Adonai Eloheynu Melech ha-olam* are the words that introduce many blessings. The most familiar English translation for the Hebrew is "Blessed art Thou, Lord our God, King of the Universe." Alternatives to this translation are found throughout this book, none of which refer to God as a male monarch.

Shabbat—The Sabbath

1. Genesis 2

2. Abraham Joshua Heschel, *The Sabbath* (New York: Farrar Straus and Giroux, 1951) p. 10.

3. Deuteronomy 5:12

4. Ezekiel 20:12

5. Talmud: Shabbat 118b

6. Exodus 16

7. Isaiah 58:13

8. Hayyim Schauss, *The Jewish Festivals* (New York: Schocken Books, 1962) pp. 11–12.

9. Samuel H. Dresner, *The Sabbath* (New York: The Burning Bush Press, 1970) p. 66.

10. Some of these may be found in a book called *Hasidic Tales of the Holocaust,* by Yaffa Eliach (New York: Avon Books, 1982).

11. The kinds of work that are forbidden on *Shabbat* are based on a list of 39 specific labors listed in the Mishna, which is part of the Talmud. The rabbis theorized that these tasks, which are largely agricultural in nature, were derived from the work of constructing the portable Tabernacle in the wilderness. Rabbis have based other restrictions—including the modern prohibition against using electricity—both on the Mishna and on subsequent codes of Jewish law.

12. Schauss, p. 33.

13. Bella Chagall, *Chagall: Burning Lights* (New York: Schocken, 1946. 1969 edition) p. 48–49. This volume is described as a "double portrait of the warm world of Russian Jewry." The text is by Bella Chagall, and the book is illustrated by 36 line drawings by her husband, the artist Marc Chagall.

14. This translation and others in this chapter come from *Vetaher Libeynu,* the daily prayerbook of Congregation Beth El, Hudson Rd, Sudbury, MA 01776.

15. Exodus 20, Deuteronomy 5

16. Herbert C. Dobrinski, *A Treasury of Sephardic Laws and Customs* (Hoboken, N.J.: Ktav, 1986) p. 231.

17. Reprinted by permission of the author.

18. Rabbi Susan Grossman-Boder has written a lovely egalitarian poem based on the traditional text. See *The New Jewish Wedding* by Anita Diamant (New York: Summit Books, 1985) pp. 231–232.

19. Genesis 1:31; 2:1–3

20. Numbers 15:17–21

21. Pirke Avot 3:17

22. Pirke Avot 3:21

23. Translation from *Vetaher Libeynu*

24. *Y'did Nefesh* was written by Rabbi Eleazar Azikri, who lived in Palestine during the 16th century. Translation from *Vetaher Libeynu*

Good Deeds

1. Pirke Avot 2:21

2. Deuteronomy 16:20

3. Talmud: Baba Bathra 9a

4. Danny Siegel, *Gymshoes and Irises* (Spring Valley, New York: The Town Mill Press, 1982) pp. 120–124.

5. In an essay entitled, "Brother, Can You Spare a Dime; The Treatment of Beggars According to Jewish Tradition: A Case in Point," New Yorker Arthur Kurzweil turned to the Talmud for help in fashioning a personal response to the daily requests for handouts he faced on the streets of Manhattan. Reading from the classical Jewish sources in translation, Kurzweil found a guide—or at least a model—for his own actions. He concludes, "The message seems clear: don't ignore the beggar, don't treat him or her with anything but kindness, don't find excuses as to why not to give. Rather give to everyone, regardless of who he or she is, but just give a little." Published in Siegel, pp. 114–115.

6. Sota 14a, quoted in Siegel, p. 126.

7. Isaac Luria's book, *Sefer Yetzirah,* is one the basic books of Jewish mysticism, called *Kabbalah.*

8. Isaiah 57:14–58:14

The People of the Library

1. See Barry Holtz, *Back to the Sources* (New York: Summit Books, 1984) p. 13.
2. Pirke Avot 1:14
3. Talmud: Shabbat 25b
4. Rabbi Lawrence Kushner, *River of Light* (San Francisco: Harper & Row, 1981) p. xxi.
5. Genesis Rabbah, VIII, 5
6. The Jerusalem Bible is distributed in the US through bookstores by: Phillip Feldheim and Co., 200 Airport Executive Park, Smith Road, Spring Valley, NY 10977.
7. *The Encyclopedia Judaica* and its yearbooks are distributed in the US through bookstores and Jewish book clubs by Chemed Books and Company, Inc. The EJ can also be ordered directly from Chemed. For information: 3709 13th Ave, Brooklyn, NY 11218.

What Jews Eat

1. Samuel H. Dresner, *The Jewish Dietary Laws* (New York: The Burning Bush Press, 1959) pp. 15–16.
2. Rabbi Hayim Halevy Donin, *To Be a Jew* (New York: Basic Books, 1972) pp. 98–99.
3. Leviticus 11
4. The rule is repeated three times in the Torah: Exodus 23:19 and 34:26; Deuteronomy 14:21.
5. The reigning liberal ruling is that cheeses made with rennet are also kosher. Rennet, an enzyme taken from the lining of calves' stomach and added to harden cheese, is considered so denatured in its processing that it no longer qualifies as meat and falls into the category of a new thing, *dvar hadash*.
6. Because wine falls into the category of things used for sacramental purposes—specifically, for making *kiddush*—the Talmud outlawed the use of any wine made by non-Jews for fear it might have been used for idol worship.
7. Rabbi Seymour E. Freedman, *The Book of Kashruth* (New York: Bloch Publishing Company, 1970), p. 3.
8. Genesis 1:29–30
9. Isaiah 11
10. "Kashrut: How Do We Eat?" by Sheila Weinberg, in *The Jewish Family Book*, edited by Sharon Strassfeld and Kathy Green (New York: Bantam Books, 1981) p. 85.
11. Edda Servi Machlin, *Classic Cuisine of the Italian Jews* (New York: Dodd, Mead & Co, 1981) p. 11.
12. Josephine Levy Bacon, *Jewish Cooking from Around the World* (Woodbury, NY: Barron's, 1986) p. 2.
13. Blu Greenberg, *How to Run a Traditional Jewish Household* (New York: Simon & Schuster, 1983) p. 109.

PART THREE: COMMUNITY

1. Pirke Avot 2:5
2. Rabbi Lawrence Kushner
3. Ta'anit 22b

Synagogues

1. These figures, from the national office of the Union of American Hebrew Congregations, are approximations only, as of July 1990.
2. These figures, from the national office of the United Synagogues of America, are approximations only, as of July 1990.
3. This figure, given by the Reconstructionist movement, is approximate as of July 1990.

A Nation of Students

1. Midrash Sefer Eliahu Rabba 7
2. Midrash Rabbah 4:11, Song of Songs
3. Strassfeld and Green, p. 146.
4. Jewish confirmation ceremonies were begun in the 19th century by the Reform movement as a substitute for *bar mitzvah* in response to the consensus that 13-year-olds were too young to be admitted as adult members of the community. Today, however, confirmation is a collective ceremony which occurs some years later than and in addition to *bar/bat mitzvah*.
5. The B'nai B'rith Hillel Foundation is named for one of Judaism's most beloved teachers. Hillel the Elder, who lived toward the end of the first century, B.C.E. engaged in a life-long debate with another great teacher, the brilliant but impatient Shammai.
   Hillel was known for his benevolence, gentleness, and humility and is credited with many famous aphorisms. Perhaps the most famous story about him involves the impatient student who asks him to explain all of Judaism while standing on one foot. Hillel answered, "Love your neighbor as yourself. The rest is commentary. Go and study." (Shabbat 31a)
6. Talmud: Eruvin 54a

PART FOUR: OBSERVANCE

Observance

1. Heschel p. 8.

Jewish Time

1. The Gregorian calendar was brought into use by Pope Gregory XIII during the 16th century.
2. This date was arrived at by calculations based on biblical references.
3. There are also agricultural and pagan sources.
4. For an excellent treatment of this subject, see "The Second Day of Festivals," in Arthur Waskow's *Seasons of Our Joy* (New York: Bantam Books, 1982), pp. 226–227.

Rosh Hashanah and Yom Kippur

1. Rabbi Lawrence Kushner
2. Isaiah 57:14–58:14
3. Micah 7:20
4. Leviticus 23:26–32
5. Leviticus 18

Sukkot and Simchat Torah

1. Rabbi Lawrence Kushner
2. Exodus 23:16, Leviticus 23:33–44, Deuteronomy 16:13–17
3. For a sample building plan see *The First Jewish Catalog*, edited by Richard Seigel, Michael Strassfeld, and Sharon Strassfeld (Philadelphia: Jewish Publication Society, 1973) pp. 129–130.
4. For further discussion of these interpretations see: Michael Strassfeld, *The Jewish Holidays* (New York: Harper & Row, 1985), Philip Goodman, the *Sukkot/Simchat Torah Anthology* (Philadelphia: Jewish Publication Society, 1973).

Hannukah

1. Rabbi Lawrence Kushner
2. According to the revisionist version of the "official" Hannukah story, the war was, in fact, a civil conflict between the devout masses in the countryside and the assimilated city-folk who had adopted Greek ways. Years after the Maccabee victory, they too became Hellenized. Thanks to Rabbi Barbara Penzner.

Tu B'Shvat

1. Dobrinski, pp. 376–380.
2. For a good description of the Tu B'Shvat *seder* of the mystics of Safed, see Waskow, pp. 108–109.
3. Avot de Rabbi Natan 31b
4. Deuteronomy 20:19
5. Rabbi Zalman Schachter-Shalomi, in Strassfeld's *The Jewish Holidays*, p. 183.

Purim

1. Rabbi Lawrence Kushner
2. Deuteronomy 25: 17–19
3. Talmud: Megilot 7B

Passover

1. Rabbi Lawrence Kushner
2. This description of Passover as the essential Jewish holiday owes a great deal to Rabbi Irving Greenberg's views, expressed in *The Jewish Way; Living the Holidays* (New York: Summit Books, 1988)
3. Actually, most of the story is not told at the *seder* table. Passover sets in motion a season of study.
4. For instructions about *matzah*-making, see *The First Jewish Catalog*, pp. 144–145.

Holocaust Remembrance Day and Israel Independence Day

1. Rabbi Irving Greenberg, p. 339.
2. Genesis 17:8
3. Rabbi Lawrence Kushner

Shavuot

1. Rabbi Lawrence Kushner
2. Exodus 23:16, Leviticus 23:15–21, Deuteronomy 16:10
3. Waskow, p. 202.

THE LIFE CYCLE

Birth

1. Alfred Kolatch, *The Name Dictionary* (Middle Village, NY, Jonathan David Publishers, 1967) p. xi.
2. Betsy A. Lehman, "The Age-old Question of Circumcision," *The Boston Globe*, June 22, 1987.
3. Rabbi Lawrence Kushner, "Save this Article," *Bulletin of the Congregation Beth El of the Sudbury River Valley*, Sudbury, MA. Vol. VIII, No. 6, Sivan/Tammuz 5742, p. 3.
4. Toby Fishbein Reifman with Ezrat Nashim, *Blessing the Birth of a Daughter; Jewish Naming Ceremonies for Girls* (Englewood, NJ: Ezrat Nashim, 1978). Quoting an unpub-

lished paper by Rabbi Marc Angel of the Spanish and Portuguese Synagogue in New York, p. 27.

Bar and Bat Mitzvah

1. Adapted from the Talmud, Berachot 17a, translation by Rabbi Lawrence Kushner.
2. Exodus 30:14; Leviticus 27:3–5; Numbers 1:3, 20
3. Avot 5:21
4. *Encyclopedia Judaica*, Volume 4 (Jerusalem: Keter Publishing House, Ltd: 1972) p. 243.
5. Sukkah 42a, Megilla 23a, as cited in *The Second Jewish Catalog*, edited by Strassfeld and Strassfeld (Jewish Publication Society, 1976) p. 62.
6. For examples of alternative *bar/bat mitzvah* ceremonies, see the appropriate chapters in *The Jewish Family Book* and *The Second Jewish Catalog*.
7. From a conversation with Karen Kushner, MSW, which informs much of the following discussion.

Marriage

1. Zohar 1:89a
2. Rabbi Maurice Lamm, *The Jewish Way in Love and Marriage* (San Francisco: Harper & Row, 1980) p. 198.
3. Adapted from a translation by Debra Cash.
4. Philip and Hanna Goodman, *The Jewish Marriage Anthology* (Philadelphia: Jewish Publication Society, 1977) p. 28.

New Traditions

1. Rabbi Aryeh Kaplan, *Waters of Eden: The Mystery of the Mikvah* (New York: National Conference of Synagogue Youth/Union of Orthodox Jewish Congregations, 1976), p. 35.
2. Rabbi Daniel Shevitz, "A Guide for the Jewish Adoptive Parent," *Response*, No. 48, Spring, 1985. pp. 107–126. In addition to being the sensitively written account of an adoptive parent, this article is an excellent source of information about traditional Jewish views and laws regarding adoption.
3. This ceremony is based on one written by Rabbi Daniel Shevitz and Susan Shevitz for their son, Noah.
4. Jewish Women's Resource Center, "Birth Ceremonies, *Brit Banot:* Covenant of Our Daughters," New York, 1983. p. 2.
5. Leviticus 12:1–5
6. From a *get* written by Rabbi Lawrence Kushner and Rabbi Henry Zoob.
7. Ecclesiastes 3:1–5

Death

1. According to tradition, Jews are buried only in Jewish cemeteries or in portions of cemeteries designated for Jews only. Thus, whenever Jews settle in a new place, one of their first communal acts is the purchase of land for a cemetery.
2. Rabbi Rami M. Shapiro, *Open Hands: a Jewish Guide to Dying, Death and Bereavement* (Miami: Temple Beth Or) p. 15.
3. Translation from *Vetaher Libeynu*, p. 119.
4. Pirke Avot, 4:23
5. Ezekiel 24:17
6. Traditionally, a *chevra kadisha* prapared the body for burial, a task that is, by and large, now performed by Jewish funeral homes.
7. Talmud: Shekalim 2:5

TIMELINE

These dates provide both Jewish and secular reference points to help readers place dates and events mentioned in the text of this book into familiar historical contexts.*

Secular Calendar		Hebrew Calendar
B.C.E.	(BEFORE COMMON ERA)	
3761	Creation of Adam, the sixth day of creation	1
2704	Birth of Noah	56
2104	The Flood	1656
1812	Birth of Abraham	1948
1764	Tower of Babel	1996
1742	Covenant between God and Abraham	2018
1712	Birth of Isaac	2048
1675	Binding of Isaac	2085
1652	Births of Jacob and Esau	2108
1589	Isaac blesses Jacob	2171
1568	Jacob marries Rachel and Leah	2192
1544	Joseph sold by his brothers	2216
1522	Jacob and his family move to Egypt	2238
1505	Death of Jacob	2255

* Sources: *The Encyclopedia Judaica, Seder Hadorot* by Rabbi Yechiel Heilpern and *Toldot Am Olam* by Rabbi Shlomo Rottenberg, as compiled by Tzvi Black

1451	Death of Joseph	2309
1428	Beginning of slavery in Egypt	2332
1392	Birth of Moses	2368
1312	Exodus from Egypt, giving of the Torah	2448
1272	Death of Moses	2488
1106	The story of Deborah	2654
950	The story of Samson	2810
879	Samuel anoints Saul as king of Israel	2881
877	Samuel anoints David as king of Israel	2883
836	King Solomon begins his rule	2924
825	First Temple completed	2935
796	Split of the kingdom of Israel	2964
586	First Temple destroyed, Babylonian exile begins	3174
356	The story of Purim	3404
352	Construction of the Second Temple	3408
312	Alexander the Great conquers Persia, beginning of Greek rule	3448
139	Miracle of Hannukah, kingdom of the Hasmoneans begins	3622
36	Hasmonean dynasty ends, Herod begins his rule	3724
32	Leadership of Rabbi Hillel begins	3728
18	Herod begins Temple reconstruction	3748

C.E.	(COMMON ERA)	
68	Second Temple destroyed by the Romans	3828
73	Fall of Masada	3833
80	Leadership of Rabbi Akiva begins	3840
93	Josephus completes "Jewish Antiquities"	3853
120	Rebellion of Bar Kochba	3880
219	Mishna compiled	3979
306	Christianity becomes the state religion of the Roman Empire	4066
325	Council of Nicea, Christians begin to celebrate Sabbath on Sunday	4075
358	The permanent Jewish calendar is instituted	4118
368	Jerusalem Talmud compiled	4128
426	Babylonian Talmud compiled	4186

476	Fall of Rome, beginning of Byzantine rule over Israel	4236
500	Babylonian Talmud completed	4260
622	Hegira-Mohammed flees from Mecca to Medina	4382
638	Islamic conquest of Jerusalem	4398
691	Caliph Abdul-Malik completes "Dome of the Rock"	4451
814	Death of Charlemagne	4574
1040	Birth of Rashi, biblical and Talmudic commentator	4800
1066	William of Normandy conquers England	4826
1096	First Crusade	4856
1131	Birth of Maimonides, "Rambam"	4891
1144	First Blood Libel against the Jews in England	4904
1205	Death of Maimonides	4965
1215	Magna Carta	4975
1290	Expulsion of the Jews from England	5050
1305	Death of Rav Moshe DeLeon, author of the Zohar	5065
1337	Beginning of the Hundred Years War	5097
1348	The Black Death	5108
1394	Expulsion of the Jews from France	5155
1480	Inquisition established in Spain	5240
1492	Expulsion of the Jews from Spain; Columbus discovers America	5252
1516	Ottoman Turks conquer Palestine	5276
1544	Martin Luther, Protestant Reformation	5304
1564	Joseph Caro publishes "Shulchan Aruch" in Safed, Palestine	5324
1569	Rav Isaac Luria comes to Safed to teach Kaballah	5329
1582	Gregorian Calendar established	5342
1588	Destruction of Spanish Armada	5348
1620	Mayflower arrives at Plymouth Rock	5380
1648	Chmelnitzki massacres in Poland; end of 30 Years War	5408
1654	First Jewish settlement established in North America	5414
1760	Death of Baal Shem Tov, the founder of Hasidism	5520
1776	American Revolution	5536
1789	Beginning of the French Revolution	5549
1791	French National Assembly grants full civil rights to Jews	5551
1791	Pale of Settlement established in Russia	5551
1804	Napoleon crowned Emperor	5564

1806	End of Holy Roman Empire	5566
1815	German Jewish immigration to America begins; Waterloo	5575
1844	First meeting of German Reform leaders	5604
1861	American Civil War	5612
1881	Czar Alexander II is assassinated; Pogroms against the Jews	5641
1882	Mass immigration of Russian Jews to America begins	5642
1885	Pittsburgh Platform (Statement by American Reform Movement)	5645
1894	Dreyfus trial (France)	5654
1897	First Zionist Congress (Basel)	5657
1902	Conservative Movement emerges in US	5662
1914	World War I begins	5674
1917	British defeat Turks, capture Jerusalem; Balfour Declaration	5677
1920	England receives mandate over Palestine	5680
1933	Hitler comes to power	5693
1938	Kristallnacht riot against Jews in Germany	5698
1939	World War II begins	5699
1947	Dead Sea Scrolls first discovered	5707
1948	State of Israel is declared	5708
1956	Sinai Campaign	5717
1967	Six Day War. Reunification of Jerusalem	5727
1972	First woman rabbi ordained by Reform Movement	5732
1973	Yom Kippur War	5734
1976	Entebbe Rescue	5736
1978	Camp David Peace Accord	5738
1979	Israeli-Egyptian Peace Treaty	5739
1982	Incursion into Lebanon	5742
1984	Operation Moses, rescue of Ethiopian Jews	5744
1987	Intifada, Arab uprising in Israel begins	5748
1988	Elie Wiesel receives Nobel Peace prize	5749
1989	Berlin Wall comes down	5750
1990	Operation Exodus: Resettlement of Soviet Jews in Israel	5750

GLOSSARY

Guide to Pronunciation

ah	is pronounced like	a	as in father
ai	is pronounced like	ai	as in fair
ay	is pronounced like	ay	as in pay
ch	is pronounced like	ch	as in challah
e/eh	is pronounced like	e	as in red
ee	is pronounced like	ee	as in meet
ei	is pronounced like	ei	as in height
i	is pronounced like	i	as in big
o	is pronounced like	o	as in open
oo	is pronounced like	oo	as in boot
tz	is pronounced like	ts	as in bets
u	is pronounced like	u	as in push
y	is pronounced like	y	as in my

Note: In general, pronunciation follows modern Hebrew usage.

Afikomen (AH-fee-ko-men) the middle MATZAH of three MATZOT used in the Passover *seder*. Greek for "dessert."

Akedah (ah-kay-DAH) The story of the binding of Isaac in Genesis 22. Hebrew for "binding."

Alef-Bet (ahlef beht) Name of the Hebrew alphabet; also, its first two letters.

Aliyah (ah-lee-YAH) To be called to the TORAH to recite a blessing; a section of the weekly Torah portion is called an *aliya*. Also, "making *aliyah*" refers to moving to the land of Israel. Hebrew for "ascent."

Amidah (a'mee-DAH) An anthology of short blessings and prayers which form the core of a religious service. The *amidah* is recited standing and usually includes some personal meditations. Hebrew for "standing."

Aninut (ah-nee-NOOT) The period between death and burial when mourners refrain from all activity except preparing for the funeral.

Apocrypha (a'PAHK-r'-fah) A collection of books, including the Books of Maccabees, that were not included in the final redaction of the Bible, but which are, nevertheless, important Jewish texts. Greek for "hidden."

Aramaic (air-a-MAY-ik) An ancient Semitic language related to Hebrew. The GEMARA was written in *Aramaic,* as is the well known KADDISH prayer.

Ashkenazic (ahsh-ken-AHZ-ik) Refering to the culture of the predominant section of world Jewry that settled throughout northwestern Europe in the Middle Ages, and later in eastern Europe. It is distinguished from SEPHARDIC JEWRY through folk and religious traditions.

Aufruf (OOF-roof) calling up of a couple to the TORAH on the SHABBAT before their wedding. Candy is usually thrown at the couple to symbolically wish them a sweet life together. Yiddish, for "calling up."

Avelut (ah-vay-LOOT) The year-long observances for the death of a parent. An *AVEL* is a mourner. Hebrew for "mourning."

B.C.E. Before the Common Era. Jews avoid the Christian designation B.C., which means Before Christ.

Baal Shem Tov (bahl shem tov) An honorary name given to Rabbi Israel ben Eliezer, the founder of HASIDISM, the 18th century mystical revival movement. Hebrew for "master of the good name."

Bar Mitzvah (bahr MITZ-vah) A boy of 13 who has reached the age of religious majority; also the ceremony marking that event. Hebrew for "son of the commandment."

Barchu (bahr-CHOO) The call to worship. The formal beginning of a service which is usually preceeded by introductory prayers and blessings. Hebrew for "blessed."

Baruch ata Adonai (bah-RUCH ah-TAH ah-do-NAI) Words that begin Hebrew blessings, commonly rendered in English as "Blessed art Thou, Lord our God, King of the Universe." This book contains many alternatives to that translation.

Bat Mitzvah (baht MITZ-vah) A girl of 13 who has reached the age of religious majority; also the ceremony marking that event. Hebrew for "daughter of the commandment."

Bench/Benching (bench) Yiddish for "bless."

Bible The Hebrew Bible. It includes the books of the Torah, Prophets and Writings.

Bimah (bee-MAH) Raised platform in the synagogue from which worship services are lead.

Birchat Hamazon (bir-CHAHT hah-mah-ZON) Grace after a meal. Hebrew for "blessing for food."

Boray P'ree Hagafen (bo-RAY p'ree hah-GAH-fen) The blessing recited over wine or grape juice. Hebrew for "creator of the fruit of the vine."

Bris (bris) Yiddish for BRIT.

Brit (breet) Covenant, and covenant ceremony. Often refers to the covenant of circumcision.

Brit Habat (breet ha-BAHT) A term applied to many modern ceremonies used to welcome baby girls into the covenant of the people of Israel. Many other names are given to this type of ceremony. Hebrew for "covenant of the daughter."

Brit Milah (breet mee-LAH) The covenant of circumcision.

Buber, Martin (1878–1965) Existential theologian, popularizer of Hasidic spirituality, bible scholar and philosopher.

Cantor A leader of synagogue services trained in Jewish liturgical music.

C.E. Common Era. Jewish alternative to A.D., which means *Anno Domini*, Latin for "in the year of our Lord."

Challah (chah-LAH) Braided loaf of egg bread, traditional for SHABBAT and holidays.

Chevra Kadisha (CHEV-rah kah-DEE-shah) The group responsible for the ritual preparation of a body for burial. In synagogues today, the CHEVRA KADISHA committee may help arrange meals, a MINYAN, and other details for mourners. Hebrew for "holy fellowship."

Cholent (CHO-lent—here the "ch" is as in "chair") A hearty stew popular among ASHKENAZIC Jews consisting of barley, beans, potatoes and flanken. Because actual cooking is forbidden on the Sabbath, this dish which simmered over night, was a traditional meal served for lunch on SHABBAT.

Chumash (choo-MAHSH) One of the terms used for the TORAH or 5 Books of Moses. From the Hebrew for "five."

Conservative Religious movement, developed in the United States during the 20th century as a more traditional response to modernity than that offered by Reform.

D'rash (drahsh) Religious insight, often based on a text from the TORAH.

D'var Torah Hebrew for "words of Torah": an explication of a portion of the TORAH. (Plural is divrei Torah.)

Daven (DAH-vin) Yiddish for "pray."

Diaspora Exile. The dwelling of Jews outside the land of Israel.

Draydl (DRAY-dl) Yiddish for a top used in playing a game of chance during the festival of Hannukah; in Hebrew a *sivivon*.

Enlightenment Eighteenth century rationalist philosophical movement that challenged previously accepted doctrines.

Erev (EH-rev) Eve, especially of a holiday. *Erev Shabbat* is Friday evening. Hebrew for "the evening of."

Etrog (ET-rog) Citron. A lemon-like fruit, one of the four species used in observance of the holiday of Sukkot.

Flayshig (FLAY-shig) Yiddish word for meat food, which according to the laws of KASHRUT, may not be mixed with dairy products; includes poultry, but not fish.

Gemara (G'MAH-rah) The rabbinical exegesis of the MISHNA, written in ARAMAIC, completed around the fifth century C.E. The *Gemara* and MISHNA together form the TALMUD. ARAMAIC for "study."

Gemilut Hassadim (g'mee-LOOT chah-sah-DEEM) Acts of loving kindness.

Get (get) Jewish divorce document.

Gragger (GRAH-ger) Noise-maker used on PURIM.

Gut Shabbes (gut SHAH-biss) A traditional Sabbath greeting. Yiddish for "A good sabbath."

Hachnasat Orchim (hahch-nah-SAHT or-CHEEM) Hospitality. Hebrew for "welcoming guests."

Haftarah (hahf-tah-RAH) "Conclusion" refering to readings from the biblical books of the Prophets, which conclude TORAH services. Unrelated to the word "Torah."

Haggadah (hah-gah-DAH) The book containing the liturgy of the Passover *seder*. Hebrew for "a telling."

Haimish (HAY-mish) That which gives one a sense of belonging. Yiddish for "homelike."

Halachah (hah-lah-CHA) An umbrella term for the entire body of Jewish law.

Hamentaschen (HU-men-tah-shen) A triangular pastry served on PURIM, said to resemble Haman's hat.

Hametz (chah-METZ) Food prepared with leavening, not eaten during the Passover holiday; anything which is not "kosher for Passover."

Hannukah (chah-noo-KAH) An 8-day winter festival commemorating the victory of the Maccabees over the Syrians in 139 B.C.E., celebrated in part by the lighting of a HANNUKIAH, an 8-branched candelabra. Hebrew for "dedication."

Hannukiah (chah-noo-kee-YAH) A candelabra with nine branches—one for each of the 8 nights, plus a helper candle—used during the festival of HANNUKAH.

Haroset (chah-RO-set) A mixture of wine, nuts, and apples used as part of the PASSOVER SEDER. It is said to symbolize the mortar the Jews used to prepare bricks for the Egyptians.

Hashem (hah-SHEM) A name used to refer to God. Hebrew for "the name."

Hasidism (CHAH-see-diz'm) Eighteenth-century mystical revival movement.

Havdalah (hav-dah-LAH) Saturday evening ceremony that separates SHABBAT from the rest of the week, also performed at the end of major holidays. Hebrew for "separation."

Havurah (chah-voo-RAH) Small, participatory groups that meet for prayer, study and celebration. Hebrew for "fellowship" (Plural is havurot.)

Hazzan (chah-ZAHN) Hebrew for "CANTOR."

Hazzanit (chah-zah-NEET) A female cantor.

Hechsher (HECH-sher) A symbol on food packaging that means its contents are kosher and were prepared under rabbinical supervision.

Heschel, Abraham Joshua (1907–1972) Scholar and philosopher who sought, among other things, to explain Judaism as a living relationship between human beings and God.

Hesped (HES-ped) Hebrew for "eulogy."

Hiddur Mitzvah (hee-DUR mitz-VAH) The rabbinic principle of adorning or decorating something used for religious purposes. For example, using a beautiful goblet as opposed to a paper cup to make a blessing over wine. Hebrew for "beautification of a *mitzvah.*"

Holocaust Remembrance Day The 27th of the Hebrew month of Nisan (a week after PASSOVER) set aside by the government of Israel as the day to commemorate the Holocaust and its victims.

Huppah (choo-PAH) Wedding canopy.

Israel Independence Day The anniversary of the founding of the state of Israel in 1948, held on the 5th of Iyar (about 2 weeks after PASSOVER).

K'riah (kree-AH) The mourning custom of tearing a garment as a sign of grief. Hebrew for "rending."

Kaballah (kah-bah-LAH) The Jewish mystical tradition. Not a single book. From the Hebrew for "receive" or "tradition."

Kaddish (KAH-deesh) A prayer written in ARAMAIC, associated with mourning. It contains no mention of death, and is understood as an affirmation of life.

Kallah (KAH-lah) Bride, and one of the names of SHABBAT.

Karpas (KAHR-pahs) A green vegetable used as part of the Passover SEDER.

Kashrut (kahsh-ROOT) System of laws that govern what Jews may and may not eat.

Ketubah (k'too-BAH) Marriage contract.

Kibbudim (kee-boo-DEEM) Ceremonial honors.

Kibbutz (kee-BOOTZ) Israeli collective farm.

Kiddush (kee-DOOSH) Sanctification, and specifically the blessing over wine recited on SHABBAT and holidays.

Kippah (kee-pah) Skull cap, worn as a sign of reverence for God. The Yiddish term is "yarmulke." Plural is *kippot.* Hebrew for "cap."

Kohane/Kohen (KO-hayn) Today, used to refer to people who trace their ancestry to the priestly family of Aaron. Hebrew word for "priest."

Kol Nidre (kol NEED-ray) The opening prayer of YOM KIPPUR, an annulment of all vows chanted to a haunting melody.

Kosher Foods deemed fit for consumption according to the laws of KASHRUT. The verb, to make kosher, is *"kasher."*

Kvatter, Kvatterin (K'VAH-ter, K'VAH-ter-in) Hebrew for "godfather," "godmother."

Latkes (LAHT-kiz) Potato pancakes, associated with HANNUKAH.

Lulav (LOO-luv) A bouquet of palm boughs, myrtle and willow branches used during the holiday of SUKKOT.

Ma'ariv (MAH-a'reev) The evening service.

Ma'asim Tovim (mah-ah-SEEM to-VEEM) Good deeds, righteous actions.

Machzor (mahch-ZOR) The special High Holiday prayer book. Hebrew for "cycle" (referring to the cycle of the year).

Maggid (mah-GEED) The telling of the story of PASSOVER at the SEDER. Hebrew for "telling."

Maimonides Rabbi Moshe Ben Maimon, also known as the Rambam, lived from 1135–1204 in Spain and North Africa. One of the great scholars and philosophers in Jewish history, he is best known for two works: the *Mishneh Torah,* and *The Guide for the Perplexed.*

Maimuna (my-MOO-nah) A joyous celebration of SEPHARDIC origin, marking the end of PASSOVER.

Matzah (MAH-tzah) Flat, unleavened bread eaten during the Holiday of PASSOVER, known as the "bread of affliction" and the "bread of haste." Plural is *matzot.*

Maven (MAY-vin) Yiddish for "expert."

Mazel Tov (MAH-zl tov) In common usage, "Congratulations." Hebrew for "good luck."

Megillah (m'gee-LAH) Usually refers to the scroll of the Book of Esther, read on Purim. Hebrew for "scroll."

Menorah (m'no-RAH) A candelabra, often used to refer to the HANNUKAH *menorah,* the HANNUKIAH.

Mensch (mench) Yiddish word meaning person; a honorable, decent person. *Menschen* is the plural. *Menchlichkeit* means "person-ness," the quality of being a *mensch.*

Mesader Kiddushin (m'SAH-der k'doo-SHIN) One who "orders" or leads a wedding ceremony, usually a rabbi.

Mezuzah (m'zoo-ZAH) A small container, affixed to the doorposts of a home containing the first two paragraphs of the SHEMA written on a parchment scroll. Hebrew for "doorpost."

Midrash (mid-RAHSH) A genre of literature consisting of imaginative exposition of and stories based upon holy scriptures.

Mikdash Ma'at (meek-DAHSH m'AHT) The Jewish home. Hebrew for "little sanctuary."

Mikvah (meek-VAH) Ritual bath.

Milah (mee-LAH) Circumcision. BRIT MILAH is the covenant of circumcision.

Milchig (MIL-chig) Yiddish term for dairy foods, which, according to the laws of KASHRUT, may not be mixed with meat products.

Mincha (meen-CHAH) The afternoon service.

Minhag (meen-HAHG) Custom. Plural is minhagim.

Minyan (meen-YAHN) A prayer quorum of ten adult Jews. For Orthodox Jews, ten men.

Mishna (meesh-NAH) The first part of the TALMUD, comprised of six "orders" of laws regarding everything from agriculture to marriage, written in Hebrew and compiled in the second century C.E.

Mitzvah (meetz-VAH) A commanded deed, a value-action. A fundamental Jewish concept about the obligation of the individual to perform commandments set forth in the TORAH and elaborated by rabbinic tradition. Often it is used to mean a "good deed."

Mohel (MO-hel) A person trained in the rituals and procedures of BRIT MILAH, circumcision. The Yiddish pronounciation is "moy'l."

Motzi (mo-TZEE) Blessing over bread recited before meals. Hebrew for "bringer" or "brings."

Musaf (moo-SAHF) An additional service for SHABBAT and holidays which comes after the TORAH reading.

Ne'ilah (n'ee-LAH) The final, closing service of YOM KIPPUR. Hebrew for "locking" or "closing."

Niggun (nee-GOON) A wordless prayerlike melody.

Oneg Shabbat (O-neg shah-BAHT) The informal gathering for conversation and community after Sabbath services. Hebrew for "joy of the Sabbath."

Orthodox An orthodox Jew is one who believes that all of Jewish law is binding.

Parasha (pah-rah-SHAH) The weekly TORAH portion read at services. The Torah is divided into 54 *parshiyot* (plural). One (and occasionally two) is read each week. Hebrew for "portion."

Pareve (pahrv or PAHR-veh) Neutral foods that can be eaten with either dairy or meat meals.

Passover The spring festival commemorating the exodus from Egypt.

Pentateuch The five books of Moses; the TORAH. From the Greek, meaning "five scrolls."

Pesach (PEH-sahch) Hebrew for "PASSOVER."

Pharisees (FAIR-i-seez) The spiritual leaders of the Jewish people during the latter part of the second Temple period.

Pidyon Haben (peed-YON hah-BEN) The ceremony of redeeming the first-born son from a priest *(kohane)*.

Purim (POO-reem) A late-winter festival that celebrates the rescue of the Jews from destruction, as told in the Biblical book of Esther.

Pushke (PUSH-keh) A coin box reserved for TZEDAKAH.

Rabbi A seminary-ordained member of the clergy. "The rabbis" refers to the men who codified the TALMUD. Hebrew for "teacher."

Reconstructionism Religious movement begun in the United States in the twentieth century by Mordecai Kaplan, which views Judaism as an evolving religious civilization.

Reform A movement begun in nineteenth-century Germany that sought to reconcile Jewish tradition with modernity. Reform Judaism does not recognize the divine authority of HALACHAH.

Responsa A genre of literature composed of the legal answers (responses) to situational questions of Jewish law, and like legal opinion in all traditions, has the weight of law.

Rosenszweig, Franz (1886–1929) German Jewish philosopher and existentialist thinker.

Rosh Hashanah (rosh hah-shah-nah) The fall holiday that marks the beginning of the Jewish year; the day on which the SHOFAR is sounded.

Rosh Hodesh (rosh CHO-desh) The first day of every lunar month. Hebrew for "head of the month."

Sabra (SAB-rah) A native born Israeli.

Safed (SAH-fed) A picturesque town in Northern Israel overlooking the sea of Galilee. In the 16th century it was the scene of the great flowering of the Jewish mystical tradition known as Lurianic Kabbalah. Pronounced "Tz'faht" in Hebrew.

Sandek (SAHN-dek) The person who holds the baby during a circumcision; godfather. *Sandeket* is a new term for a woman performing the same function.

Schmaltz (shmaltz) Yiddish for melted or rendered chicken fat, schmaltz is used in English for "corn" as in excessive sentimentality; also as an adjective, *schmaltzy* (corny).

Seder The PASSOVER talking-feast. *Seder* can also be used to describe the order of rituals at other meals; for example, the SHABBAT *seder*, and the TU B'SHVAT *seder*. Hebrew for "order."

Sedra (SID-rah) Another term for the weekly Torah portion. See *Parasha*.

Sephardic Referring to the culture of Jews who are descendants of the Jews of Medieval Spain, and now used to describe Jews of the Mediterranean region. Sephardim are distinguished from ASHKENAZIM (see above).

Seudah (s'oo-DAH) Hebrew for "feast," "banquet" or "festive meal."

Seudat Mitzvah (s'oo-DAHT mitz-VAH) The festive celebration of a milestone. Hebrew for " a commanded meal."

Sh'chitah (sh'chee-TAH) Laws governing the KOSHER slaughter and inspection of animals.

Shabbat (shah-BAHT) Hebrew for Sabbath. In Yiddish, *Shabbos* or *Shabbes*.

Shalom A universal Hebrew greeting which means "hello," "good-bye" and "peace."

Shalom Aleichem (SHAH-lom ah-LAY-chem) A popular Hebrew greeting meaning "peace unto you." Also, the pseudonym of Sholom Rabinowitz (1859–1916), one of the greatest Yiddish writers of all time.

Shalom Bayit (SHAH-lom BAH-yit) The principle of a peaceful home. Hebrew for "peaceful house."

Shamash (shah-MAHSH) The ninth candle on a HANNUKIAH used to light the others; also a synagogue sexton. Hebrew for "helper."

Shanna Tova (shah-NAH-to-VAH) Popular Jewish New Year greeting. Hebrew for "good year."

Shavuot (shah-voo-OT) The late spring harvest festival of first fruits, which also commemorates the giving of the TORAH on Mt. Sinai.

Shechinah (sh'-CHEE-nah) God's feminine attributes, often referred to as a separate entity; God's presence in the world.

Sheheheyanu (she-heh-cheh-YAH-nu) A common prayer of thanksgiving. Hebrew for "has kept us alive."

Sheloshim (shlo-SHEEM) The month following the burial of a loved one, a period during which mourners attend services and refrain from joyful activities. Hebrew for "thirty."

Shema (sh'mah) The most often-recited Jewish statement that declares God's Oneness: Listen, Israel, Adonai our God is One (Deuteronomy 6:4).

Sheva B'rachot (SHEH-vah b'rah-CHOT) Seven marriage blessings. Hebrew for "seven blessings."

Shiva (shi-vah) The seven-day mourning period that begins on the day of a funeral. From the Hebrew for "seven."

Shmooz (shmooz) A Yiddish word that means "to chat."

Shoah (sho-AH) Hebrew for Holocaust.

Shochet (SHO-chet) A person trained in the rituals and procedures of KOSHER slaughter.

Shofar (sho-FAHR) A ram's horn, blown on ROSH HASHANAH.

Shtetl (shteh'tl) Small town, especially one in Eastern Europe inhabited by ASHKENAZIC Jews before the Holocaust.

Shul (shool) Synagogue.

Siddur (see-DOOR) Prayerbook.

Simcha (seem-CHAH) Joy, also a celebration of joy or party.

Simchat Torah (seem-CHAHT to-RAH) The holiday at the end of SUKKOT which marks the beginning and end of the annual TORAH reading cycle. Hebrew for "rejoicing over the Torah."

Siman Tov U'mazel Tov (SEEM'N tov oo-MAH'ZL tov) A song of good wishes sung at joyous celebrations, especially weddings. Hebrew for "a good sign and good luck."

Sofer (SO-fehr) Scribe. A person who is trained in the writing of TORAH scrolls and other religious documents.

Sukkah (soo-KAH) A temporary hut or booth erected for the holiday of SUKKOT.

Sukkot (soo-KOT) The fall harvest festival (also plural of SUKKAH).

Tallit (tah-LEET) Prayer shawl. A four-cornered shawl with specially tied fringes worn generally at morning worship services. Yiddish pronunciation is "TAH-lis."

Talmud (TAHL-mood) Encyclopedic compilation of rabbinic thought, lore and law consisting of the MISHNA and GEMARA (and commentary) completed around the 5th century C.E.

Tanakh (tah-NAHCH) The Hebrew acronym for the BIBLE. It stands for TORAH (five books of Moses), Nevi'im (Prophets) and Ketuvim (Writings).

Tashlich (tahsh-LICH) A ceremony that takes place on the afternoon of ROSH

HASHANAH where sins (bread crumbs are often used) are symbolically cast off into a body of water. "You will cast their sins into the depth of the sea" (Micah 7:19).

Tefilah (t'fee-LAH) Hebrew word for prayer. Also another name for the AMI-DAH.

Teshuvah (t'shoo-VAH) Repentance. From the Hebrew for "turning."

The Temple The first building associated with Jewish worship is often referred to as "The Holy Temple." It was built in Jerusalem by King Solomon around the 10th century B.C.E. The first Temple was destroyed by the Babylonians in 586 B.C.E. A second temple was built, but it was destroyed by the Romans in 70 C.E. The Temple was the physical symbol of God's presence on Earth, and prayers for its rebuilding are a symbolic call for the coming of the messiah.

Tikkun Olam (tee-KOON o-LAHM) Taking responsibility for correcting the damage done by people to each other and to the planet. Hebrew for "repairing the world."

Tisha B'av (tee-SHAH b'ahv) The 9th day of the Hebrew month of Av which commemorates the destruction of both temples in Jerusalem.

Torah (to-RAH) First five books of the Hebrew BIBLE (Genesis, Exodus, Leviticus, Numbers and Deuteronomy), portions of which are read every SHAB-BAT. "Torah" is also used to refer to Jewish learning in general.

Tractate A treatise, which usually refers to a section of the TALMUD. The TALMUD is divided into 6 "orders" or major divisions, and further sub-divided into 63 tractates.

Trafe (trayf) The opposite of kosher. From the Hebrew for "torn."

Tu B'shvat (too b'SHVAHT) The 15th day of the Hebrew month of *Shvat*. A festival celebrating the New Year for Trees.

Tzedakah (tz'dah-KAH) Righteous giving, charity.

Ulpan (ool-PAHN) An intensive course in conversational Hebrew.

Yamim Noraim (yah-MEEM no-rah-EEM) The High Holidays of ROSH HASHANAH and YOM KIPPUR. Hebrew for "days of awe."

Yarmulke (yar-mool-keh) Skull cap. Yiddish for *"kippah."*

Yarzeit (YAHR-tzeit) The anniversary of a death, when it is traditional to light a 24-hour candle. Yiddish for "a year's time."

Yeshiva (y'shee-VAH) An academy of Jewish learning; usually used to describe Orthodox institutions.

Yichus (YICH'es) Yiddish word that means family status or lineage.

Yiddish Language spoken by ASHKENAZIC Jews; a combination of early German and Hebrew.

Yizkor (YEEZ-kor) A prayer in a memorial service that asks God to remember the souls of parents and other deceased relatives and friends. It is customarily recited on YOM KIPPUR and at the end of SUKKOT, PASSOVER and SHAVUOT. From the Hebrew for "May [God] remember."

YMHA/YWHA Young Men's Hebrew Association/Young Women's Hebrew Association: The Jewish versions of the YM/YWCA.

Yom Ha-atzmaut (yom hah-ahtz-mah-OOT) Hebrew for "Israel Independence Day."

Yom Hashoah (yom hah-sho-AH) Hebrew for "Holocaust Remembrance Day."

Yom Kippur (yom kee-POOR) Day of Atonement, the holiest day on the Jewish calendar. A day of fasting and repentance.

Zohar (ZO-hahr) "Book of Splendor." The major work of Jewish mysticism, probably written by Rabbi Moses De Leon in the 13th century. The *Zohar* is a mystical commentary on the TORAH.

INDEX